ONE TOUGH DAME

HOLLYWOOD LEGENDS SERIES
CARL ROLLYSON, GENERAL EDITOR

ONE TOUGH DAME

THE LIFE AND CAREER OF DIANA RIGG

HERBIE J PILATO

FOREWORD BY RUPERT MACNEE

INTRODUCTION BY RAY AUSTIN

UNIVERSITY PRESS OF MISSISSIPPI / JACKSON

The University Press of Mississippi is the scholarly publishing agency of
the Mississippi Institutions of Higher Learning: Alcorn State University,
Delta State University, Jackson State University, Mississippi State University,
Mississippi University for Women, Mississippi Valley State University,
University of Mississippi, and University of Southern Mississippi.

www.upress.state.ms.us

Designed by Peter D. Halverson

Frontispiece courtesy mptvimages.com.

The University Press of Mississippi is a member of
the Association of University Presses.

Library of Congress Control Number: 2024016818
Hardback ISBN 978-1-4968-3797-4
Epub single ISBN 978-1-4968-5280-9
Epub institutional ISBN 978-1-4968-5281-6
PDF single ISBN 978-1-4968-5282-3
PDF institutional ISBN 978-1-4968-5283-0

British Library Cataloging-in-Publication Data available

Dedicated to the equality, freedom, acceptance, and diversity of all human beings of every gender, culture, vocation, economic level, and good religious or spiritual belief or creed.

CONTENTS

Courtesy Classic TV Preservation Society (CTVPS)

Rupert Macnee (right) with his father, Patrick Macnee. Courtesy of Rupert Macnee.

FOREWORD

RUPERT MACNEE

IN THE HISTORY OF THE WORLD, 1964 WAS AND REMAINS A PIVOTAL YEAR. Amidst one tragedy after the next, there was hope with a decade of change in style, technology, and social and political expectations. Beyond the era's horrific assassinations of John F. Kennedy, Martin Luther King Jr., Bobby Kennedy, the Vietnam War, the racial disparities, and other challenges, there was a glimmer for something better.

The wave of change was intensively evident in relationships between men and women and their ability to make life and career choices. For Diana Rigg and Patrick Macnee, my father, who I affectionately referred to as both "Daddy" and "Patrick," 1964 was marked in the way episodes of *The Avengers* were created and produced in the old-school style of multi-camera techniques, which were exciting, dangerous, and often hilarious at the same time.

For most, it mattered who wore the pants in the family. But Diana broke such rules with the courage and admiration of a generation of both men and women wrapped into one. As Mrs. Emma Peel on *The Avengers*, she burst onto the scene with seasoned experience, and immediately became a worldly, perfect match opposite her decade-older, on-screen male partner of Mr. John Steed, the role played by Daddy.

In portraying Mrs. Peel and Mr. Steed, Diana and Patrick maintained a physical and theatrical athleticism with diverse training that was honed by a British crack team of established and professional writers, directors, designers, trainers, stunt fighters, and other creative sorts who found themselves in a perfect storm of success. It was a success that swept the world with *The Avengers*.

I first met Diana in 1965 at Elstree Studios, where *The Avengers* was filmed. She was friendly, open, and witty, and Patrick adored her. He liked the downhome side of her, as they were both fond of being in the country. Daddy respected Diana from day one, even after she left the show. Both she and he knew it was time for a change.

Some years later, in Los Angeles, I was in the audience when Diana performed live on stage in the play *Abelard and Eloise*. In the early 1990s, I saw her on Broadway in *Medea*, and she was extraordinary. After the performance, I went backstage and asked her if I could conduct an interview with her for CBC Radio in Toronto. It was an intelligent, intending experience during which she revealed a remarkable, dynamic side of herself—a dynamic I had recognized from *The Avengers*, but which had expanded beyond measure.

With compelling performances, stories, and unyielding imagination partnered with sleek, sophisticated leather suits, bowler hats, and canes, *The Avengers* no doubt struck (sometimes literally!) an immediate chord for the male and female population at home. The show teamed a man and a woman as equals, partners working together to make the world a better place. It presented in context and in content various themes and a look that was harvested and made internationally famous, right alongside two outstanding individuals in the guise of Daddy and Diana. One, who I knew more intimately as his son. Another, who I admired from afar yet close enough to know and observe just how diverse, charismatic, talented, and strong a woman she really was, physically, emotionally, and psychologically, all wrapped within a daunting humanity.

Both Diana and Patrick were tremendous readers, each with a unique ability to bring a word sailing off the page. As such, they would have enjoyed *One Tough Dame: The Life and Career of Diana Rigg*, which explores, to full capacity, her humanity, fearlessness, endurance, tenacity, her most beloved performances, and so much more.

INTRODUCTION

RAY AUSTIN

I HAVE KNOWN AND BEEN FRIENDS WITH SOME OF THE MOST COMPELLING, dynamic, and intelligent women in the world, including my wife Wendy, the most remarkable woman of them all. My lovely Wendy and I have been married for over forty years, and we have rarely exchanged a cross word. We are one lucky couple, and I am one lucky man.

The other remarkable women I have known and befriended over the years include a number of glamorous stars of the stage and screen—those with whom I have worked with in television, either as a stuntman, director, writer, or producer. I even fell in love with a few of them along the way. Who wouldn't? For example, 1952 was a very good year, as I met Judy Garland, Sophia Loren, Barbara Stanwyck, and others. And I would go on to enjoy many laughs and good times with each of them in ensuing years.

Today, I live in Virginia, but one of the last terrific experiences I had in Los Angeles took place quite a few years back at a Thanksgiving luncheon held at the home of my dear friend Roddy McDowall. I had attended the event with Robert Wagner and his beautiful wife Jill St. John. While there, we mixed and mingled with other dear friends from across the decades, including Elizabeth Taylor, Maureen O'Sullivan, Ann Miller, Stefanie Powers, Eleanor Parker, among others. It was a Thanksgiving lunch to end all Thanksgiving lunches. It was a gift to be able to sit and listen to magical Hollywood memories and stories of the past with legends who lived them.

But such a grand celebration would have been even more magical and meaningful had Dame Diana Rigg been seated my table. A fine and accomplished actress, Dame Diana gave grace to every room she entered, to every party she attended, to every stage she set foot upon, be it the live theater or any television or motion picture studio lot. I can say this because I saw it happen.

Ray Austin captured Diana's attention and respect as stunt coordinator on
The Avengers. Courtesy of Ray Austin.

I had worked with Dame Diana on the hit 1960s TV show, *The Aveng-ers*, on which she played secret agent Mrs. Emma Peel. I was the fight and stunt coordinator for the show, and from the very first day I met Diana, we battled, once, twice, sometimes three times a week. It was a real physical kind of fighting. We would throw punches, and shove and kick each other all over the place. And this went on for three years, minus any Marquess of Queensbury rules.

I share this particular memory with tongue-in-cheek because, fortu-nately, the fighting was fake, though the mesmerizing woman with whom I was fighting was all too stunningly real.

Here's how it came to be: in 1965, I was instructed by *The Avengers'* producer Albert Fennel and the show's producer-writer Brian Clemons to spend thirty minutes with five extremely attractive young ladies, and to report back with an assessment of each. One by one, I invited each woman to a special dressing room, with mattresses covering the floors and walls. No, no. It's not what you're thinking. Each of these young ladies were contenders to play Mrs. Peel opposite the show's male star Patrick Macnee, who played the dashing John Steed.

After just one day of attempting to teach Judo to those five attractive young actresses, I was black and blue, with a twice-bloody nose and a cut lip. They couldn't remember the moves, and I was the one being thrown, over and over again. These intelligent performers had already passed their on-camera screen tests for acting and dialogue abilities. But now the most important skill for the potential new female partner of Steed's was to see if she could be capable of the physical regimen the show required. My predecessor, Doug Robinson, had elected to use Judo with actress Honor Blackman, Patrick's initial costar in the original black-and-white episodes of *The Avengers*. But now it was time to do something different.

While sitting in my dressing room, bruised and sore, I had planned to inform Fennel and Clemens that no matter which actress was selected, it was going to be hard work. But, I was going to say, we had a chance with at least one of the five women who had remembered the routine I had mapped out.

At which point there was a loud banging on my dressing room door. It was Brian Clemens, telling me that they had tested one more girl on camera and were happy with her and wanted me to put her through her paces. He stepped aside, and there stood Diana Rigg, then only in her mid-twenties. Brian introduced us, Diana entered my dressing room and my life, and the rest is history.

That first day, we worked out a routine. I showed her the moves. She repeated them, no-nonsense, without any trouble, and without any more harm to me.

I then took Diana to the second-floor dressing room, which was allotted for her screen test on *The Avengers* stage. Subsequently, I reported back to Fennell and Clemens with my assessment of Diana: she was flat-out terrific. My colleagues were pleased with my findings and asked me to bring Diana to their office.

As Diana and I walked in the corridor to that destination, I could feel her excitement mounting. Suddenly, she tugged on my arm and said, "Do you think I've got it? Do you think they liked me? Did the director like the test?"

Though I had become her pipeline at that stage of the game, I didn't have the answers. I had no idea what was being said behind closed doors.

But by the end of the next day, indeed a deal had been bartered, a contract had been signed, and Diana Rigg had become the new partner to Patrick Macnee in *The Avengers*.

From the first afternoon we met, rolling around together on the floor, Diane and I became the closest of friends for the next three years. At that moment in time, I was the only friend she had at ABPC studios in Borehamwood. She did not know anyone connected with *The Avengers*. She had met Fennell, Clemens, and one of the directors. She had been in front of the camera and peered out beyond the lights at the faces of strangers and crew watching her with critical eyes. But beyond that, I was the only friendly face she recognized.

When Diana won the role of Mrs. Peel, everyone was thrilled that the show would continue. She was excited to be on the show, and I was thrilled to be creating, coordinating, and supervising the fight sequences.

Early on, I had convinced Clemens and Fennel to dump Judo as the main display of martial arts, and replace it with kung fu, which was little known at the time. Kung fu was new to the martial arts world—that which existed in England, anyway—and Fennell and Clemens agreed to a demonstration of new form. Thanks to Doug and Joe Robinson, I was a black belt in Judo, having attended their classes at the YMCA in London. I had then drifted into karate with Gerry Crampton, another stuntman who was extremely proficient in that particular martial art.

But then I achieved a black belt in kung fu, which became my chosen technique. I studied under Master Chee Soo at his dojo in Dunstable for over three years. Chee Soo came to my aid and helped me develop the key elements of the martial art moves into fight sequences with Diana, which were always fun to work out.

As everyone on the set of *The Avengers* got to know her, it became apparent that she was a shy person. Many thought she was a bit toffee-nosed (British slang for *snobbish*) and did not want to befriend the likes of the crew and others. But I am sure that was due to shyness at this stage, not distancing herself from her fellow workers.

After only her initial three episodes of *The Avengers* aired, Diana's boat was truly rocked. No one expected the reaction that she received from her skintight leather suits, with her long legs kicking out and her arms flying this way and that. No one expected the world's reaction to her appearance on *The Avengers* and beyond. But within just three weeks, Diana Rigg as Mrs. Emma Peel had become an international sex symbol. This shocked her. She had no idea that this could happen to her because of a television show. She did not know how to handle it. Men being men, as we were in those days (including myself), thought it was great fun to have our star be a sex symbol and on our show. We joked about it even with Diana. The first few times she laughed along with us. But it very soon went pear-shaped and became a taboo subject on the set.

One particularly challenging day comes to mind. We were on location for an episode that was directed by Bob Day. Diana and I were sitting in the back of the Bentley that was used as John Steed's car, waiting to shoot the next scene. Right out of the blue she said, "I hate this fucking sex symbol crap. I keep all the unopened fan mail in the boot of my car. Most of it is obscene, and I'm going to dump it."

I told her not to do that, because someone would get hold of it, and it would wind up in the press. So, I suggested she burn it. A few days later, Diana told me she had handed the mail over to her mother, who was now also her secretary, and that she was going to handle it.

With that issue resolved, by the end of *The Avengers'* first season, Diana had become rattled by other issues. She had very much missed the theatre and performing with the Royal Shakespeare Company. Television to her was not like being on the stage in front of a live audience. She had enjoyed a measure of fame with her appearances on, for one, the internationally syndicated BBC television production of *The Comedy of Errors* and *King Lear*. She had spent much of 1964 with the RSC, touring Europe, the Soviet Union, and the United States.

But then came *The Avengers*, for which Diana later told me, she had auditioned just for fun. I reminded her of our initial walk to the producer's office—when she was wracked with anxiety, concern, and excitement as to whether she had gotten the part. But she never responded to my memory.

Another issue arose on *The Avengers* set after only twelve episodes when Diana discovered she was earning less than the cameraman, Alan Hume. Her salary was £90 per week. He was making £120. To put it mildly, she was infuriated, and that created a tense atmosphere on the set towards the end of that first season. And none of us knew if Diana was going to return for another year, or if the show was going to come back at all. Adding salt to the wound, she found little support in the industry, much resentment from the press, and no encouragement at all from her costar Patrick Macnee. Patrick was a super-nice man, but never wanted to ruffle any feathers. He sought only a quiet life without any interruptions, which was his way until the end.

Fortunately, during the hiatus, Diana participated in salary negotiations that resulted in her receiving a raise to either £180 or £200 per week. So, that calmed the waters—at least for a while. But, in the long run, thank

God Diana had the guts to stand up for what she thought was right, on behalf of all working women in the entertainment industry—and working women in every industry.

With that said, the last time I saw and spoke to Diana, she told me a funny thing. During her tense pay negotiations decades before, she explained how tempted she was to ask me about *my* salary. But out of respect for me and the fact that I was in front of the camera like her, she never did. And a good thing, too, because she would have been pissed-off. I was receiving a great deal more than the cameraman.

After the run of the show, we never again saw each other or even chatted on the phone. And with tongue-in-cheek, and in jest, I can only attribute that to one thing: she was an extremely attractive woman who I taught how to fight. I made her look good and *sexy* with the moves I choreographed for her.

So, maybe she blamed *me* for making her a sex symbol?

But in all seriousness and truth, as far as I'm concerned, I'm nothing but overjoyed and honored that she was in my life. I liked her very much and will always have pleasant and fond memories of her. During our years working together, through all that transpired, she and I remained buddies: true, good friends.

We held many wonderful conversations and would spend a great deal of time alone, especially working out and discussing the fight sequences as they were presented in the scripts by Brian Clemens and the other writers of the show. All the writers were instructed to pay special attention to describing the fight sequences in detail, to make them as sexy and tantalizing as possible, with every possible emphasis or innuendo. "Emma's arms are forced back behind her"; "Emma is dragged back across the leather sofa as her nails scrape along the leather"; and so forth.

This, too, had been my briefing, but Diana and I went on in our usual way and I choreographed some terrific fight scenes that to this day are enjoyed by the fans.

In addition to playing Mrs. Emma Peel, Diana experienced other fascinating moments behind and in front of the camera and the curtains of the live theatre she so very much adored. Herbie J Pilato explores those experiences in *One Tough Dame: The Life and Career of Diana Rigg*, an honest, in-depth, compelling, and straightforward chronicle of one of the most remarkable, courageous, and talented women I was ever privileged to know and work with—and who ever lived.

PREFACE

"I HOPE THERE'S A TINGE OF DISGRACE ABOUT ME. HOPEFULLY, THERE'S one good scandal left in me yet." So noted Dame Diana Rigg with her sometimes caustic but always funny and charming no-nonsense view on life. She said things like that all the time, for shock value, or just because she could. Even if she denied the intention. Rigg frequently used four-letter words in public, once suggesting it was her Yorkshire upbringing that inspired her to call "a spade a spade." As she told the BBC-TV's Mary Parkinson, "The fact that people find it shocking is because they have probably called a 'spade' a 'shovel.'" Or as she much later told CBS News correspondent Anthony Mason, "I came from a Yorkshire family, and compliments were never given. Their way of loving you was telling you what was wrong with you."

An outsider at every stage of her demonstrative life and career, Rigg rarely played by the rules. She was best known as the leather-clad supersleuth Mrs. Emma Peel in ABC's 1960s-era British import *The Avengers*, and for her Emmy-winning role as the sharp-tongued matriarch Olenna Tyrell in HBO's *Game of Thrones* (2013–2019), she stood out and remained firm on her convictions with regard to artistic venues, practical matters, and social causes. She shook the status quo and dropped jaws with a blunt delivery of lines that blurred reality and performance.

Scripted or otherwise, the actress owned each of her moments, and hardly suffered fools gladly. Her tough exterior armored the softer side of a complex but dynamic and engaging personality that kept those about her at bay and on their toes. Like the best of jazz, you never knew what note she was going to hit, and it was always a surprise. She bemoaned not making more feature films and was open to expanding her TV and stage wheelhouse. For her, "being doomed to the classics" was as limiting as being stuck for a lifetime in a TV series. She celebrated *Game of Thrones* but rejected signing photos of *The Avengers*. As she told the *New York Times* in the 1970s, "It would have been death to have been labeled forever by that one TV series."

A subsequent fashion icon by way of Mrs. Peel, Rigg unwittingly utilized that role as a trailblazer for gender economic equality, and other inclusive rights. She was a trumpeter for humanity in ways that could never have imagined. Though hesitant to share her political views, Dame Diana held liberal leanings. She supported Barack Obama, protested the war in Iraq, and was entranced but then felt duped by Labor prime minister Tony Blair: "Did he seduce me? Yes. He courted my profession. But now I disavow [him]." She called Blair's replacement, Gordon Brown, "the understudy who got the role but didn't understand it."

In a BBC-TV *Newsnight* interview with Steven Smith in 2019, on International Women's Day, Rigg addressed why filmmakers prefer British actors of her ilk: "We're very undemanding. We turn up and know our lines. We don't ask for too much money and we certainly don't want caviar and champagne in our caravans." She rarely requested or required exuberant paydays but was sure the amount was fair and equal with any male counterpart or co-worker.

That standard began on the imbalanced set of *The Avengers* alongside Patrick Macnee during a tumultuous decade upon learning she made less than a cameraman. As she told Smith, "I was a lone voice in the wilderness. Nobody backed me up. Pat Macnee kept his head well below the parapet when I stepped forward and said, 'I think it's quite wrong that I'm getting less than the cameraman.' And, of course, I was painted as this sort of mercenary woman and hard-headed, you know . . . money-grabbing and all the rest of it. But it struck me as being unfair. So, I spoke out. I've always said that I thought equal pay gets you a long way to being treated equally by a man."

In another interview from 2015, this time with the *Daily Mail*, Rigg stated, "I don't understand women getting angry about men opening doors for them, but obviously I'm a feminist if feminism is about economic equality. You have to have the same power to lead the life you want as a man does and that means earning the same amount of money. We still have a battle on our hands with that."

According to Rigg, by then strides had been made for women in the workforce, although "the sleazier side of things was horrible." In the 1960s, there was "more of that around. Hands on your knees, that sort of thing. I was propositioned lots of times. I was extremely good-looking in those days. I don't think I am anymore."

With an unwavering badge of courage, a preordained Dame Diana was at the unforeseeable but inevitable forefront of the #MeToo movement. Assaulted early in her career by a "very powerful" director, she "simply acknowledged it was happening. Scorn is quite a powerful tool. And I would urge women to use scorn whenever possible, because it sort of scorches the gentlemen."

Though never permanently bitter or burned by romance, Rigg held a torch for at least three men in her life. And one of those relationships resulted in the light of her life: daughter Rachael Stirling, a respected actress in her own right.

To care for Rachael, Diana took a hiatus, but then returned to acting, as she always did. Though passionate about her craft, she was also compassionate, and strong-willed behind the scenes, with a near-diabolical dash of humor on the side. Unwilling to easily compromise, be reckoned with, or beckoned to, Rigg called the shots before, during, and after *The Avengers* with a full life and career. She was witty, spry, talented, smart, fierce, and remained current with every generation. Like TV's Laura Petrie, as played by Mary Tyler Moore on *The Dick Van Dyke Show*, Rigg's signature character Emma Peel was a slacks-wearing female pioneer. Diana *wore the pants in the family*, literally and figuratively, on and off set—even if that meant being asked to leave a hotel restaurant for a dress code violation.

Though she eventually made her mark in the global pop culture, during the immediate post-*Avengers* years, Rigg was not fully appreciated by mainstream America. As she noted to Anthony Mason, she guarded her private life. "I've just got stuff I don't want to talk about, it's very simple." But was the first to fight for a public cause. She played the acting game by her rules, and earned the veneration of peers, critics, and millions of fans.

Before Léa Seydoux would play Mrs. James Bond (opposite Daniel Craig in 2021's *No Time to Die*), Rigg was the first actress to do so, opposite George Lazenby in the 1969 feature *On Her Majesty's Secret Service*. Though this was Lazenby's sole performance as the iconic superspy, it was Rigg's portrayal of Countess Teresa di Vincenzo that captured the attention of moviegoers.

A Shakespearean-trained artist, Rigg's career culminated with a stunning portrayal of a cunning and troubled character: Miss Collins, in director Edgar Wright's enigmatic film *Last Night in Soho* (which premiered one year after her demise). Set in London of the mid-1960s, *Soho* would have been a lesser movie without her presence. She enjoyed playing protagonists like Mrs. Bond and Mrs. Peel, but preferred antagonistic roles like Ms. Tyrell and Miss Collins. From Rigg's perspective, those characters were no less heroic in their challenge and interpretation.

In like manner, and for the reader's benefit, this book covers the full spectrum of Diana's life and career. This chronicle combines insight from rare archived interviews she granted (on video, via the University of Kent and Oxford Union conversations, and several print discussions), applicable recollections culled from various media outlets through the decades, all-new, never-before-published recollections from those who knew her best, and fresh perspectives from several leading entertainment historians and sources.

With exclusive commentary from those like Rupert Macnee and Ray Austin, actors Samuel West, Bernie Kopell, Barbara Barrie, Juliet Mills, John Schuck, Damon Evans, and director Bruce Beresford, and director/producer and James Bond documentarian David Naylor, *One Tough Dame: The Life and Career of Diana Rigg* delivers an in-depth perspective of the beloved, brave, brilliant (by American and British standards and definitions), and no-holds-barred thespian of the highest degree.

PART ONE

BEFORE

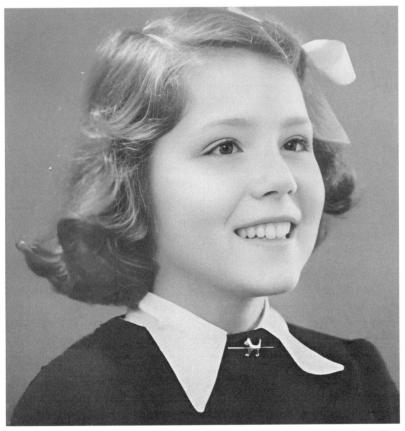

Diana in her starry-eyed youth. Courtesy Classic TV Preservation Society (CTVPS).

CHAPTER 1

RIGGED

If you have a good inner life, you don't get lonely.
I've got a good imagination.

—DIANA RIGG

WHEN DIANA RIGG WAS "SMALL AND PUT TO BED IN THE AFTERNOON," there were "yellow curtains blowing in the breeze and lit by sunshine." As she once told *The Guardian*, that was her first memory of life, a life that stemmed from an eclectic family.

Louis Rigg, a pale, skinny Yorkshire lad of twenty-one, decided to follow in his father's footsteps and become a railway engineer. Arthur Rigg invested almost six months of wages to make certain his son would receive a top-level apprenticeship with Nigel Gresley, the designer of the *Flying Scotsman*, an express passenger train. After studying at the Institute of Mechanical Engineers, Louis passed the requisite examination on December 11, 1924, and graduated. Two years earlier, the British government had decreased the number of railway franchises from 122 to only four. Louis, seeking employment elsewhere, responded to an advertisement in the *Times* calling for railway engineers to work in India. On December 18, with an engineering apprentice scholarship with the title of Assistant Locomotive Superintendent, Louis boarded the RMS *Maloja* in London, bound for Sydney. He gave colonial India as his intended future permanent residence.

By 1929, Louis decided it was time to marry. Granted six months leave, he returned to his homeland to find a wife. At a local Doncaster tennis club, Louis met and instantly fell in love with twenty-one-year-old Beryl Hilda Helliwell (born February 24, 1909), daughter of master tailor Percy of Hebden Bridge, Yorkshire, and Annie Helliwell, of Triangle, Yorkshire. Though engaged almost immediately, it took Louis nearly three years to convince Beryl to make the six-week voyage to India. Finally, on October 7,

1932, Beryl, now twenty-three, boarded the RSM *Strathaver* as a first-class passenger from London, with Bombay, India, as her destination.

Louis and Beryl were married on October 28 in Bombay Cathedral, and lived in a sprawling, one-story bungalow at Bikaner, in Rajasthan, on India's west border. Two years later, their son Hugh William Rigg arrived during a hot, traumatic stay at an Indian military hospital.

In 1938, Beryl became pregnant again but, this time, while Louis remained in India, she insisted upon giving birth in England. Enid Diana Elizabeth (registered as Enid D. E. Rigg) was born that year on July 20 in what was then in the West Riding of Yorkshire of Doncaster (now in South Yorkshire). Doncaster rests at the core of the industrial North of England, on the East Coast railway that links London with Edinburg.[1]

On September 24, Beryl, twenty-nine; Hugh, four; and two-month-old Enid boarded the SS *Narkunda* from London back to Bombay. On May 31, 1939, the Riggs then sailed the *Cilicia* from the Karachi port to Liverpool, where they remained for a short time. Under the column, "Permanent Residence," the ship's passenger list read: "Other part of the British Empire."

Diana considered her time in India as an adventure, with some frights for her mother who shrieked whenever anyone journeyed outdoors without their topee.[2] Snakes and other varmints ran rampant, particularly in the bathrooms. In one serpent's nest, even snake eggs were in full view. But through it all, Diana's parents were revered by the locals, some of whom were taught the waltz and foxtrot by Beryl. Tall and trim like her father, if tomboy-tough from the outset, Diana was graceful and loved to dance. Her mother would read to her and her brother by the fireplace. Louis would flop down in his favorite chair at night, and a servant would bring him a whiskey and soda. Doncaster had provided the patriarch with a career in engineering. His wife circulated in high social standings. Diana and Louis enjoyed an intrepid, privileged, intellectual, and open-minded, if rigid, upbringing.

When the Riggs moved to Leeds, Diana attended a Moravian school just outside of town. The almost Quaker mindset of the school proved too draconian for the girl's tastes. She rebelled against what she called "mindless" disciplines, like having to walk on the left side of the corridor, keeping her tunic three inches below the knees, making sure that her hair only touched certain portions of her blouse, and remaining silent at specific intervals. "Communication between teacher and pupil was practically nonexistent," Diana told Trevor Fishlock of *The Guardian*. Professors were the "establishment," students were "considered something pretty lumpish and stupid," and sincere, noble bonds, or one-on-one connections between student and teacher were not allowed. As a result, Rigg found it difficult to treat her teachers with "the degree of respect that they demanded . . . simply because they were the teachers."

In the school of life, she relied more on the roots of her heritage. Diana absorbed a seemingly eternal connection between India and Britain, with no animosity to the monarchy that reigned for two hundred years. Some came to rule but many were like her father, resulting in a mutually gracious bond between two different cultures. Diana's father lived a life of service. As Maharana of Udaipur, owner of the Gajner Palace India, once observed (to Trevor Fishlock of the *Telegraph*), "He was a boss but not a ruler."

The Rigg family resided close to the train stations that kept Louis employed and served everyone from the homeless to the British upper class. Though Diana once referred to her servant-laden upbringing as very British Raj, in terms of the Raj hierarchy, her father was not classified as being in the upper tier. But his eventual promotions did allow him and his charmed brood to attend elegant banquets. Diana recalled the aroma of exotic foods and train stations. "This was Dad's kingdom," she said. "He loved it so much."

Though her father was not born into money, Diana said her parents led happy, opulent lives, with his career on the rails ultimately resulting in a leap in status. Beryl learned swiftly the ways to supervise a home with servants and adjust to the social conventions of the Rai, which were stern, merciless, and unsympathetic. Diana's father was an excellent shot, golfer, tennis and squash player, all of which also contributed to his welcome into the realm of the upper class. It didn't hurt that he also happened to be witty, handsome, charming, and at times, down to earth. For one thing, he liked to fish, an activity Diana herself took on as an adult. "I'm quite good at seeking out the gentlemen fish . . . the one that isn't actually sitting up and begging to be caught," she recalled.

But back in time, the Riggs captured their summers in Nainital, also known as the Lake District of the Himalayan foothills, where Diana and Hugh ran free. "We disappeared every day, though we came back for lunch," she recalled. She would suck on the toffee her mother made and read Jim Corbett's *Maneaters of Kumaon*, with rain drops blistering on the roof. She'd listen intently as her father recited passages from Kipling's *Just So Stories* and Tolkien's *The Hobbit*. "India gave me a glorious start to life," she said, "an independence of spirit."

In their bungalow, Diana and Hugh were cared for by a nanny, or ayah, who taught them Hindi. The ayah would tell Diana, "*Aap bahut hi badmash ladki hain*'," which translated means, "You're a very bad girl." Her mother thought Diana sounded too much like an Indian and tried to keep things British by serving her children the closest thing to English food fit for a king and queen. Diana thought most of it, packaged in tins, was disgusting, although the sardine kedgeree was delicious.

Although Diana dearly loved her family, there were times that she felt somewhat disconnected from them. Her father may have taught her how to fry those fish they caught, but he was also aloof and distant. She perceived her parents as Edwardian and saw little of them beyond the summer months. She spent more time with her nanny and reading alone.

World War II ended in 1945, and Tupperware and Slinky toys were beloved by housewives and children in America. But the erudite Diana, unfamiliar with the simple pleasures of life, became despondent and, at just eight years old, was sent back to England for boarding school. India may have had its colonial ways doused for good, leaving Diana adrift and worse for the wear. She felt abandoned by her new school and her young parents. It was not their intention to be cruel, but they were. "It was a matter of convenience," she later recalled to the *Sunday Times*. "They thought they were doing the right thing."

With the first, nonstop around-the-world airline flight only two years in the future, and Diana's parents three weeks away by boat, and unreachable by phone, she knew no one and therefore started from scratch. To make matters worse, the weather was bleak and frigid, and she was diagnosed with an earache and lice. "With an experience like that your life changes," she said. "There is a sense of rejection, and you have to take care of yourself. You are never reliant on your parents again."[3]

Diana Rigg was always a bit of a ham, but she was never an exhibitionist. She may have been an introvert, but she pushed herself to try new things. She made her acting debut as a "lumpish eleven-year-old" in a stage production of *Goldilocks and the Three Bears*. "I happened to be a very *big* Goldilocks . . . but [I] took the role very seriously," she said. So seriously, in fact, that her parents began to worry. In the large United Kingdom city of Leeds, her West Yorkshire hometown, a female thespian was branded a scarlet woman, automatically promiscuous, suspect socially, and even stupid. She imagined her parents' dilemma of having given birth to a child who suddenly wanted to be an actress: "It's rather bewildering and puzzling for them. They can't help you. Parents really want to be able to help their children. They couldn't help me; I had to help myself."[4]

Actor Samuel West came to know Diana through her early work and by way of his parents, actors Timothy West and Prunella Scales, who were friends with Rigg. He would also work with Diana a few times through the years. As he observed, "Diana is part of that extraordinary generation of people who weren't from posh backgrounds. She wasn't particularly poor, I don't think. She was from Doncaster. We still have, in some cases, an extraordinary group of people who, postwar, in Britain, kind of redefined the class issues without necessarily being really posh themselves."

CHAPTER 2

FIRST SIGNS OF ROYALTY

I never relied on my beauty for anything.
—DIANA RIGG

DIANA RIGG WAS A PRODUCT OF DELIGHTFUL COMPLEXITIES. FROM A THE-
atrical standpoint, those came in handy in class, where she was easily bored
and often caught daydreaming. She was unimpressed by the strict guid-
ance and distant personalities of boarding school. However, at least one
visionary theatrical instructor proved inspiring: Silvia Greenwood. As she
told the *Appleton Post Crescent* on February 9, 1969: "Mrs. Greenwood was a
brilliant dramatic coach with a great capacity for engendering enthusiasm
for the stage among her pupils. I owe everything to her."

Indeed, Greenwood proved to be an indelible force in young Diana's
life and foray into theater. It was she who introduced the girl to poetry,
which Diana called "the magic of words." As she became more comfortable with reciting poetry in public, Greenwood suggested that the young
thespian audition for the Royal Academy of Dramatic Arts (RADA). But
she needed to make the request in writing, which was then the standard
for initial communication.

Diana followed suit, was accepted into the prestigious school at just
seventeen, but later regretted the decision. She lamented not selecting a
traditional university education. "I am terribly conscious of great morass
in my knowledge. Great gaps."[1] In her eyes, not continuing with a more
formal higher education created a barrier to her learning French, a favorite
language, which she did not fully embrace until much later. Though eventually conquering her incapacity for retention of what she read, Diana also
believed early academic shortcomings compromised that process. She
eventually caught up as best she could but thought it all a bit late.

Thus was the proverbial fork in the road. Before she contacted RADA,
Rigg was engaged. Her father insisted she choose between marriage or

dramatic academia. She opted for the latter. But he couldn't afford the tuition, and that's when she composed that letter to the Leeds Council, which, in those days, granted scholarships. As she later revealed to Gavin Esler at the University of Kent, "I went to the town hall . . . walked through [what seemed like] miles, of . . . flooring to a table at the far end with a lot of very serious old men who said, 'What makes you think you could be an actress then?'"[2]

"I don't know," she recalled thinking. "I must have found the words, because they found the money and thank God to them."[3]

During this time, Diana found cigarettes, which she began inhaling upwards of a pack a day. As she once noted, "I do a lot of wrong things: I smoke, and . . . drink wine." In the same breath, she joked, "People might be horrified at my eating habits. I eat when I'm hungry, and if I'm not, I don't."[4] Although her smoking habit ultimately contributed to her demise, it was, at present, beginning to add gravel to a deepening voice and artistic approach. As she later expressed to Esler, she had wanted to act from the time she was thirteen. She had a goal, a purpose, which, she believed, many actors of a later generation lacked. All she could do was wish those souls the best of luck.

Assuredly, fortune was on her side as training with RADA began in 1955. In July 1957, as part of the York Festival, Rigg made her professional stage debut at age nineteen as Natasha Abashwilli in the Academy's production of Bertolt Brecht's *The Caucasian Chalk Circle*.

But there was an issue. Rigg later told journalist Jay Sharbutt of the Associated Press that she had "spent opening night in a hospital, a victim of shingles, a virus infection." Fortunately, as Sharbutt noted, Rigg exhibited the "solid confidence of one for whom total disaster is a temporary disturbance, survived the shingles, likewise the hospital."

As such, Rigg made her stage debut a mere one year later in *The Passing of the Third Floor Back*, which she described as "an allegorical tale of Christ—who visits a rooming house. It was a creaky old play. I did it in repertory."

Between March and May 1958, she served as an assistant stage manager for the Chesterfield Repertory Company. The following summer, while in repertory at Scarborough, she was cast as Vivian in Jerome K. Jerome's *The Passing of the Third Floor Back*.

Rigg admitted to Esler that she never had "a huge amount of ambition." That may have sounded silly coming from someone so accomplished, but she never thought, "Oh, I've got to get there!" For Rigg, it was all about appreciation, which was once clarified by a lifelong friend who told her,

"*Not* ambitious. You've always been *grateful.*" Years later, she affirmed as much to Esler. "I have been. I'm grateful for the joy of the profession that I found myself in . . . for all the . . . jobs that happened along the way, starting with Rep in Scarborough."[5]

Diana was eager to share her own experience as an actress with aspiring thespians, but only if they asked. She insisted that the only path to career longevity was through proper lifelong training: learning breath control, studying voice, elocution, and projection: "You have to work on yourself all the time," she said, encouraging others to learn and keep learning, "experimenting and throwing yourself into whatever came next."[6]

After graduating RADA in 1957, Diana became an understudy for the Shakespeare Memorial Theatre Company in Stratford-upon-Avon in 1959. In 1960, the Tyrone Guthrie- and Peter Hall-led company transitioned into the Royal Shakespeare Company (RSC). She signed a five-year contract with this troupe, which included, among others, Paul Scofield, Ian Holm, Judi Dench, Dame Edith Evans, Ian Richardson, and Laurence Olivier. (Olivier, incidentally, would later call Diana "a brilliantly skilled and delicious actress.")[7] She began with a walk-on part as a spear carrier and soon graduated to more prominent roles.

According to Ray Austin, Rigg's future director/stunt coordinator on *The Avengers*, the RSC "was either a downfall or an *upfall* in Diana's career, depending on which way you look at it."[8] But Rigg viewed her five years with the company as an opportunity to express herself; to learn and hone her craft in a safe, yet challenging, environment.

Prior to her arrival at Stratford, Diana's repertory in Chesterfield began with a stage manager apprenticeship. In a later interview with the *Oxford Union*, she described the experience as "deep" and "incredibly valuable."[9] But that position could also prove challenging at times, especially if she was prompting actors backstage. For example, while awaiting her cue to appear in a play, a stagehand would grab the prompt book from her hands. All the behind-the-scenes signals, including the lighting cues of amber (which translates as "stand by") or red (for "go," as in "performance in process," or "in sessions"), were inscribed in the prompt book that she was no longer holding. Behind her was something called a Brunswick Panatrope Phonograph, which supplied whatever sound effects were needed, such as cars arriving or leaving, or entrance and exit music. As a trained professional, she had been familiarized with the Panatrope as part of her apprenticeship. Rigg likened it to latter-day technology used in Broadway productions, including headphones, walkie-talkies, and glinting lights, all of which allow the crew to instantaneously communicate not only with the actors on stage but the entire production team throughout the theater.

Rigg once relayed her archaic stage-managing experience to a modern tech team and, as she recalled, "They simply could not believe it. That at one stage, as a nineteen-year-old, I was doing what they were doing, and I was in fact in charge of the production."[10] She occasionally reflected "with great pleasure" on several such moments in her early life and stage career. One faux pas she shared during a question-and-answer session at the Oxford Union occurred during a performance of an Agatha Christie play: "I was supposed to play on the Panatrope, as the curtain came down on the first act, 'The Ride of the Valkyries,' and I'd got the wrong record on the turntable, and it turned out to be 'Jimmy Shand and his Dancing Dustmen.'"[11]

Despite such snafus, Diana felt fully prepared for her eventual Stratford theatre experience, following what became her one year of repertory with Chesterfield. "I was incredibly lucky," she said, because it was the last year for director Glen Byam Shaw. He decided to go out with a bang . . . inviting a huge and stellar cast of people."[12] Her initial performances included productions like *All's Well That Ends Well* and *Othello*, the latter with Paul Robeson in the lead. "I was not even playing small parts," she said. "I was simply a walk-on in all these productions, and what a privilege that was."

In addition to Robeson, the *Othello* cast included Mary Ure (then wed to future film star Robert Shaw of *From Russia with Love* and *Jaws*), Sam Wanamaker as Iago, Albert Finney, and Peter O'Toole. "Listening to that text with Paul Robeson's absolutely astonishing voice was amazing," Rigg said.[13] The second production was *A Midsummer Night's Dream* with the legendary Charles Laughton portraying Bottom. Rigg played Helena, one of the mortals entranced by the pixie Puck while wandering the woods. The third production, *Coriolanus*, featured Laurence Olivier, Dame Edith Evans as Valumnio, and Vanessa Redgrave in a minor part.

"If you can imagine," Rigg observed, "that was how I learnt . . . by watching and listening [to such icons]. And I couldn't have had better teachers because each night you'd note a subtle difference in the performance and different inflection. And each night you were hearing consummate actors dealing with verse, and the way they dealt with it, the way they turned it to their personal use. Still observing the verse but making it entirely personal within the character was a very profound early lesson for me."[14]

But it was working with the legendary Laurence Olivier that remained one of her most cherished memories: "He was so glamorous. I mean, my

God . . . he had a quick-change room off the stage, where he had the big-gest bottle of Mitsuko perfume in it you have ever seen. And we used to walk past it and go, 'That's two years' wages . . . in liquid.'"

One evening, Rigg was behind the scenes watching Olivier enact a sword fight that had gone terribly wrong. "I was standing with my friend Mabel, both of us deeply humbled, dressed in rags. And he threw the sword into the corner and then he saw Mabel and I standing there, and he [said], 'Oh, ladies,' a very rude word followed, 'forgive me.' And, my friend Mabel, who was madly in love with him, said, 'Shit, I don't care.'"[15]

Rigg continued: "What happened, later at Stratford, was that after Glenn Byam Shaw left, Peter Hall stepped in. He was young, extraordi-narily passionate, and he instigated lessons in verse speaking, lessons in movement, lessons in singing, and he actually nurtured young talent. Something which has never been done subsequently, alas, and something that I benefited from immeasurably."[16]

Such theatrical troupes "don't exist anymore," she said. "It's shifting, and they don't take people on and train them up, allow them to fail. I have to say, I have failed many times in my profession. And I'm being perfectly honest . . . when I [say] that I learnt more from within my failures than I ever learnt from my successes. . . . Actors in those days, were given the license to fail and I think that has now disappeared.[17]

She viewed her success as a fine mixture of stage academics and grati-tude. She treasured her classical training and the desire to learn and keep learning, and experimenting and throwing yourself into whatever came next. She was always grateful for whatever part she was offered and, as she said, if in particular, "it expanded me in a way, anyway, I would embrace it. Because there is simply no point in standing still. In whatever you do, you have to keep moving and learning."[18]

Diana Rigg paid her dues, and she frowned upon artistic complainers, no matter their economic level. As she told Esler, "It's rubbish. I do hate it when actors moan. . . . They say, 'Oh, all the Toffs are getting the parts.' Well, no, it's not true. I mean, I've been around a very long time, and I remember when . . . the Toffs were the last people to get the parts. In the early sixties it was . . . people who spoke with [a British] accent. So, its cyclical."[19]

During her RADA days, Diana worked at a coffee shop located near Cambridge Circus called Hanway Street, which was frequented by many Greek sailors. "There were a lot of tarts around" who tripped her while serving tables. She worked "from half past five until half past eleven," and then she'd catch the last underground train home to Clapham South. It was "not a glamour life."[20]

But she would not have changed a thing. It was as if she knew all the while that her struggles were preparing her for something more—not just with her acting career, but as a mentor for aspiring actors. She would never discourage those who chose a similar path, or who would seek to follow in her footsteps. Diana embraced the opportunity to inspire, because she cherished her own mentors. In the process, she encouraged actors to patronize the theaters they hoped to perform in. "Buy as many cheap seats as you can, and go and see . . . performances," she suggested. "Because *I* did that when I was a student and certain performances are engraved."[21]

To enhance the experience, Diana also encouraged aspirants to "read as much as possible. I don't necessarily mean plays. I mean *read*." As in "some good literature . . . found and shared in book groups and clubs." In her youth, she would find the time, one way or the other, to gather with fellow aspirants for group readings to discuss plays, or as she said, "to keep those juices flowing."[22]

Diana understood that steady acting jobs and worthy parts were few and far between. Her upbringing was far from ordinary, but her career path was not any smoother because of it. She still grieved about and empathized with aspiring actors mostly due to her early artistic struggles. "Unless the young have a strong foothold in the truest part of theater . . . they're going to be so bemused," she said,[23] and find themselves lost and astray. She encouraged actors at all levels and ages to form group discussions, and recommended theater clubs in London that provided space for such forums, among them Arts Theater and the Actors Centre, which she described as "terribly important."[24]

"Go there," she said. "Never lose sight of [the physical body] being your instrument. You've got to play on it as often as a pianist would play on a piano. You've *got* to."[25]

As she later explained at Oxford University, Rigg also encouraged actors to join touring companies like she did, pre-*The Avengers*, with the Royal Shakespeare Company. She traveled with the RSC behind the Iron Curtain in the 1960s. For her, Russia, specifically Moscow and Leningrad, proved to be the most intriguing places to perform. And though the experience was "a nightmare," she even performed at the Lens Soviet Palace of Culture, which had the capacity for a large audience. "There were little ladies in booths in the front doing simultaneous translation. And you can imagine simultaneous translation spreading over two thousand people and the playback was listening to budgerigars literally."[26]

But performing in Moscow still proved fascinating for her, mostly because the RSC was the first Western company to remain there for a lengthy period. It was also thrilling because, as part of the performance, students would hide themselves throughout the theater, ducking in dressing rooms or any accessible area they could find. Some found themselves in the gantries, unable to see and only hear performances. But as Rigg said, "They were so hungry for the theatre," and the benefits were widespread. Case in point: Diana recalled meeting Madam Fretsiba, the minister of culture, who became another mentor of sorts. "She was extraordinary."[27]

Art galleries, for better or worse, also played a role in Rigg's early training. She'd frequent museums that showcased paintings selected by the Central Committee, with eight copies, each rendering placed under the original. Upon seeing those, Diana thought to herself, *Where's the creativity? Gone?*

During this same period, she also met Khrushchev, whom she and fellow students viewed as "this very imposing gentlemen." For their performance of *The Comedy of Errors*, Khrushchev visited the cast backstage and seemed perplexed. "I think he must have been very confused by it," recalled Diana, who thought he "didn't have much of a sense of humor, anyway."[28]

Playing the courtesan in that production of *The Comedy of Errors* was Elizabeth Spriggs, whom Diana remembered as "a wonderful actress," with a "very revealing" costume. "She had very generous breasts and Khrushchev was absolutely fascinated by [them]," apparently accented at times by a bowl of sweets on a table nearby. "And the Russian sweeties are big, you know . . . Quality Street," Rigg said. "They're big Quality Street sweeties. And . . . [Khrushchev] kept on putting these sweeties down [Spriggs's] cleavage."[29]

• • •

Actor-turned-author Margaret Drabble was Diana's understudy at the RSC. As Drabble recalled to *The Guardian* in 2020, Rigg went on to stardom after a "lucky break in *The Comedy of Errors* in 1962." For Drabble, Diana's role as Adriana revealed "a fine Shakespearean actress and a fine comedian . . . and the stunningly sexy costumes by Anthony Powell hinted at other possibilities ahead."

Drabble mentioned her discontent with the word "sexy," and said she had never used it before, but then added, "For once there is no option." She also understudied for Diana's Cordelia in Peter Brook's *King Lear*, adding that she sat in either the auditorium or a dressing room every night of the run. "Never did I tire of watching this astonishingly powerful production," Drabble explained. "Diana was splendid and her wicked sisters, Irene Worth, and Patience Collier were equally memorable. I can hear them all now. The last scene, where Paul Scofield as Lear mourned his daughter, was almost unbearably moving. Diana was quite tall, but Scofield carried her dead body unflinchingly, as I recall, and without too many irreverent jokes."

The entire cast, including the understudies, traveled to Paris when the play was on tour and witnessed Rigg being embraced backstage by an effusive Marlene Dietrich. "These were days of high glamour," Drabble noted. It was her first time on a plane, and traveling with the RSC troupe was "a heady experience."

"Diana's demeanor in real life was most unlike Cordelia's," Drabble said. "And her vocabulary was racy and rich." She copped to inserting one of Rigg's more colorful remarks about a fellow actress in a novel. Even though her "squeamish [male] editor" begged her to remove the passage Drabble believed she left it in. "But," she said, "I wouldn't know where to look for it.

"Like her colleague Judi Dench," Drabble explained, Diana "knew how to make people laugh, and she was good company." Drabble had understudied Dench as Titania in director Peter Hall's 1962 production of *A Midsummer Night's Dream*, in which Diana played Helena. That was a role she reprised in the 1968 adaptation with Helen Mirren as Hermia. "Again," Drabble said, "it was a magical performance, in which Diana's height was more of an asset than it had been as Cordelia. Her comic timing was faultless."

Actress Juliet Mills also performed with Rigg in Hall's live stage version of *A Midsummer Night's Dream*. In her interview for this book, Mills had similarly kind remarks to share about Diana. "She was very pretty and had beautiful red hair. She had always been a good actress, and she proved as much when I worked with her. She had that marvelous voice and a wonderful sense of [Hall]. She was very professional and passionate about the work."

Additional cast members of this *Midsummer* edition included Michael Williamson who, as Mills recalled, "was not yet Judy Dench's husband but would be"; Brian Murray, who Mills described as "a very, very good English actor"; Barry Foster; and Robert Stevens, who would later marry Maggie Smith (another of Rigg's contemporaries). "It was a glorious experience . . . because Peter Hall was directing and he was brilliant," Mills said. "He was an expert on the Bard [William Shakespeare], so to be working with him was a joy. We had a lot of fun in that production. We rehearsed for ten weeks, and in that amount of time, you get to know your fellow actors quite well by the time you open [premiere a given play].

"We toured with that production together in several cities in England," Mills continued to explain, "in repertory with another play. Diana stayed on with the company, and remained with them for quite some time, playing all sorts of classical roles. But I did not."

Like Diana, Mills would soon find fame on TV in an American series on ABC. But whereas Ms. Rigg would become the mortal (but near-superpowered) Mrs. Peel opposite Patrick Macnee on *The Avengers*, Mills would be cast as the magical lead opposite the mortal-playing Richard Long in the supernatural sitcom, *Nanny and the Professor*. That show would ultimately air on the then-called "Alphabet Network" from 1969 to 1971. Mills did continue to perform on the London stage after working with Diana in *A Midsummer's Night Dream*. But then she filmed the pilot for *Nanny and the Professor*, which received the green light for a weekly series. "So, at that point," Mills intoned, "I left England, and never really went back to live there. I would travel therefore work, but that would be it. That's where my life and Diana's separated."

Although Mills would "hardly see Diana again over the next thirty or forty years," there would be significant times when the two famed stars would cross paths. "I'd sometime see her at an event here and there and we'd have a quick word," Mills said. "I and other actors like the great Charles Dance [with whom Diana would later perform more than a few times] and Nigel Hawthorn had appeared in a play, *The Heiress*, that was produced by her first husband, Archie Stirling. But that was pretty much it."

CHAPTER 3

GREAT EXPECTATIONS

I was very young . . . practically untouched by human hands.

—DIANA RIGG

THE UNCONFIDENT HELENA OF SHAKESPEARE'S *A MIDSUMMER'S NIGHT Dream* was quite opposite to the bold nature of Katherine, the leading character in the Bard's *The Taming of the Shew*, which seemed a better fit for Diana Rigg's sensibility in real life. And she would have *killed it* in the role. But early in her career, in the fall of 1961, she was instead cast as Bianca, younger sister to Katherine, who was played by Vanessa Redgrave in the same production. As Redgrave's understudy, Diana refused to show any jealousy concerning the casting. As she told Gavin Esler, "It was a wonderful production. It really was such fun." No doubt. *Shrew* is a rambunctious comedy about the courtship between Katherine and Petruchio, who misbehaves toward the object of his affection. Although "he treats her badly," Diana observed, *Shrew* is "really about two people finding each other and eventually falling in love."[1]

Diana's *Taming* was staged by Maurice Daniels at the Aldwych Theatre in London. According to the October 4, 1961, issue of *Variety* (for a September 14th performance), Daniels, unique approach to the play "with gusto" was, at times, excessive. The trade paper noted, "There is too much broad slapstick . . . and knockout business with actors falling down, endlessly hitting each other, guffawing and prancing around."

The young actress later found herself cast in British television renditions of such classic plays as Jean Giraudoux's *Ondine*. The original Broadway production of the show had featured Audrey Hepburn, who won the Tony for Best Actress in a Play. That version opened February 18, 1954, at the Forty-sixth Street Theatre in New York City and ran for 157 performances. The Bristol Old Vic then hosted the British premiere on October 18, 1955 (which ran for a limited three weeks). But the original West End/BBC production with Diana opened January 12, 1961, at the Aldwych Theatre in London. Written by Maurice Valency and directed by Peter Hall, this adaptation, along with several other RSC TV productions, were grouped together under the title *Theatre Night*. In *Ondine*, Diana played Violanta, a silent mermaid, opposite Leslie Caron in the lead. Others in the cast included Patrick Allen, Mavis Edwards, Richard Johnson, Wendy Gifford, Derek Godfrey, Yvonne Bonnamy, Roy Dotrice, and Ian Holm. The music was composed by Raymond Leppard, with sets and costumes designed by Tanya Moiseiwitsch.

Ondine, Diana explained, is the story of "a mermaid who comes up out of the sea, falls in love with the prince, takes human form, but, in the end, tragedy of tragedies, she has to go back into the sea again. Not if it's Leslie Caron playing Ondine. No tragedy there, believe you me. Anyway, I'm being rude."[2]

But she was brutally honest. Caron was then married to the director, which, according to Diana, "was the only reason she was in [the play]."[3] Meanwhile, the wardrobe was one of two main reasons the experience was less than enthralling for Diana. The other was because she didn't have any lines other than the countless crisscross figures on her outfit, which she described as "deeply, deeply unfortunate."[4] In brief, her dress had fins at the bottom, and zipped up the back. In front, three seashells from the seashore were strategically, if not so subtly, placed over her groin and over both breasts. She also wore a floppy hat, with more seashells, and some seaweed. This forced Diana to clomp around with her legs and feet woven together, up and down the stairs to her dressing room.

Once on stage, Rigg and Gifford, in character, were to seduce a character played by Allen, whom Diana called "wildly handsome . . . and very naughty."[5] To properly reach their characters' objective, Rigg and Gifford were perched at a balcony window, peering down to Allen, whose back was to the audience. As Diana explained, Allen "was looking at us and pulling the sort of face to say, 'Are you out of your mind?' So, of course I started laughing, and I laughed every single night [for every performance]."[6]

Eventually, Rigg was summoned to Caron's dressing room.

"Diana," the actress told her, "I hear you every night. I wanted you to know you are laughing."

To which Rigg replied, "I'm sorry, Ms. Caron. I'm really sorry. It's a weakness of mine."

"I had that weakness," Caron returned. "I cured myself. Think of something sad. Think of being fired."[7]

Caron was nothing if not blunt, which Rigg respected and, to some extent, mimicked. Even so, their bluntness did not sideline either of their careers, and certainly not Diana's.

Also, during this period, Diana performed in a TV production of *Women Beware Women*. Not one to watch herself on-screen, Diana did so with *Women* only because she was invited to a special screening at the National Theatre located in the Southbank of London, many years after the show's original airdate. As she said, the production was "rather better than I remembered."[8]

It was then May 18, 1962, when Rigg began her three-week gig at the Lincoln Center's New York State Theatre with *The Comedy of Errors* (a special command performance that she also delivered at Windsor Castle). *Errors* alternated with *King Lear*, in which she played Cordelia to Paul Scofield's Lear. ("It was a wonderful production . . . quite extraordinary," she recalled.)[9] According to how the *Appleton Post Crescent* later described it on February 9, 1969, Diana's "greatest acclaim" came for her portrayal of Cordelia opposite Scofield in *King Lear*.

As it were, both *Lear* and *Errors* were directed by Peter Brook. She claimed to enjoy working with Brook (whom she described as "a very chilly man, indeed"),[10] particularly in *Lear*, even if he proved, at times, to be a handful and distracting.

Though that would change, to some extent, with her interactions with Brook.

Before each performance, she would be in her dressing room above the stage, preparing her wardrobe. In what became a nightly routine of sorts, Brook would make the steady climb up the backstage stairs to her dressing room. Bracing for the incoming storm, Diana hurriedly applied her favorite Number 9 lipstick. Standing behind the actress and looking at her image in the lighted mirror, Brook would deliver some opinionated notes. Following this, he would tip her head up, kiss her on the mouth, and then lean forward, grab a tissue, remove the Number 9 from his lips, and make his exit. This transpired "nearly every night," she said. "Nowadays, of course, you know, he'd be sued, wouldn't he?"[11]

At the time of Brook's indiscretion, Rigg was "too young, and too frightened, and too everything" to do anything about it. But Brook was "absolutely wonderful" in the overall production of *King Lear*. "So, possibly . . . there are penalties to be paid when you're directed by . . . a very good director."[12]

The penalty was more than worth the price because, she said, "It's a cliché, I know, but my favorite play is *King Lear* . . . because it's the greatest play."[13] She had performed in three different productions of the work. The first involved a mere walk-on role alongside Charles Laughton ("That's how long ago it was!"). Next came her turn as Cordelia, opposite Paul Scofield. And third, her portrayal of Reagan to Olivier's Lear. "God, I loved it," she said.

Diana never appeared in a gender-bending edition of the play, which has been performed for centuries. That included a recent twenty-first century production of *Lear*, starring Glenda Jackson in the lead. There was also a Shakespeare Globe Theatre production of *Othello*, which cast a female as the intended male role of Casio. As Rigg never saw either production, she did not offer her opinion on the casting. She did feel comfortable, however, commenting on the basic idea of it: "We're at a stage now where all sorts of lines are being blurred, and if that's what the current audience wants, then I say, 'Go there.' I mean, why not? It either succeeds or it doesn't. And if it doesn't, then we'll move on to another form of experiment . . . I wouldn't shut the door for anything that might . . . bring in a new audience. It's all about bums on seats, isn't it?"[14]

Additionally, Diana pegged the female-geared adaptation of *Lear*, like similar versions of *Othello*, *Julius Caesar*, and the like, "a symptom of the March of Women." Uncertain if such productions were created for mere shock value or just gimmickry, Rigg refused to bring feminism into the fray. For her, interpretations of any play, TV show, or film should rest with the audience to make up their minds about it.

Then, of course, there is the current unpopularity of the term "actress," which has in recent years been replaced by the gender-neutral "actor." Rigg's response: "I just love our language. We've got the richest language in the world. And I love it to be precise, and I am an 'actress.' I ain't got balls!"[15]

One thing Diana did have was stamina. In June of 1963, she appeared in a Royal Shakespeare Company revival of *A Midnight's Summer Dream*, staged by Peter Hall at the Aldwych Theatre. According to the July 3, 1963, edition of *Variety*, which reviewed the production on June 14: "A staunch favorite with London theatergoers, *Dream* cries out for imaginative staging, and Hall has not only pulled out every ace in the pack, but added a few extra professional tricks. He makes excellent use of the large Aldwych stage, and his scene changes from the Duke's castle to the forest avoid any let up in the action."

Again, just like Diana. On November 23, 1963, she switched gears to play Francy Wilde in "A Very Desirable Plot," an episode of the television series *The Sentimental Agent*. A television drama series spinoff from *Man of the World*, this *Agent* was produced in the United Kingdom in 1963 by

Associated Television and distributed by ITC Entertainment. In her segment, Diana played opposite star Carlos Thompson (as an Argentinian import-export agent, Burt Kwouk), Clemence Bettany, and "a few shivering potted palms" in the background. That was so viewers would think the series was shot in some exotic locale. In fact, it was filmed in the borough of Runnymede, Surrey, England, less than twenty miles southwest of central London.

Others who guest-starred on *Agent* (title for which in retrospect, seems a slight foreshadow to Rigg's role on *Avengers*), included a pre-*M*A*S*H* Donald Sutherland and actor Patrick Magee (not Macnee, though that, too, in looking back, seems another irony).

Also in late 1963, premiering December 14th, to be exact, and on into 1964, Rigg portrayed Adriana (sister to Julie Christie's Luciana), in a Royale Shakespeare/UK small-screen revival of *The Comedy of Errors*, presented at Aldwych Theatre in London.

A review in *Variety* described the production as "buoyant . . . for a three-week Christmas engagement at its London headquarters." Regarding Rigg, the famed Hollywood trade observed, "Diana Rigg repeats her success as the fluttering wife who finds herself with a couple of husbands."

Minus the *fluttering* part, that assessment was somewhat of a foreshadow of Diana's future reality.

• • •

Diana's career was fast catching fire at just the right time. The Beatles were leading the British invasion in the US, and suddenly, everything with a British accent had currency.

Circa 1967, Rigg was performing a double duty. She would commute between Stratford-upon-Avon and don the requisite regalia for such RSC productions as *Twelfth Night* (as Viola), and the Borehamwood Studios, where she squeezed into leather catsuits as Mrs. Peel. It was *The Avengers* by day, theater performances by night, she told *TV Guide*. But she was on a mission. She wanted to prove that she could succeed on all levels, at any pace. "To be without money, is to be without anything," she said, even if that was "a bad comment on the world."[16]

As Rigg also once observed, she was "nourished and nurtured at Stratford as a very young actress. They guided me and forgave me!" But in her early years, she had grown weary of performing the masterpieces of theater. "The trouble with staying with a classical company . . . is that you get to be known as a 'lady actress,'" she said. "No one ever thinks of you except for parts in long skirts and blank verse."[17]

When Diana then integrated herself into television, the medium was not as significant as film, theater, or radio but, as she said, it "proved to have far greater powers than those." Suffice it to say, her first powerful TV appearance occurred in a mid-1960s production of *The Hot House*, costarring Harry Corbett, replacing the director's wife who dropped out. But by no means was it smooth sailing from there.

Diana's father Louis (top left), mother Beryl Hilda (top right), brother Hugh, and friends (bottom). Courtesy Classic TV Preservation Society (CTVPS).

All's Well That Ends Well, 1959. Photo by Angus McBean © RSC.

The Winter's Tale, 1960, the Shakespeare Memorial Theatre. Directed by Peter Wood, designed by Jacques Noel. PICTURED: Mamillius (Dennis Waterman) and attendants: 2nd Old Gentleman (Ian Richardson), 1st Old Gentleman (Roy Dotrice), 2nd Lady-in-Waiting (Maroussia Frank), 3rd Lady-in-Waiting (Diana Rigg), and Emilia (Mavis Edwards). Photo by Angus McBean © RSC.

Diana Rigg was indeed a true student of the theatre, as this image from early in her career attests. Courtesy Classic TV Preservation Society (CTVPS).

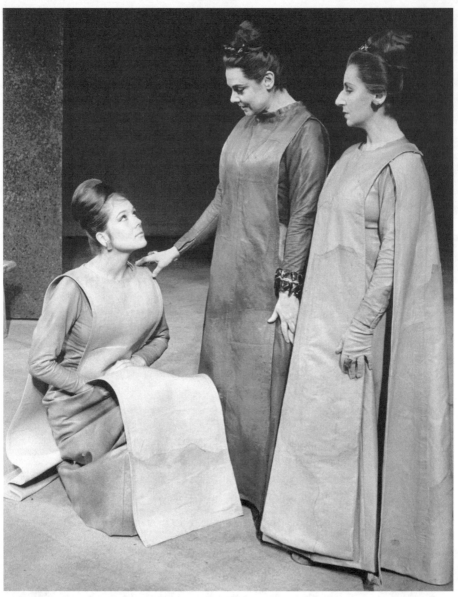

Diana Rigg (as Cordelia), Irene Worth (as Goneril), and Patience Collier (as Regan) in *King Lear*, directed by Peter Brook, 1962 at the Royal Shakespeare Theatre. Photo by Angus McBean © RSC.

Diana as Helena and Barry Macgregor as Demetrius in Royal Shakespeare Company performance of *A Midsummer Night's Dream* at the Aldwych Theatre in London, 1963. Photo by Reg Wilson © RSC.

PART TWO

DURING

Diana catapults to fame via *The Avengers*. Courtesy Classic TV Preservation Society (CTVPS).

CHAPTER 4

EMBRACING EMMA

There is always one thing that turns you into an icon,
an iconic image. In my case, a catsuit.
—DIANA RIGG

"IF SHE DOESN'T WASTE HERSELF ON SILLY STUFF, SHE COULD BE QUITE good." So noted Tony Award–winning theater and film director Peter Brook, regarding Diana's early TV career choices. Essentially, that was a back-handed comment on her portrayal of Emma Peel on *The Avengers*. But that move proved more brilliant than fluff, even if she called it "a perverse decision in a long line of perverse decisions."

Diana played Peel on what was then a relatively new medium, which gave credence to each of her early acting choices. As she once observed, "TV was regarded as something that wasn't as great as film or theater or radio. But it has proved to have far greater powers than those." She never thought the medium would boost her stage presence, but that's what hap-pened, following her exit from the Royal Shakespeare Company. When performing with the RSC, and other related stage or classics-geared TV performances, she figured prospective directors and producers perceived her as only a dowdy, serious actress. When cast as Mrs. Peel, she felt confined by second-rate film types who categorized her as merely a sexy superspy.

In 1969, Diana debated the public's perception of her dueling screen personality on earth. As she told the *New York Times*, "The twain never seem[ed] to meet. It's really absurd."[1]

Her brash statement proved ominous. Decades later, she'd perform with David Suchet at London's Almeida Theatre in Edward Albee's *Who's Afraid of Virginia Woolf?* That's a play on words, if there ever was one, eas-ily categorized in the Theatre of the Absurd. With its stylized sci-fi-like storytelling, and Rigg's steamy high-fashion garb, *The Avengers* might be considered Television of the Absurd. Brilliant, quirky, and groundbreaking, the show made its British premiere in 1962, the same year Sean Connery introduced James Bond in *Dr. No.* Four years later, ABC brought *The Avengers* to America.

In 1966, the first twenty-six episodes of the series aired in the States, with Rigg replacing original female lead Honor Blackman, opposite Patrick Macnee as John Steed. The show was sold to the US network for $2 million, with potential increases to $45 million, if optioned for more. With the largest dollar-earning TV barter for its time, fifty-one additional episodes were filmed, the last twenty-five in color (and without Rigg).

Several other pivotal, high-concept TV shows made their debut that year, including *Star Trek, That Girl, Batman, The Green Hornet, Mission: Impossible,* and *Dark Shadows.* With the exception of NBC's *Star Trek* and CBS's *Mission,* each of these, along with *The Avengers,* aired on ABC, the most youth-oriented of what were then just three networks. In one capacity or another, such programming contained some measure of the sci-fi/fantasy, action/adventure, and "girl power" elements presented on *The Avengers* (with or without Rigg).

But it was indeed Diana's presence that helped place *The Avengers* on ABC's map, and the viewer's radar. Stunt coordinator-turned-director Ray Austin believed that her appeal was more cerebral than physical. He once observed, "As an actress, playing a character, and as a real person off-screen, she listened. If you had a conversation with her, she would listen . . . not just to me because I was the director, and it was her time to listen. But when she had a conversation with someone, she would listen to the other person's point of view."[2]

Early in his career, Austin learned to pay attention to what he called "people's body English" [as in "language"], and Diana's "body English" was brilliant. "Her gestures and mannerisms were always good. She would 'get into' watching others at work. And if you were talking with her about something, she was intent on hearing you, so much so, that you felt you were having a conversation with someone who knew exactly what you were talking about."[3]

"That is to say," Austin continued, "you expect an actor to be able to drop into a character, immediately . . . very immediately . . . because it's what they do, especially in television, [where] you haven't got time to coax an actor to get into character. You say things like, 'You're Jim Brown. You're going to kill that person,' or, 'You're the detective and you're going to do this or that.' Let's go."[4]

On a TV show set, the director does not have the luxury to motivate an actor with elaborate details on the character's background, development, or storyline. The actor has to come prepared before the cameras roll. Or as Austin explained, "You haven't got time to sit down and say, 'Well, I think your mother was really an invalid in a chair and she sort of saw this vision of God,' and that's the setup. No. In television, you don't get to give that kind of direction. The actor is paid to act, and to act quickly. And Diana did that superbly."[5]

Rigg's physical appeal as Mrs. Peel did not go unnoticed, either. *New York Times* critic Vincent Canby once described her avenging Emma as "a tall, lithe, Modigliani of a girl, with the sweet sophistication of Nora Charles and the biceps of Barbarella," providing "a good reason to stay home on Friday night for a group melt of TV dinners."[6]

Rigg's core-centric allure on *The Avengers* had to do with her apparel, which included various colorful editions of her famed leather catsuit. Diana's Peel was the nimbler, but no less formidable, half of a dynamic duo, completed by Macnee's bowler-hatted old-school, more traditionally garbed spymaster John Steed. "Subliminally it was quite kinky,"[7] she later admitted to author David Story for his companion book to *The Avengers*. The compromising positions in which Peel would find herself, literally and figuratively, were provocative. More often than not, she would be strapped to props and set pieces like a dentist's chair with her feet in the air, while the camera focused on her high-heeled boots.

Diana saw no point in defending her recognized eroticism as Emma. Nor was she in the least embarrassed by her performance on the show. In her conversation with Story, she pegged Peel a trailblazer, "a new type of heroine [and quite] good for leather fetishists."[8]

For example, in one episode, "A Touch of Brimstone," which premiered on February 19, 1966, in the UK, Steed joins the Hellfire Club, while Emma adds to the visual shock-value by becoming the "Queen of Sin." Wearing a spiked dog collar, a whalebone corset, and tall leather boots, she is whipped five separate times. It's a sensationalized sadomasochistic segment that originally shook, rattled, and rolled the waves across both sides of the Atlantic. According to what show producer Brian Clemens conveyed in Story's book, two of the whippings had to be removed for the British airings, while America banned the sequence altogether. "But then we found out that . . . ABC [executives] used to run it every year at their convention."[9]

For "Brimstone," Rigg was instructed to wear a snake on her arm for an entire day. The serpent's handler, who was "terribly sweet,"[10] warned of her potentially and suddenly being micturated upon. *Oh, please, no*, she thought. *I don't need that.*

In the less stressful but no less stimulating episode "Honey for the Prince," which premiered the following March 3, Steed joins the natives and Emma joins the harem of an Arabian potentate, with her bejeweled belly button on full display. Unable to belly dance, Rigg was able to at least approximate some moves. In those days, she and other TV actresses like Barbara Eden (*I Dream of Jeannie*) and Dawn Wells (*Gilligan's Island*) were not allowed to expose their navel cavities on American television. But when *The Avengers* prop men attempted to gingerly insert the jewel inside Rigg's navel, they could not find the right kind of glue. "So, the jewel kept popping out," she said—most likely, right along with the eyeballs of many in the audience watching that episode.[11]

The Avengers was pure escapist entertainment during the turbulent 1960s, a time when fantasy pervaded television and film. As a small-screen secret-agent response to Sean Connery's big-screen Bond, *The Avengers* proved to be an immediate hit. Periodically psychedelic for its time, with a surreal sense of self and humor, the series paired Peel and Steed against all manner of evil geniuses bent on world domination. With its improbable gadgetry, absurd situations, witty dialogue and interplay, the series was ABC's entertaining espionage answer to NBC's *The Man from U.N.C.L.E.*, or more appropriately, *The Girl from U.N.C.L.E.*, the former's first female-geared, if short-lived, sequel.

But unlike *U.N.C.L.E.*, ABC's *Honey West* (with Anne Francis), or NBC's spy-com *Get Smart*, *The Avengers* was known for its extensive cast changes. It began as a live, straightforward adventure show called *Police Surgeon*, starring Ian Hendry as Dr. David Keel, a man on a quest to find his wife's killers. The male Keel (as opposed to the female Peel) was joined in his plight by Macnee's refined Steed. Eventually, the bereaved Keel, who never completed his search, was replaced by a female character named Cathy Gale, played by Honor Blackman.

The irony of Rigg's Peel portrayal, and, ultimately, Blackman's early participation in *The Avengers*, was that the show's initial focus was on its original two leading male characters. As Diana relayed to Gavin Esler, when Hendry "dropped away at the very last minute," Blackman was hired, and the original script went unchanged concerning character gender. She "was doing all those things that men do," Rigg said, and the producers "didn't have a clue" and "couldn't believe their luck" when the show introduced what eventually became two female pop-culture phenoms.[12]

Beginning with Blackman's casting, Steed and his new female partner had become government agents. But the dialogue remained the same for Gale as it had been for Hendry and, in the process, paved the way for non-gender-specific and stronger female roles. By the time *The Avengers* reached American shores, Blackman had been cast as Pussy Galore in the James Bond film *Goldfinger* and left the series. Another actress, Elizabeth Shepherd, was hired to replace her. But producer Brian Clemens was displeased with Shepherd's performance. "She's not a bad actress," he later recalled. "But she just didn't have a sense of humor at all—that was essential in *The Avengers*."[13]

Consequently, any footage with Shepherd was scrapped, and she was fired. In stepped Rigg, whom Macnee once described as "a dazzling actress with an equally dazzling body [as Blackman's]."[14] With great pause, that isn't to infer that Macnee held women in any disregard, especially women with a powerful presence on any level. According to his son Rupert, it was quite the opposite. "My dad grew up around mainly strong women. And he brought that experience to working on *The Avengers* without any threat to his masculinity. He could be a man, in a non-dominating way, while having a great deal of respect for women."[15]

Patrick Macnee proved to be as debonair off-screen as he was on. During an interview with *The Lady* magazine in 2014, Macnee was put on the spot. He was asked to select the most alluring of his three female *Avengers* costars: Honor Blackman, Linda Thorson, or Diana. "The very first thing you learn if you're a gentleman," he replied, "is that you never compare one woman to another. That's the way of all death. You get a pointed high heel in your groin, and you'll never walk again!"[16]

In the same breath, Macnee expressed his delight with the show and how, due to Diana's presence, it blazed the TV trail for female independence. "The wonderful thing was it made women feel they didn't just belong in an apron in front of a stove, cooking for the kids. It made them delight in the awareness that they could get out there and do it all; fight men, take on villains; all kinds of stuff we showed in *The Avengers*."[17]

"I'm very proud of what we achieved for women," he continued. "I don't think we knew that we were doing it at the time; it just seemed that a woman would make the ideal foil to my John Steed. And so, she did."[18]

CHAPTER 5

AVENGING ANGEL

Patrick [Macnee] was a very dear man,
and I owe him a great deal.
—DIANA RIGG

DIANA TOOK "NO CREDIT AT ALL" FOR *THE AVENGERS'* SUCCESS; SHE WAS merely grateful to play Mrs. Peel. "It was a wonderful part, and Patrick was adorable to work with," said Diana. "And I think it came through that we really did love each other. No sex. But we loved each other."[1]

She meant the fabricated on-screen relationship between Peel and John Steed, and not her association with Patrick Macnee. Off-screen, the two actors maintained a professional and platonic relationship. "It helps if you've got mutual respect," she said, "and we did have that."[2]

On-screen, Peel was introduced as the widow of a test pilot, while her relationship with Steed was never fully explained. And that proved intriguing for viewers. Many wondered if Peel and Steed consummated their relationship. For producer Brian Clemens, the answer was obvious and opposite to what Diana believed. "If you ask me," he said, "they certainly have—they've been to bed together."[3]

It was all about keeping the mystery alive. As Diana revealed to David Story, "Quite often, it's the distance between two people that's the most interesting. It's never the clinch. It's always the dialogue before the clinch, or the silence before the clinch. There was never any full stop put on the relationship [with Steed], and I suppose people find that interesting and beguiling." Peel's physical relations with Steed were "at times, to put it mildly, ambiguous," Rigg continued. "They're certainly not active—they might have been in the past or, then again, they might be in the future. They were extremes. Steed was the archetypal English gentleman. Emma, on the other hand, was a prophecy of what women would become."[4]

Rupert Macnee likened the Macnee/Rigg chemistry to that of Bruce Willis and Cybill Shepherd on ABC's 1980s-era hit, *Moonlighting*. "There was great balance and dynamic, which implies elasticity, between the two characters in both shows. There's a push and a pull to their relationships, a tension about their interactions that made both shows work."[5]

While Diana made Mrs. Peel work, she was an actress who settled for nothing less than respect across the board. Her sense of assurance is what helped get her the job in the first place. Or as Brian Clemens said, she "was head and shoulders above everybody else."[6]

But that audition proved haphazard. Diana had never seen *The Avengers* but tried out anyway. "I didn't have a telly," she told *TV Guide*, "so I didn't know what it was."[7] She felt awkward and thought she was wasting her time, and initially, the producers agreed. Years later, Diana had the first of three interviews with the BBC's legendary TV host and journalist Michael Parkinson, who died in August 2023, and who actor Michael Caine at that time described as "irreplaceable" and "charming." In other words, Parkinson was someone who Diana could trust. In her initial chat with him, she reflected on her *Avengers* audition: "I hadn't seen Honor on the telly because I'd been doing theater all the time, and I turned up [at] the studios to do a test along with five hundred other ladies all dressed in basic black trousers and a sweater."[8]

Rigg tested with Macnee and Ray Austin who, as she recalled, "was clouted over the head with a handbag five hundred times. And when it got to my turn—I mean, he's punch-drunk and fell to the floor. They obviously thought, 'Well, *she's* the strongest,' and gave me the part,'" she mused, if with a slightly different recollection to Austin's but to the delight of Parkinson's audience. It was the kind of welcoming response she received wherever she went. That's why, as Parkinson observed, she was "the ideal interviewee, in that she was frank, quick-witted, and funny. And she looked as if she enjoyed being asked questions no matter how daft they might be. Or perhaps she was just demonstrating her talents as an actress."[9]

According to Rupert Macnee, it was director/stunt coordinator Austin who added sheen to Diana's shine. Austin had cut his teeth on *The Avengers*, and would later helm countless hours of American TV, everything from *Barnaby Jones* and *The Fall Guy* to, fittingly, *The Man from U.N.C.L.E.* TV reunion movie, *The Fifteen Years Later Affair* (1983). But, as Rupert recalled, before any of that, it was Austin who choreographed that famous photo of Diana throwing someone over her shoulder.

While that image represents, at least in petrification, Diana's literal and lateral position on *The Avengers*, Austin himself remembered the events, the pomp and circumstance that led to her, and his, involvement with the series in the first place. He had been approached by producers Albert Fennell and Brian Clemens, the latter of whom was a childhood friend. As Austin remembered it, Blackman "didn't want to do it anymore, and went on to star in *Goldfinger*." He recalled working with leading producer Julian Wintle, who became ill, and the initial replacement casting of Elizabeth Shepherd, whom he described as "a very sweet, nice, and super person. I taught her some Judo ... and the first few episodes with her were ready to shoot. But Elizabeth had a mind of her own, and she was her own worst enemy. She shot herself in the foot. One day, Elizabeth walked down the staircase at the studios in Borehamwood Studios in England, came face to face with Julian and immediately told him, 'I don't like this outfit I'm wearing. I am going to have to have this changed.' That's something you don't say to a producer like Julian Wintle, especially when you're a young actress just starting out."[10]

Nonetheless, *The Avengers* began filming, and upon viewing the daily rushes, Wintle decided to remove Shepherd from the series. "And that was the end of that," Austin said. "Very quietly, Julian recast the part."[11]

The search began for a new actress, a process Austin recalled as "an absolute nightmare. Whoever it was they were going to consider and ultimately select would not only have to be a good actress, but they had to be very physical to do the Judo and actions scenes."[12]

Austin was a black belt in Judo, and one of the first in the industry to practice kung fu. "No one in England ever heard of that," he said. Although "into it," he remained silent about naming the elaborate martial art; one that would later expound in the seventies, via Bruce Lee in the movies, and David Carradine on TV's *Kung Fu* series. In the post-Shepherd *Avengers* period, aspirants were nowhere near the martial arts caliber of Lee or Carradine. According to Austin, those in the potential Shepherd-replacement pool were "the worst," mostly because they were thrown into unfamiliar territory in both the verbal and action sequence territory.[13]

Still, the process trudged on. Austin filmed a screen test with each potential Peel player, and carefully coordinated fight sequences supervised by director Roy Moore Baker. Those auditioning included Mary Peach, whom Austin considered a top choice; Tracy Reed, the daughter of director Sir Carol Reed; Eleanor Bron; Shirley Eaton, yet another Bond Girl from *Goldfinger*; and Katherine Woodville, who was then married to Patrick Macnee. With each session, Austin mustered a measure of physical prowess and endurance. To contend with the continuous blows, rehearsed or accidental, he placed a line of mattresses in a designated rehearsal room. From there, he instructed each candidate in varied martial arts positions.

But no matter how planned or precise the moves, this audition process proved painful for Austin. Every film, TV, or stage fight sequence is rehearsed, but that doesn't prevent tragic accidents from occurring. With *The Avengers'* screen tests, no matter how many times Austin ducked or tried to protect himself, some yet-to-be fully trained actress still somehow punched him in the head, the stomach, or another, more delicate, area. As he recalled, "I'd go down in a crouch, and be hit with a right hook. I'd fall to the ground, and then be jumped upon with feet in my gut. I would be thrown over shoulders, hit in the jaw, and kicked in the balls. No one ever stuck to the routine I outlined. By the end of the day, I was black and blue, with a black eye and a bloody nose."[14]

Adding to the physical trauma was the emotional, psychological, aesthetic disappointments. Most of the actresses "were terrible," he said. "Shirley Eaton was the worst of the lot. I worked out a right cross, a left cross, a knee to the stomach, a head butt, a knee butt into the head, and a shoulder-throw. We started the sequence, she kneed me straight in the stomach, and tried to head-butt me." Eaton's audition became so brutal that Austin was forced to yell, "Cut!"[15]

"What was that?" he'd ask her. "Where's the routine we worked on?"

According to Austin, she said, "That's it!"

"No, it's not," replied Austin, who in retrospect, found his experience with Eaton to be humorous, even if it nearly drove him "stark raving mad."

Then, amid chaos, a calming presence arrived. Or, as Austin put it, "This young, pretty [young woman] named Diana Rigg walks into the audition and does the screen test with me."

Soon after, Rigg and Austin walked to the gym. "She was nervous as hell," he said, and asked things like, "Do you think that they liked the screen test?"

"I don't know," he'd tell her. "I suppose they would."[16]

And they did, especially Brian Clemens, who described Diana as "good," "with long, lanky legs," and "very pretty."[17]

As a result, Diana and Ray worked out what he called "this little fight scene, Judo style. And God, she *nailed* it. She was just marvelous . . . lots of high kicks and one thing and another. She was excellent, and the producers were very pleased."[18]

Austin was especially happy with the fight sequences. "*More* than happy," he said. As he told his colleagues, "She's very good, and she listens." He rarely altered the fight sequence from rehearsal to filming. But when he did, it was never a problem for Diana. "It takes a lot of time on the floor, doing fight sequences. You can lose a lot of screen time when you're on a tight budget, which was the case with budgets in England for ten-day shoots."[19]

With most American TV shows during the sixties, filming or taping usually required five days, which at first intimidated Austin. But making *The Avengers* was more relaxed, despite its limits to the fight sequences. For years, rumors circulated that Austin was not allowed, under any circumstances, to utilize any other martial art than Judo, and that he secretly had to teach Diana kung fu. The truth is however, Austin had a black belt in karate and wanted to incorporate kung fu into the show, via Les Gibbs, a kung fu champion under whom he had studied. Upon his and Gibbs's arrival at the Borehamwood studios, they enacted a fight sequence for the producers, including Clemons. "Brian said, 'God, let's go for this . . . because it's great," Austin recalled.[20]

So, that puts to rest any behind-the-scenes gossip regarding other aspects of the fight sequences. Most of the hearsay was in regard to Austin allegedly being prohibited to teach Diana kung fu was, as he put it, "a load of bullshit. It's so wrong, and not true in the least. She took to it very well—and liked it. The only mistake I made, and which I learned about later, was that I did not coordinate the kung fu sequences in high-speed."[21]

Such was the case later, with American-made martial arts films starring Chuck Norris and Bruce Lee overseas, whereas the slow-motion effect was utilized (at 110 fps) with David Carradine on *Kung Fu*. Had the fast-motion process been utilized with Diana's fight sequences on *The Avengers* "she would have been incredible," Austin said. "Though she'd have probably hated being that incredible."[22]

According to Austin, Rigg looked forward to rehearsing the fight sequences, most of which featured his stunt men subbing for her. Except for one day when, in a kung fu class, he stumbled upon a stunt woman named Cyd Child, whom he then hired for the entirety of the series. But overall, Diana was there, directly in the mix. As Austin said, "We got on like a house on fire. We really had a super time. She herself was super, and never ever gave me any problems as a director, or as a fight arranger."[23]

Diana's TV persona at times proved intimidating for fans and even some potential suiters. "Socially, it can be terribly difficult," she said. "They think you're infallible and they think this is sort of a great butch creature, you know, which I'm not, either. And neither I am going to work my head off to try and sort of dissolve that whole image . . . I expect people to accept me as I am. That's that."

Viewers never knew what to expect from Mrs. Peel, which was a good thing for the show and the ratings. Not exactly a secret agent, she was instead a talented amateur with a thirst for adventure. Without question, she was one of the most liberated TV characters of the 1960s, female or otherwise.

CHAPTER 6

DEFENDING MRS. PEEL

The essence of Emma Peel is oneself. All those accessories like
being able to fight and knowing everything about engines
and computers, is very far away from me.
But . . . what she represents, in a way, is quite close to me.
—DIANA RIGG

WITH DIANA AND PATRICK MACNEE LEADING THE WAY, *THE AVENGERS*
became the first British series broadcast on American television. Sometimes hampered by limited plots, the show nevertheless embodied a unique
style. Peel and Steed encountered a litany of strange characters and surreal
adventures not regularly seen on TV at the time. But early on, that proved
a challenge for ABC, especially with certain initial black-and-white episodes the network considered too over the top. Two such examples were
"Honey for the Prince" (March 26, 1966) and "Epic" (April 14, 1967), which
only later made the cut for syndication.

In "Epic," the evil, whip-swishing, megalomaniacal German movie
mogul Z. Z. von Schnerk (Kenneth J. Warren) pays tribute to Peel, perfectly
describing her character, if also, too, a few elements of the actress: "You
are a woman of courage, beauty, and action. A woman who could become
desperate, yet remain strong, become confused yet remain intelligent, who
could fight back, yet remain feminine."

But no matter what strides the show made for women, with episodes
like "Epic," *The Avengers* rattled ABC's nerves. As Ray Austin recalled,
"Number one: they said we were too violent. But in my eyes, it wasn't a
violent show. Neither Diana nor Patrick ever shot a gun, ever. They never
even handled a gun. In fact, they would be seen tossing them away."[1]

While Austin instructed Diana in the ways of kung fu, he also taught
Macnee how to handle an umbrella with "panache," or what Webster

defines as "a grand or flamboyant manner." Austin learned the technique from a Frenchman who fought with one simple weapon. "He was incredible. He'd make you fall over, and trip you [up] with just a stick." Macnee followed suit with Steed's graceful umbrella wielding and a few other items. "We even used ping pong balls," Austin said, "or anything we could muster, except nasty weapons. We would never kill a character. We knew characters would die. But Emma Peel or John Steed would never kill a character. You never saw *anybody* getting killed, only wounded.[2]

"There was no obvious sex in the series, ever," he continued. "And sad to say, we never showcased African or Caribbean American Englishmen either. That just bloody didn't happen—to our detriment."[3]

But the show still presented a measure of violence, which was carefully monitored.

According to an interview with then-ABC executive Alfred R. Schneider for the periodical *Mass Media and Violence*, "The general standards enunciated for controlling the portrayal of violence at ABC are: violence for the sake of violence or shock value is not permitted and the use of violence must be necessary to the development of the plot or character development. The relevance of violence to the plot or character development varies proportionately to the network estimate of number of children in the audience. One interesting characteristic is that each program is judged separately and on the basis of its time zone in the program slot."

Among the more specific criteria that Schneider listed:

1. No sensationalism merely to attract audience
2. Concern and awareness of the public's feelings.
3. Questions of public taste.
4. Desire not to generate a negative reaction in viewers.

Interestingly, with regard to social science literature on the effects of violence on viewers, the report concluded, "ABC does not deem it helpful in formulating specific policy recommendations on how violence should be portrayed in concrete cases—there are too many different points of view."

That included the discussion of *Avengers* episodes like those written by David Spooner. A prolific British TV writer and script editor, Spooner worked in, among other creative venues, children's television. And he maintained loyal associations with several screenwriters and producers in the UK, including Brian Clemens.

According to Austin, in one scene from a Spooner-penned *Avengers* segment, "This guy goes up against the back wall of the garage and gets shot . . . not dead. But *shot*. The network saw it, and complained, 'We can't have that . . . an unarmed man, backed against a wall, and getting shot."[4]

That's when complaints were filed by Clemens who, according to Austin, said: "Fuck 'em . . . We're gonna keep it. He's gonna stay shot. We'll re-shoot it, and I know what we'll do."

To resolve the matter, tins of different colored fake paint were placed high on a shelf, out of frame. The man was shot. He flew back against the wall. The shelf collapsed, and the fake paint poured down on the man, who was left amid a deluge of bright colors on and surrounding him. According to Austin, "America *loved* it. They said, 'Wonderful, lovely.' The network may not have wanted the man to be shot, but in fact, we turned it around by doing just that . . . camouflaging the moment by pouring paint all over him. We did so many things like that . . . including slapping people . . . but not in direct and obvious ways."[5]

Scenes with Mrs. Peel were also restricted by the network's mild assault command. As Austin also recalled, "She could not be too violent with men. 'Mrs. Peel mustn't hurt men'—that was the edict from the network," one to which Clemens objected. "What do you mean she can't hurt men? That's crazy," Austin recalled his producer telling ABC.

A compromise, of sorts, was reached. According to Austin, "If a man had pulled a gun on Emma Peel, she would take it away from him, and probably throw him over her shoulder, with him landing on his head, slightly unconscious. But anybody who became unconscious always moved after the fact. That was always made clear in any such scene we did like that. There was always the implication that the person being shot, or whatever, was not dead."[6]

Either way, Mrs. Peel "had to defend herself. Or she had or wanted to defend Steed or Mother [the supervising spy played by Patrick Newell]."

The obligatory fight scenes became par for Peel's course. Most were comedic and closed with a bit of business, like having her pick up her knitting where she had left off. As Diana later noted herself, Peel "didn't mind fighting people and neither was she apologetic about her achievement."

Besides Ray Austin, there were others who choreographed the various fight sequences, including Gerry Crampton, Lee Crawford, Cliff Diggins, Joe Dunne, Peter Elliot, Frank Henson, Denny Powell, Eddie Powell, and Terry Richards. According to what Diana told Story, each scene was orchestrated "very carefully. . . . They didn't want me to be biffed."[7]

The battle scenes became so popular, even British pop star Betty Boop, decades later, mimicked Peel's moves in a music video, while clad in a leather jumpsuit. But in the sixties, Peel arrived with a more serious impact when women, according to Rigg, "were getting a pretty bad deal on the face of this earth, and they had to change things." For Diana, Mrs. Peel became "the embodiment" of female empowerment, paving the way for women who "now have an extended life professionally, sexually and socially, and about time, too."[8]

But as Austin clarified, "Most importantly . . . Diana didn't want any part of the violence. Yes, she enjoyed the fun of throwing a guy over her shoulders. She certainly threw *me* over a desk and such many times, and I would land sitting in a chair with a phone in my hand. But that was the extent of it."[9]

In Austin's view, such sequences were not violent but merely action-adventure moments that amounted to "just silly fun," such as when Steed drove a Bentley on a road littered with nails that were intended to puncture his car tires. He steers and maneuvers around every nail. "We would have had the tires blow up or something like that. It was all much more clever than violent."[10]

There was one scene with Peel and Steed which just so happened to be their last moment together on-screen. They are enjoying a steak dinner that Steed prepared on the engine of that Bentley. "I mean, how silly can you get?" Austin suggested. "To cook a steak dinner, medium rare, of all things, on a Bentley in the middle of a beautiful field? Where did Steed get the steak from? Who knows? We never knew where he or Mrs. Peel got the champagne from either. Brian would say, 'It doesn't fucking matter where the champagne came from.' They had got the champagne and that's the end of it, and *chink* go the glasses and they toast each other. It was heaven."[11]

Once ABC hit the jackpot with *The Avengers*, the network lessened its grip on censoring violence, with the show's tamed or camouflaged assaults no longer an issue. From the beginning, it was always Clemens's intention to focus on the style and substance of *The Avengers*. "We're not going to make the show violent anyway," Austin recalled his saying. "It's not that type of show."[12]

That said, the show's violent tendencies were presented within the confines of what Austin described as "a heightened reality," a pall came over the set when more than a few creative disagreements with the network resulted in Brian and Albert being fired. Before they were eventually rehired, John Bryce came aboard as producer, right about the time Linda Thorson replaced Diana. "But John didn't know what he was doing," Austin said. "They employed him because they wanted to bring the series back to realism, which had nothing to do with Brian and Albert's vision for the show."[13]

That's when the series became *The New Avengers*, with Austin's last episode involving Diana aptly titled, "Have Gun, Will Haggle." That segment positioned, literally, Newell's Mother character in all kinds of places, including his office, in bed, and in a swimming pool. "Then I put him on top of the bus."[14]

After that, and with Bryce's involvement, "There were going to be real gunfights, like in real life," continued Austin, who also recalled the displeasure felt by mainstay producer Julian Wintle about such developments. "Julian said, 'I cannot for the life of me, see Diana Rigg or Patrick Macnee pull out a machine-gun and kill anyone. I cannot see Diana Rigg take a knife from a man and accidentally stab him in the stomach. It's not going to happen, and it won't work.'"[15]

Along with Bryce and Albert, Julian knew "they understood the show's audience," Austin said. "They understood the characters of Mrs. Peel and Steed."[16]

• • •

While none of this was part of any master career plan on Diana's part, once she debuted as Mrs. Peel, the actress and the character became a twin trailblazing voice and body for what would become the Women's Liberation movement a few years later. Emma Peel's adventure-girl allure, coupled with Rigg's husky voice, the result of a pack-a-day cigarette habit, brought the actress a legion of admirers of every gender.

Such notoriety may have been a dream come true for other actresses, but for Rigg, at least, when it came to donning Peel's leather catsuit, it was a nightmare, requiring forty-five minutes just to unzip it, as if she were stepping in and out of a wetsuit. Once the wardrobe switched to jersey catsuits, they were easier to wear. Dubbed "Emmapeelers," the new-and-improved jumpsuits, made of Crimplene and available in eight colors, were designed by T. B. Jones, Ltd., of London. Diana, for one, approved of the change. She may have had to watch for baggy knees now and then, but nothing worse.[17]

Becoming a sex symbol almost overnight was a shocking experience for the actress. She went from anonymity to suddenly being mobbed. She once had to hide in the lavatory at a motor show, while German police resorted to using batons to hold back the crush of fans. She kept fan mail unopened in the boot of her car because she did not know how to reply to the often-salacious letters; nevertheless, she thought it rude to throw any of them away. Her mother, Beryl, would field the more explicit correspondence from pubescent males by replying: "Those aren't very nice thoughts. And besides, my daughter is too old for you. I suggest you take a run around the block."

It all came with the territory. As Rigg expressed in her interview with Oxford Union, she did not take to all the attention naturally. "In those days, the huge publicity machine that concentrates on television stars now, it didn't exist . . . at all. So, to be well known . . . to be recognized was a . . . strange experience. And coming from Yorkshire, as I did . . . to be called a sex symbol was absolutely extraordinary, and I simply didn't know how to handle it. Because you didn't talk about sex in Yorkshire. Ever. Still less, flaunt your sexuality. So, I was not very good at flaunting, and . . . rather sort of walked away from that aspect of my fame. Yes . . . nowadays . . . it's such a different world. . . . Without sounding dreadfully old-fashioned."[18]

For Rigg, the challenging aspects of her new image were "hard to explain." For example, the female youth of her era did not wear jeans. "You were dressed as a middle-aged lady," she said. "You know, you wore skirts and twin sets. There was a sort of dresses called *Horrocks* that you wore in the summertime, which middle-aged ladies still wear. But they wore the only things available to you. There was no pop music, not really. Chubby Checker. That was about it. So, it was . . . completely different, and I was, in those days, completely at sea."[19]

In comparing her sex symbol status to that of contemporary stars, and the undue sensualizing of women and young actors in general, Rigg said it was "a choice. You can either go into it, and use it, and a lot of young actresses do, and as a result are very successful. Or, you say, 'I have certain priorities and my sexuality isn't at the top of my list. My profession, as an actress, is the part of me that I wish to concentrate on. And that is the part of me that I will develop.'"[20]

Rigg made a similar point to Gavin Esler at the University of Kent: "I know it sounds terrible to turn your back on the gift of fame, when it *is* a gift. Because suddenly you're well known all over the world. But I find it's such an intrusion . . . to be a sex symbol!"[21]

Assuredly, her notoriety in general took its toll on her love life, as is the case with countless individuals subject to any form of public inspection. In the mid-1960s, she, with "little desire to be respectable," had a scandalous affair with the older, and then-married, actor/director Philip Saville.[22]

In 1972, when BBC-TV journalist Michael Parkinson asked Rigg why she chose to first live with a man without marrying him, she answered that she had reached her decision through what she called "a very personal process." As such, it was "a very personal decision," one she had no desire to share. She abhorred the idea of "affecting anybody, and saying, 'Marriage is out,' and all that."[23] She was simply talking about herself, and how not being married for her meant that she consciously committed herself to someone daily. She found, in fact, that she was "more faithful . . . loving and caring" than if she were married. Although her first marriage was still a few years away, for the moment at least, she preferred to keep trying to succeed in an intimate relationship.

"You can have a permanent companionship outside marriage," she said. "The mistake is to think that living outside marriage with somebody can *be* a marriage, but simply without the ceremony. That's all."[24]

She also talked with Parkinson about how much she had learned by then. "I don't mean, basically," she said. "I mean, I have many more accessories and I suppose I've got more money and more things. But the qualities that existed as a Yorkshire girl are still there." That was her "sense of reality," she more than anything else. It's the awareness that, even though one may be a success, it's the Yorkshire voice at the back of one's mind, which is saying, 'Ah, but not . . . but just. You've still got to keep working at it, you know."[25]

That she did. Rigg continued to mature emotionally with each life experience. She also continued to expand her reach as an actress. While conversing with Parkinson, she credited her upbringing, specifically mentioning her parents. "They love you very much," she implied in generic terms of anyone's mother and father, "and if they think you want to do something like crazy, like being an actress, they're behind you. But there's always a reason. They always, in some sense, rationalize it. I heard my mother's rationalization only last week. And she said, 'Well, of course. . . . Somewhere, sometime ago, one of your forebears was illegitimate!' And that seems to explain the fact that I became an actress."

The discussion then turned toward morality, debating the potential lies or truth of what Diana recalled as "the days of the casting couch . . . if they ever did exist." She thought they must have been "very much exaggerated because nobody's asked me to take off my clothes for a while. I mean, I don't know whether to take that as a sort of knock or what."

As to Rigg and Saville, that was a different story altogether. While together, Diana never had any intention of marrying him (or anyone else) at the time.

On October 1, 1972, she told reporter Clive Russell of the *San Antonio Light*, "I can't promise that I'll still be with the same man at 50. I have made no promises." As Russell observed, "That was before it became fashionable to say such things."

"Good Women's Lib stuff," Russell continued to note, "but Diana Rigg has never seen herself as part of the bra-burning scene."

"What I do," she said, "is a result of my own personal beliefs. The way I live is the way I believe is right for me. It's nothing to do with anybody else."

Diana mentioned all of this while promoting her performance at the National Theatre in the Tom Stoppard's play *Jumpers*, which Russell described as "a kind of science fiction, philosophical farce." Here, she portrayed, as Russell put it, "a sexy nightclub singer married to a university don, and who can keep up with him intellectually. It is difficult to think of another actress who so completely fits the bill."

The next month Diana would play Lady Macbeth in the National Theatre's production of *Macbeth*. She had been waiting forever to play the part, from the moment she became an actress. "I dropped enough hints," she told Russell, who said, "Gelling such a plum part in a big, prestigious production is a remarkable achievement for a thirty-two-year-old, and an actress who has diversified her talents so widely."

"I consider the times I'm not working to be just as important as the time I am," Rigg added. "I don't see myself acting for rest of my life. I'd like to do something else—but I've no idea what."

"Just as she has no time for the formula ballyhoo that so goes with being a recognized star," Russell noted, "neither does Diana Rigg crave status." At the time, she lived in what she described as a bohemian flat in London's Hampstead, a residence that once belonged to artist Augustus John, with Saville and a parrot which has a ripe line in repartee. "I have no jewelry to speak of, and what I have I sling round the neck of a lady statue in the bedroom."

Femininity, she declared, bored her. "My closest friends, [purely in the platonic sense], are men. I get on well with women, but the sort of straight-talking women I like are few and far between." And to her most contented moments? "Each night behind the locked door of my bathroom in the bath with a glass of wine."

Rigg eventually left Seville for what would be a three-year marriage to Israeli artist Menachem Gueffen. But as Laurence Laurent observed in the *Washington Post* on August 27, 1973, "In the days of *The Avengers*, Diana was fiercely determined to remain single. She was quite happy, she said, with a flat in Knightbridge," an upper-crust district just in central London.

To Paul Henniger of the *Los Angeles Times*, she touted, "I'm not available for marriage. But that doesn't mean to say that one's hard-headed or fantastically ambitious. It's not a philosophy. I advocate for other people, but for myself, I don't think the state of marriage is a particularly good idea."

She later told Rosanna Greenstreet of *The Guardian* that "life itself" was the greatest love of her life, while she believed that love itself felt like "firing on all pistons." She cowed to the indiscriminate overuse of the term, "I love you," in her youth. But "never now." And in looking back, she would have made different choices with "a couple of lovers." But when asked how often she had sex, Rigg replied, "My business."

She cherished the simple treasures of life, such as "a cooked breakfast, about twice a year." But other things, such as "people leaving litter and dog shit in lovely parks," depressed her. She would have apologized to "anyone I would have hurt thoughtlessly." But she frowned upon "most politicians . . . for their lies and treating us like idiots," and the "gratuitous bitchiness women visit upon each other. Particularly journalists." In fact, she pronounced women "more bitchy then men" and "dangerous and competitive" about their looks and attractiveness to the opposite sex. She berated women for complaining about men holding doors open and pulling chairs out for them, which she said was "good manners," not sexism. Though men patting women's derrieres was not allowed; men "deserved to be slapped for that," she said.

That said, Diana's personal opinions and intimate life may have simply been challenged by her public sex symbol status. She likened the predicament to the press she received in France for her performance as Cordelia in a Paris production of director Paul Scofield's *King Lear*. As she recalled to Gavin Esler, "The Paris Olympia . . . I mean, the 'tutte Paris' were there." Because Diana was a junior member of the company, she had "a very scrubby dressing room," situated at the top of the building. "I think people had to sort of dry their hands on the curtains."[26]

But it was during a particular curtain call that another legendary actress, whom Rigg described as "this extraordinary golden creature," had been positioned in the audience approximately four tiers back from the stage. "And the stage light just sort of reflected on her, and she had this aureole of golden hair . . . [and] . . . a gold lamé coat. . . . It was the most beautiful thing I'd ever seen. My eyes riveted on her."[27]

When the curtain fell, Rigg and the rest of the company dispersed to their separate dressing rooms and were bidden to the British ambassador's home for a soirée. And Diana wondered, "How was I going to get there," with her "best dress . . . not very grand . . . hanging in the corner?"

Then, suddenly, there was a knock at the door. Diana opened it, and there stood that golden creature. It was Marlene Dietrich, confirming the recollection from Rigg's understudy Margaret Drabble.

As Rigg relayed to Esler, Dietrich told her, "I've come to take you to the British ambassador's."

"I promise you," Rigg mused to Esler, "I'm not kidding. I'm not making this up. She then said, 'I will help you dress.' And so, she unzipped my leather costume. And I was standing there in my bra and pants. She said, 'Your body is beautiful. You don't need underwear."[28]

Rigg asked, "Not even a bra?"

"No!" Dietrich replied.

"So, she zipped me into my dress, and I went to the British ambassador's [home] in her chauffeur-driven car. I was sort of like this [*arms across chest*], the whole time."

"Any person of that age nowadays wouldn't be like that," Rigg said.[29]

But she couldn't help it. Inside, she was still that shy little Yorkshire girl.

The brazen side of Diana, however, was living very much in the present. When she learned that her male costar was making much more than she was, she blamed her agent for the iniquitous arrangement. "This girl isn't going to go very far," is what she remembered her then-representative saying. "Let's sell her cheap."

"I made a bit of a fuss about it and got this reputation for being mercenary, which I wasn't at all," Diana insisted.

In one sense, she enjoyed working on *The Avengers*. "I love the fact that we had to make-do," she said, to pretend the danger was "around the corner instead of presenting it on the screen." But the show's workload did take its toll on her. Each day of filming, a car would be sent to pick her up at six in the morning and take her home late at night. "It was very tiring," she said. She also grew weary of the show's repetitiveness. "Oh, 'Another dead body . . .' What do you *say*?"[30]

And just as she had grown bored with the Royal Shakespeare Company, Diana would opt to leave *The Avengers*. Her final episode, "The Forget-Me-Knot" (which aired in America on March 20, 1968), features Patrick Kavanagh, Jeremy Young, Alan Lake, Patrick Newell, and introduces twenty-year-old Linda Thorsen as new operative Tara King. At the close of "Forget," Mrs. Peel retires after learning her husband, thought killed in a plane crash, is in London, where she decides to join him.

When "Knot" premiered, a friend asked Rigg if she could visualize Mr. Peel. She could not, but when the character finally surfaces at the end, he is donning a derby and carrying a brolly, the very image of Steed.[31]

But none of that mattered to Rigg. As far as she was concerned, Emma Peel remained unemancipated. As she told *TV Guide* at the time, Macnee's real Steed periodically patted her on the head "like a good horse," which compelled her to leave the series. *The Avengers* was fun, she said, but it began to feel claustrophobic, like the show was "taking over."

Into the mix, the studio frowned on Rigg's interaction with the press and what she revealed to the public in the process. She would always try to speak the truth, while the show's increasing success made it more difficult for her to leave. Had Diana stayed with the series, she would have been pressured by "forces outside" herself to do so. Instead, she reasoned, "Why wait till I was stale if I could leave on a high note?"[32]

• • •

Once more, she retreated into the world of live theater, which contributed to a certain double exposure: two different kinds of notoriety. In this way, fame did not annoy Rigg, but she was conflicted about it. As she expressed to Esler, it once more had to do with a kind of double exposure on the screen and the stage. She felt "split, because on the one hand you realize that it is important to be known."[33]

Or as Rigg noted to the *Appleton-Post Crescent* in 1969, the term "classical actress" is frequently misunderstood. The description is not necessarily that of one who performs heavy drama. Some of William Shakespeare's plays, for example, were comedic by definition, and she performed in many such productions.

As she also told the *Appleton*, Rigg had no "best side" when it came to facial features, but she indeed felt she had two different personality profile. A reporter for the *Appleton* explained one as being the before-mentioned "classical," the other, "modern, provocative, lively and, in [then-]mod-British, 'Very gear,' as exemplified by her [then-] recent television portrayal of Emma Peel in *The Avengers*."

At 5 feet, 8 inches, Rigg (who once, in a deadpan manner, described herself as "tall") was, as the *Appleton* continued to chronicle, "of a stature that makes it difficult to believe that she could be the same judo-expert detective who romped through the Emma Peel portrayal."

Before Diana was deemed as thespian royalty, the *Appleton* assessed further, "Miss Rigg is neither an op-art symbol nor a *grande dame* of the classical theater. Her clothes tastes run to simplicity, and she has the directness of her Yorkshire upbringing, the majesty and independence of Britannia and the Statue of Liberty rolled into one, and a witty sense of humor."

"Diana Rigg is Diana Rigg," the *Appleton* journalist concluded. "The fact that she has resolutely stuck to this most untheatrical of names is an indication of her independence."

Or, as producer, director, and James Bond documentarian David Naylor assessed, "There is no doubt Diana was a national treasure. Laurence Olivier called her 'brilliantly skilled and delicious,' but she was so much more than that. Not just a pop culture icon, but a deadly combination of intelligence, culture, coolness, and sexy sophistication—above all, a potent influence on women claiming their place in the world."

"Legend has it," Naylor continued, "that her [*Avengers*'] character's name was intended to draw more male viewers to the series—'M Appeal.' But her interpretation of Emma Peel—aided by numerous re-writes she did with Patrick Macnee—which made the show even more popular to so many people who wanted to see her in action. Mums felt liberated by her. Dads drooled over her. Girls and women of all ages wanted to be like her, because they loved her fearlessness. And lots and lots of boys adored her.

"It is impossible for anyone under a certain age to understand what a revolutionary character Emma Peel was," Naylor added. "Viewers had never seen a female character like her. She was the first person who gave many people hope that their life choices were not as restricted as they might have believed. She was the original liberated woman and set the standard for all who followed.

"While it was a new kind of thrill to see a woman beat a man in a fight," Naylor said, "it wasn't always her badassery that entranced viewers; it was how intelligent, and educated she was. Her influence was unique in the sense that viewers found their own self-assurance grew with every episode. She showed them what they could be and what they could do in life. She gave them confidence: something which was unique on TV in the mid-'60s when viewers mostly got dizzy girls trying to get a guy.

"She not only brought so much to the role," Naylor concluded, "she elevated it. Her scenes with Patrick are an absolute masterclass in chemistry and sexual tension. And he was clearly devastated when she left the series. The tears you see in his eyes in their final scene were real. He knew instinctively the *lightning in a bottle* they'd captured was a very rare and precious thing and was about to be extinguished, and sure enough, the series began a slow, steady decline once she left."

• • •

One of the first things Diana did after *The Avengers* was return to the Royal Shakespeare Company and perform in *Twelfth Night* because she, by then, was able to "put bums on seats." She thought that was important, if only to put the theater to "good use."

But Rigg was not completely certain that her presence on-stage, post-*The Avengers*, had increased audience attendance in theaters for *Twelfth Night* or any other classic play, by Shakespeare or anyone else. "I hope so," she thought. "Certainly, maybe younger people."

Diana was one of the first stage performers to find success in the new medium. But she recalled an observation director Peter Hall made that echoed a sentiment from director Peter Brook: "You know she's going to waste herself on stupid films and television." But there were so many variables involved in comparing the theater and television of yesterday. In the sixties, the medium, sometimes referred to as "the boob tube," was not held in the high regard it is today. Though it was an innovative and exciting form of entertainment, if anything it was perceived as a threat to feature films. And as Rigg observed, those like her who appeared on television were "considered to be *slumming it.*"[34] (This was a common assertion about stage actors of the Edwardian era who took jobs in the dreaded "flickers.")

Years after *The Avengers* ended its original run, Rigg and her authentic self would still be sent photos of Mrs. Peel to sign. But by that point, Diana refused such requests because, as she told Esler, "I felt like a phony. That is not me. That is another person."[35]

Again, it all had to do with the dichotomy of time. "Fame was different then," Rigg said of her days as Emma Peel. In modern times, Diana believed aspiring actors or performers sought what she referred to as "Big Brother-type" notoriety, along the lines of the Kardashians and so forth. When filming *The Avengers*, Diana, and other actors like her, did not know how to court fame, and not everyone had publicists. Sean Connery—in a sense, Diana's big-screen male spy counterpart—did not want a publicist, nor did he believe he needed one.

Rigg looked at it this way: "I just hope the people getting their fifteen minutes now are [investing their money more productively in things like] the building of society."

Whether hollow or rewarding, Diana viewed her Peel popularity as merely an adjunct to her career. She tried to avoid any vestige of it touching her private life. She stepped into a character in her public life and felt sorry for those who could not, or simply did not, make that distinction. There was still a small part of her that was untouched by fame, never photographed, written about, or even discussed. She enjoyed that. "When I sit next to a stranger at a dinner party and they feel they know something about me, I know they *don't,*" she said.

By the same token, Diana acknowledged that she could have enjoyed her original *Avengers* fame more than she did. "I should have handled it better. Had more fun. Not naughty fun. But just, you know. I sometimes think, when I look back on those days: why didn't I have more confidence? Why didn't I know I was pretty good-looking? It is probably to do with my Yorkshire upbringing. Always thinking that people might be saying, 'Who does she think she is?'"

But no one had to wonder about the impact Rigg made by way of *The Avengers*. There was little doubt that her Peel persona helped to alter the

TV landscape. "There were no prototypes for me," she said. "The telly was full of little blonde juveniles. We had no idea it would be defining . . . it was nose to the grindstone—working all hours that God gave."

In the process, Rigg was frequently left with little time for play or romance, the latter of which had always proved to be a challenge for her independent spirit.

Diana and Patrick Macnee commence their iconic pairing on *The Avengers*. Courtesy mptvimages.com.

Ray Austin (left) brought in martial arts master David Chow (right) to help Diana train in kung fu for the fight/action sequences on *The Avengers*. Courtesy of Ray Austin.

Diana, as Mrs. Peel, flattens stuntman Ray Austin playing the villain. Courtesy of Ray Austin.

Diana, as Mrs. Peel, spikes controversy "A Touch of Brimstone," a controversial episode of *The Avengers* that originally aired on February 19, 1966. Courtesy Classic TV Preservation Society (CTVPS).

Diana begins romance with Philip Saville at *First Night of Film* in June 1968, when she had break from shooting *A Midsummer Night's Dream*, which was delayed until the fall. Courtesy Classic TV Preservation Society (CTVPS).

PART THREE

AFTER

Diana blossoms beyond *The Avengers*. Courtesy Classic TV Preservation Society (CTVPS).

CHAPTER 7

FROM THE BUREAU TO BOND

We were both naked and cold.
And I got the worst notices of my life.
—DIANA RIGG

ONCE THE *AVENGERS*-MANIA SUBSIDED, DIANA CONTINUED TO WORK ON stage and television.

In early February 1969, she returned to *A Midsummer Night's Dream*, this time costarring Michael Jayston in a CBS production by the Royal Shakespeare Company for director Peter Hall's more contemporary take on the play. By now, she was reluctant to discuss her star-making role of Mrs. Peel, but did so, when prompted. As she told Mark Shivas of the *New York Times*, "I'm not really a star type." Because of Patrick Macnee's tenure with the series, she thought "his should be the most important part."[1]

Though the ghost of Mrs. Peel still haunted her, Diana was not driven enough to banish it. Nor was she fond of self-promotion, and "the star business . . . premieres and autographs and things."[2] She preferred the low-key, steady stage work that the Royal Shakespeare Company and other such theater troupes provided.

But she still struggled with the "split image" screen/stage identity that sometimes confused her fans and critics. While that perception was difficult for her to escape, she did not believe actors have a prescribed route to success to performing on stage or before the cameras. As she relayed at the Oxford Union, "It just depends on you and how lucky you are. I mean, I was immensely lucky."[3] And pragmatic.

Rigg trained one year in repertory theater, followed by five years at Stratford. She was then cast in *The Avengers*, before going back to Stratford. She was off and running because *The Avengers* had catapulted her public persona. She became "famous," a feat that would have otherwise taken her "twenty years on the stage to reach that degree . . . if that." For her, television was "incredibly powerful, incredibly important," but she also felt it restrictive—to the degree that she wanted to keep her options open. For the sake of longevity, Diana frequently felt pulled back to theater, where she found "the most faithful audiences of all." Such consistent returns to live performing may have periodically perplexed her *Avengers* fans, but it also set the stage for broader horizons, soothed her soul, and allowed her to flex her artistic muscles. On *The Avengers*, Emma Peel and John Steed regularly escaped peril, often allowing Diana and Patrick Macnee the luxury of directing themselves. But with live theatrical productions such as *A Midsummer Night's Dream*, Rigg did what she was told, even if that decision did not always prove productive. (For example, the *Dream* cast was instructed to perform at a much slower pace than normal, which Rigg found burdensome.)

Also in 1969, Diana, at a relatively high point in her career, with regard to film and television, was just about to be seen in the extravagant period movie *The Assassination Bureau* and *On Her Majesty's Secret Service*, the latter a James Bond production. But for some reason, she opted to perform in inexpensive, dialogue-less, German-produced movies like *Minikillers*, which was produced in Super8 format and filmed in Spain.

As one reviewer, "VeeBee2," suggested on IMDb, "My personal guess is that she needed to prove some kind of legal reason or need to be a resident of Spain in order to buy property there. So, she made this couple of quickies to say to the authorities: 'Look! I work in Spain so I have a right/need to live here.' Then she bought her holiday home."

"None of which is a review of the film," "VeeBee2" continued, "so I will just say [it is] cheap but not without a kind of amateurish charm. Diana Rigg is by far the best thing about [it] and looks wonderful. To her credit, she does not just go through the motions but fills the screen with charm and charisma whenever she appears."

Such is certainly the case in making what ultimately became Diana relatively more legitimate big-screen debut in *The Assassination Bureau*, a British period comedy also starring Oliver Reed and Telly Savalas. Directed by Basil Dearden, *Bureau* premiered on March 23, 1969, and was adapted for the screen by producer/production designer Michael Relph from the Jack Lord novel (with help from Robert Fish). As Rigg relayed to Mark Shivas, Relph and company were "stuck with the rather awkward-for-America title and hasn't made up its mind what to do."[4]

In another interview, she said that "it wasn't a good film" but nonetheless considered Dearden an accomplished director. "Absolutely wonderful," she said, with a "huge string of English movies behind him. Nice man, really nice man." And though she also praised Savalas as "a very good actor," when it came to Reed, her sometimes-brutal honesty was in full swing. "He was a man who liked his booze," she asserted. "It's sort of weird when folks [with] intemperate become heroes, because there's a side of intemperance which is deeply ugly. He was rather fond of getting hold of the poor little third assistant [as opposed to just] getting him drunk. The boy couldn't say no. Then he'd be on the set with a godawful hangover the following day."

Like much of her film work, Rigg did not watch *The Assassination Bureau*. But she was sympathetic to the cause, even when it was all but lost. She recalled meeting an accountant at a cocktail party years later, "a very cross little person," who invested in the movie, which failed at the box office. In hindsight, she observed, "I can't tell you much about *The Assassination Bureau* other than that. Doesn't help, does it?"[5]

Not really. But at least Diana was impressed enough with a first read of the movie's fanciful script that she selected it as the ideal follow-up to *The Avengers*. This time, she played liberated journalist Sonya Winter, who, in an ironic nod to Mrs. Peel, planned or otherwise, says things like, "There can be no sexual equality whilst women exploit their physical appearance." Vincent Canby of the *New York Times* labeled the part "much too small" in a flawed film that he dubbed "middle-brow entertainment" but "still fine and pure and very funny." Another *Times* critic described it as "never as funny as it looks," but "a pleasant enough ride if you like companions." In his book *America on the Rerun*, David Story describes the movie as "a lark" of a tale about a secret club that eradicates unworthy members until "greed takes precedence over deduction."

Then, nine months after the premiere of that movie, Rigg appeared in her second mainstream theatrical endeavor, *On Her Majesty's Secret Service*, directed by Peter Hunt. This adventurous film, which debuted December 19, 1969, helped to distance Diana from Emma Peel—while still retaining her presence within the super-spy genre. *Her Majesty* also granted Rigg what many consider her second most-recognizable role, that of Mrs. James Bond.

According to Wikipedia, Brigitte Bardot was originally invited to play the part, but after that famed French actress signed to appear in the Western *Shalako*, opposite, ironically, Sean Connery (with whom she would later star alongside in 1994's *A Good Man in Africa*), the deal never panned out, and Diana was cast instead. Rigg said one of the reasons for accepting the role of Countess Teresa "Tracy" di Vicenzo (the first Bond girl to wed the British superspy) was that she always wanted to be in an epic motion picture.

With yet another film that was once considered unremarkable but now viewed as a cult classic, *Her Majesty*, like *The Assassination Bureau*, also happened to feature Telly Savalas (just four years shy of his 1973 CBS debut as the bold and bald detective *Kojak*). In the Bond film, he plays the villainous Blofeld, who heads the evil SPECTRE organization. With Diana as Tracy, both the actress and the character brought to Ian Fleming's 007 film franchise an elegant measure of feminine mystique, class, distinction, and an artistic level previously unseen in the series.

Tracy was raised by a Corsican father and British mother within the Union Course, an affluent criminal brood. After her mother dies, twelve-year-old Tracy and her father become estranged. Eventually marrying into royalty, she becomes Countess di Vicenzo, but is eventually widowed. At the time of her meeting 007, she's suicidal. Her father Marc-Ange Draco, played by Gabriele Ferzetti, thinks an arranged marriage to Bond would prove beneficial. Though James initially rejects the idea, he and Tracy grow closer, and things move swiftly, and dangerously, from there.

For general film and specific Bond aficionados, some of the best scenes in the movie involve Rigg, including her arrival in Mürren to rescue 007, who is being hunted down by Blofeld's underlings. In one memorable scene, Tracy skates up to Bond on a slippery ice rink, falls into his arms and, sensing danger, helps him escape with her red Mercury Cougar. Other pulsating developments find Tracy and James toppled by an avalanche, and battling Blofeld, one on one. In each instance, she proves capable of tackling the task at hand.

Shortly after marrying Bond, however, Tracy is brutally gunned down by Blofeld's right-hand woman, Irma Bunt (played by Ilse Steppat, who died of a heart attack the year of the film's release).

Though heart-wrenching and violent, such sequences inspired the rugged-minded Rigg to be a Bond girl. As she later told CBS News correspondent Anthony Mason, "Oh, come on! I mean, it was fun to do. That sequence where I'm driving around this ice rink. I did drive! It wasn't a double. Yeah, that was fun—not for the cameraman!"[6] As she also relayed to Vincent Canby in 1969, "It's nice to do [the movie] because you keep having fortnights off while they fix up the next piece of enormous machinery or move locations."[7]

Rigg acknowledged and accepted, with good reason, that *Her Majesty* was similar in style to *The Avengers*. When offered the role of Elizabeth opposite Lee Marvin and Clint Eastwood in director Joshua Logan's film adaptation of *Paint Your Wagon*, she opted instead to care for her ailing mother. Rigg later agreed to do the Bond movie because, as she told Canby, there "had been a long gap with nothing of mine seen."[8]

In her conversation with Gavin Esler at the University of Kent, Rigg described Tracy as a powerful female character, not unlike Emma Peel, in that she was the first Bond girl to come to 007's rescue. Regarding the opportunities then available for young actresses (including her own daughter), she said optimistically, "I think the parts are getting stronger. There's more recognition now," and "a huge market" for aspiring actresses. Not so much in feature films, she admitted, but television is "steaming ahead with really good parts for women."[9]

For Rigg, it was all about the market, and how important it was not to ignore the 50 percent of the population that goes to the movies or watches television. But whether first-run on the big screen or a rerun on the small screen, *On Her Majesty's Secret Service* remains a fan favorite. As she explained in her interview at Oxford University, "Everybody asks about it." In the canon of Bond mythology, the movie is primarily known for having actor George Lazenby replace, if only temporarily, the iconic Sean Connery as British secret agent 007.

Connery had long been dissatisfied with the 007 films, due to their lack of character development. So, when *On Her Majesty's Secret Service* was suggested as Bond's follow-up film to *You Only Live Twice*, which premiered in 1967, Connery opted not to return to the part. In retrospect, that may have been a mistake. The very thing that the actor was seeking for James Bond—a deeper exploration of his past, a new layer of heart—is exactly what transpired with *Her Majesty*, by way of Rigg's performance as Countess di Vicenzo.

In her review of the film on www.CrimeReads.com, Julia Sirmons awarded the film five stars. Sirmons credited Hunt for making the movie "a visual treat" and doing "inspired stuff" with the archetype of the Bond girl, considering her subplot to be "both sizzling and romantic, leading to a real emotional wallop. *Secret Service* is one of those rare treasures of genre fiction, one that manages to be a witty send-up of its norms while remaining a great example of the thing itself."[10]

According to Sirmons, Rigg ruled and steals the film before we even get a glimpse of Lazenby's face as the new James Bond: "We see Tracy's in his rear-view mirror as she overtakes him in a hairpin turn. An intrigued Bond follows her to the beach. To get a better view, he stares at her through a scope. This framing evokes that trademark button that introduces Bond before the opening credit . . . it positions her at Bond's level, as his compatriot."[11]

Describing Tracy as "a poor-little-rich-girl with a death wish," Sirmons writes that Rigg imbues a clichéd backstory and character with "wounded passion and fiery pride beneath her porcelain exterior. Despite her baggage, in the inevitable Bond–Bond Girl seduction, she is no easy conquest, and matches him beat for provocative beat. She gazes at him with the same bald sexual appraisal with which Bond usually looks at his 'girls.' It is she who propositions Bond. 'I hope it's worth it,' she says, with cool bemusement, and she's the one who flies in the night afterwards, leaving Bond pleasantly intrigued."[12]

It's because of Rigg, Sirmons asserts, that Lazenby shines as 007, "selling Bond's more romantic side."

Producer and Bond historian David Naylor, who has worked on several Bond documentaries, described Rigg's involvement within the James Bond arena as being "notable in a number of ways"; it was also a challenging time for the producers, the studio, Connery, and Lazenby. "A new actor had to be found who could not only fill some pretty big shoes," Naylor said, "but also deal with the enormity of a Bond production and all the associated demands that marketing it entailed."

The epic scope and scale of *Her Majesty* is what appealed to Rigg, Naylor said. "She knew the film would also raise her profile beyond the UK," where she had found her initial success with *The Avengers*.

As Rigg later confirmed during her interview with Oxford Union, she did indeed do much of her own stunt work for *Her Majesty*. "There was a charming girl who would stand in for me from time to time," she said. But, in those days, "I was quite . . . quite fit. I used to do quite a lot of the stuff myself."

But that stuff did not include some of the wintery scenes that required skiing. "I didn't ski," she said. "I couldn't ski."

So, when push came to shove on the mountain, in stepped a gentleman named Willie Bougne, from the renowned Alpine family, all of whom skied. As Rigg recalled, Bougne was a champion skier who one day asked her, "Would you like to know how it feels to ski?"

To which she replied, "Yes, but how?"

"I'll give you a piggyback," he told her.

For Rigg, that action became "the sexiest thing . . . [I've] ever done . . . in life." Meaning, the duo piggybacked down the mountain. In doing so, she found herself moving "with him as one," in "rhythm, and all that. Oh, God it is absolutely wonderful. It didn't end in a carnal relationship, but it was the closest thing."[13]

Beyond that particular incident, and as Diana noted in her conversation with Gavin Kesler and the University of Kent, she had never been involved with such a "huge production" as *On Her Majesty's Secret Service*: "It was astonishing. . . . They flew me to Paris . . . to choose a fur coat. . . . They sent down . . . a watchmaker for me to try on a watch that I just glanced at once, which they gave me."

The plentitude of these sort of films left her impressed. Coming from the Royal Shakespeare Company, she was "completely gob-smacked. It was terrific. Of course, we had our problems with the leading man, but there you go. I had my watch and my fur coat."

Assuredly, it was all worth it—for all parties concerned. In a recent fiftieth-anniversary tribute to the film, *Yours Retro Magazine* called Rigg's performance "stunning . . . arguably one of the best Bond Girls to date. Most likely due, in no small part, to her being the first actress to give real depth to the role, rather than just looking good in a bikini."[14]

When Gavin Esler asked Rigg who her favorite Bond girl was, throughout the entire 007 franchise, she responded, "Shirley Eaton . . . and Ursula Andress. She was beautiful."

In his book with Mark Altman, *Nobody Does It Better: The Complete Uncensored, Unauthorized Oral History of James Bond*, author Ed Gross further validates Rigg's place in the Bond universe. Until Eva Green's three appearances in future Bond films with Daniel Craig, there "was probably not a better Bond Girl than the brilliant and resourceful Diana Rigg, if you can even get away with calling her a *girl*."[15]

Following her run on *The Avengers*, Honor Blackman, like Rigg, had also appeared in a Bond film, 1964's *Goldfinger*. But next to Blackman's Pussy Galore, opposite Connery, Rigg's Tracy, opposite Lazenby, was, from Gross's perspective, "the first real . . . capable, smart" woman to appear in a Bond movie. For him, Rigg "represented a genuine evolution of the Bond Girl" and the first female Bond-counterpart with a legitimate story arc, providing a new template for future adventures.[16]

In time, producer Barbara Broccoli, daughter of the famed Albert "Cubby" Broccoli, inherited creative control of the 007 mantel. Barbara once referred to Rigg's performance as "exquisite," worthy of the title Mrs. James Bond. "She's a totally captivating, beautiful, extraordinary woman, and a magnificent actress. She certainly will be remembered for many things, and obviously, for being Tracy in this film."[17]

With Rigg as Mrs. Bond, the father Broccoli and his producing partner Harry Salzman made 007 history. They hired an established actress in a leading role, someone they believed would enhance the performance of the fledgling Lazenby, an ex-model turned actor, while expanding upon the romantic elements of the film series. As Rigg years later observed, "They wanted an experienced lady with a certain degree of glamour to help along a totally inexperienced actor." Another time, she said, "They got me on board because I was the gravitas to George Lazenby."

Other than that, Rigg had no illusions as to why she was hired to play Mrs. Bond. "They got me, and I did what I could [with the role]. I have to say, though, that the money was wonderful. It was a mammoth production, an epic, and I'd never done an epic before, so I rather wanted to know what it was to be in an epic."[18]

While filming the movie, rumors circulated in the press of a feud between Rigg and Lazenby.

According to Ray Austin, Rigg didn't even want to make movies, 007 or otherwise. "She wanted to go back to the stage and absolutely didn't want to do Bond. She wasn't looking forward to it because of George Lazenby. But in the end, Diana and George did not get along at all."[19]

"George had come up from [lesser] beginnings than Diana," Austin continued. "He was a male model; a big, handsome muscular guy who did a TV commercial carrying a great big, chocolate bar on his shoulder for ice chocolate or something or the other. But that was the only thing he had done. He never did anything else. He'd done small little bits but his main trade was being a model.[20]

"George was a lovely, nice guy," Austin continued. "My wife, Wendy, and I spent a lot of time with him. But he always knew he was the weak link in the Bond film he did, and I think Diana was probably unfair to him in looking down her nose a little bit at the way he performed, the way he acted. I just don't think she thought he was up to her, and the other actors', standards in the movie."[21]

There were also rumors of an affair between Diana and George. But according to Austin, these were "absolutely 100 percent not true. I promise you. I swear my life on it. I know George so well. And I knew Diana very well, though not at that stage in her career. But she was a very choosey lady when it came to men. She didn't even want to get married."[22]

But she *did* want to be Mrs. James Bond. In her conversation with Oxford, she said she "knew exactly" why she was cast: for publicity value. Lazenby, the former model with no acting experience had, as she observed, "just done advertisement [photo shoots]. And I was there as a professional to sort of guide him through, which I was very happy to do, up to a point. It didn't end entirely happily."[23]

Although the film itself is "much loved," she continued, and even though Lazenby was "pretty good" in it, he was also "extraordinarily difficult" to work with. As a result, Rigg relayed, "they didn't ask him back. And I think he must deeply regret it, because he truly wasn't [a] bad [actor] at all."[24]

Years later, Rigg said, "I could never understand why George behaved as he did. He was given such a glorious opportunity and he threw it all away.

I'm sorry for him, if you really want to know. At some stage, it just went to his head." Another time, she told the *Daily Mail*, "He'd really throw his weight around. Oh, he was ghastly, and I had to marry the man!"[25]

While she refuted the chilly chatter of their alleged affair, according to what Lazenby years later told the press, their association was nothing but warm, fuzzy, and funny. The gossip began, he recalled, before principal photography began in Switzerland, when Lazenby was in Rigg's quarters, with her boyfriend, who invited the former-model-turned-actor to play a game of chess.

Almost immediately, Lazenby shouted, "CHECKMATE!" After he won a second time, Lazenby said Rigg's boyfriend tossed the board in the air. "And that's the first time Diana took any notice of me," Lazenby said. Next thing he knew, he was in Switzerland, with Rigg telling him, "If you have nothing to do with any of the other girls, we may get something going."[26]

"So, here she's giving me instructions and I lied," Lazenby said. Just one week on the set, he was "fooling around" with a receptionist in the stuntman's tent, which was laden with mattresses. Just as Lazenby and the receptionist were as, he called it, "getting a little cuddly," Rigg walked by. A stuntman lifted one side of the tent. Without missing a beat, Diana quipped, "Oh my God . . . there he goes again."[27]

Another, less provocative incident apparently transpired in the UK's famed Pinewood Studios commissary on a Wednesday afternoon. Lazenby and Rigg were about to shoot their love scene. As Lazenby remembered it in a recent interview with the press, midway through their lunch Rigg called over to him, and shouted with a smile, "Hey, George . . . I'm having garlic with my pâté. I hope you are, too."

Lazenby smiled back and continued his meal. The next day, headlines around the world read, "Diana Rigg Eats Garlic Before Kiss with George Lazenby."[28]

"The press kept feeding the fire to keep the story going," Lazenby said. "Contrary to the newspaper accounts, Diana and I didn't hate each other. But Diana *did* have a big ego. After all, she had been around a while, and I was just an upstart. I'm sure she didn't like us being treated on the same level. Also, the press was very interested in me because I was new, while they had all done interviews with Diana before. Even Telly Savalas was affected. He kept saying, 'Why am I the best-kept secret on this picture?'"

Another time, Lazenby admitted, "I could have done better [as a person and performer]. But I didn't want to become an actor. It was not in my blood."[29]

Lazenby and Rigg had not seen the movie in years, nor did they stay in touch.

"I don't think one way or the other about Diana," he said.

"Oh goodness, no, he wouldn't come near me!" she said.

Rigg eventually, and fortunately, found a measure of peace in playing opposite Lazenby as Mrs. James Bond. "I hope I did help him," she said. "For someone who had never done a movie before, he was quite good."

That's essentially what she said even before Lazenby was finally, and formally, chosen for the role of 007. According to David Naylor, just two weeks before the film's principal photography began, Peter Hunt asked Diana her opinion of Lazenby. "I think he's fine. I think he'll be fine," she said.

"So, clearly, she was a great ally for him," Naylor observed. "I'm not saying that her endorsement was the clincher, but it definitely was a key part of the equation, for the simple reason that her vast acting experience made up for the fact that her soon-to-be-leading man had absolutely none at all.[30]

"If you're an actor," Naylor clarified, "The wise thing to do in a situation like this would be to absorb and learn as much as you can from the person you're doing critical scenes with. But the pressure of, not so much the role, but what came with it, as well as the unrelenting glare of the tabloids, caused so many problems."[31]

And that was true for all parties concerned.

Consequently, what may well have been an offhand attempt at humor during lunch about eating garlic before a love scene was, according to Naylor, "blown all out of proportion."

"And then it just snowballed," he added, "and took away a lot of attention from the fact that Diana and George were doing some really good work in their scenes together."[32]

Naylor also said that Diana proved to be "an incredible sport on set," and performed some of her own stunts, specifically those involving driving. But he "felt very bad for her in a way." That is to say, many of Rigg's contributions were overlooked because the press frequently hounded both she and Lazenby once Connery was no longer "a target."[33]

As to the movie itself, Rigg assessed to the *Daily Mail*, "The Bond organization really turned their back on that film. They never mention it because it's the film they consider a failure because of George. But as far as the public is concerned, it's not a failure. It's up there among the fans' favorites and it's really been reappraised as a film."

In one interview, John Cork, who has produced more than thirty James Bond documentaries for MGM DVD releases and other outlets, noted,

"Diana Rigg is one of the great actresses of her generation. She out-acts everyone else in *On Her Majesty's Secret Service*. She lifts the film up every time she's on screen and illuminates how ill-prepared George Lazenby was for taking on the leading role in a motion picture. Any actor thrown into that situation would be ill-prepared, and . . . Diana Rigg tried to help George in every way she could."

In his book, *The Making of "On Her Majesty's Secret Service*," Charles Helfenstein calls the movie "remarkably similar to the book. Minor differences here and there. No chronology jump/flashback." But it's biggest deviation, "would probably be Tracy." For him, Rigg's casting changed the script, specifically with regard to additional fight scenes at Piz Gloria between she and Grunther, played by Yuri Burienko. Due to her physical training on *The Avengers*, "she's a bit more capable, a bit less damaged than the Tracy of the book," Helfenstein said.[34]

In her book *For His Eyes Only: The Women of James Bond*, Lisa Funnell observes, "The women in Bond films have changed over time, which only makes sense because you're interacting with different politics. You have the Women's Movement of the '60s, the feminist backlash of the '70s and '80s, and you've got post-feminism in the '90s. You see Bond and his relationship with these women changing as the broader politics for women are changing."

Along those lines, Diana would have welcomed an alternate 007 on-screen, with certain restrictions. "A Black Bond would be lovely," she told the *Radio Times* in one of her later interviews. "I wouldn't like to see a female Bond, because we wouldn't want to lose the Bond girls. But we could have a lesbian Bond, why not?"

As she told Gavin Esler years later, Rigg had stopped caring about the Bond movies. For her, they simply "ran out of steam." But as she also concluded to Michael Parkinson in 1972 (or '74), regarding her work in movies, in general, "I wish I had one really good film that I could be proud of and say that I had succeeded in that. But I have not succeeded in any of the movies [I've done]. My face, actually, is not too good for movies. Even with *The Avengers*, I got away with it. But . . . I am better on stage because I have got a big face.

"And all the film stars that I have met—and I have met most of them—they have tiny features which photograph exquisitely. Me? I have big features and they don't work."[35]

With that said, movies were rarely a comfortable fit for Diana. She first attained fame during the 1960s, a decade when there were movie actors and television actors—but never both at once. The general attitude of that time was: why should we pay money to see someone in a movie theater when we can see them for free in our own living rooms? Television, at best, was viewed as a sort of training ground for future movie stars. Actors like Steve McQueen, James Garner, Burt Reynolds, and Clint Eastwood got their start in TV Westerns before being elevated to movie stardom. And once that happened, there was no going back to the small screen—that is, unless their careers had gone into an irreversible decline. To the public at large, Diana Rigg was that sexy British actress who was on that spy show. And once an image like that is established, it is virtually impossible to change it. Hence, the once-welcome starring vehicle leads to the actor's curse of typecasting.

Diana, too, was not especially interested in being a film star. Of course, when and if a worthwhile script—or simply a lucrative contract—presented itself, she committed to it 100 percent. Ever the professional, she showed up on time and she knew her lines; in short, she was ready to go to work. But privately, she found the whole process of filming to be slow, endlessly repetitive, and boring—so bloody boring.

"Theatre is more familiar to me," she decided. "And I think you love working in the most familiar [settings]. And I love people being there. It is the truest sign of whether you are succeeding or failing, because immediately you get feedback from the audience. Quiet; they are listening. If they laugh, *you* have made them laugh."

CHAPTER 8

HAILING CAESAR, THE HOSPITAL, AND BLOOD

I love walking, but I won't march.
—DIANA RIGG

ROBERT S. RAY IS AN ENTERTAINMENT AND FILM HISTORIAN WHO HAS
served as an assistant programmer for the prestigious Friday Film Forum
in Long Beach, California. He has contributed articles to the *Past Times
Newsletter*, which has catered to all things retro media and for which he
was as video critic. Ray was also on the board of directors for the Classic
TV Preservation Society, a 501(c)3 nonprofit organization dedicated to the
positive social influence of classic television programming. When it comes
to classic television series and legendary cinema, Ray knows his stuff, and
when it comes to Diana Rigg, he had this to say:

"Diana Rigg was successful because she had it all. In addition to being
beautiful and talented, she exuded an intelligence, poise, and extraordinary
charm that made her something far more than the typical sex symbol.
On *The Avengers*, Emma Peel was clearly Steed's intellectual equal while
looking great in tights. She had a steely resolve and cool demeanor that
served her well playing everything from the graceful Mrs. Bond to the icy
Mrs. Danvers in *Rebecca*. She used her intellect, poise, and charm to great
advantage throughout her long illustrious career."

Certainly, that is the case with *The Assassination Bureau*, and other films
Diana made in the 1970s, including Stuart Burge's provocative adaptation
of *Julius Caesar*.

In the 1960s and '70s, Burge transformed the Nottingham Playhouse
into one of the leading theaters in Britain, rescued the Royal Court in
London from bankruptcy (while helping to retain its creative vitality), and
was a prolific TV director who helped pioneer the BBC's single plays in

75

the 1950s, some of which Diana appeared in. Two decades later, he was guiding her as Portia in *Julius Caesar*, which also featured Charlton Heston (in the lead), alongside John Gielgud, Robert Vaughn, Christopher Lee, Jill Bennett, Richard Chamberlain, Richard Johnson, and Jason Robards (as Brutus, the betrayer).

Apparently, the latter's involvement was good casting. Diana explained the big picture to Gavin Esler, saying that the movie "was alright. But it wasn't an entirely successful film at all. It was made on a shoestring. You might notice people leaning up against pillars which shake from time to time, and we were all dressed in sheets. It was Charlton Heston's dream to do it and we did it, I think it was in Madrid. Jason Robards wasn't happy. He wasn't a happy bunny. He looked like Widow Twankey with those curls. He looked sort of—what's the word? Harried. Worried. [As if to say], 'What am I doing here?'"[1]

And indeed, Robards's energy in the film does not jibe with the rest of the cast. He speaks his lines as if reading them from the phone book, emoting not a drop. But, as one casual reviewer observed on IMDb, "The stellar performances of Heston, Gielgud, Vaughn, and the others make up for Robards's inadequacies; and Burge's direction, while not really on par with a [Orson] Welles, [Laurence] Olivier, or [Franco] Zeffirelli, is solid enough. Clearly, this isn't the most successful adaptation of The Bard. But given how hard it is to pull Shakespeare off cinematically, it is worth a 7 (out of 10)."

Rigg, it must be said, is in top form. As with every role she played, she gives her all to her Portia portrayal. Her early public speaking/poetry training with Sylvia Greenwood serves her well in this film. She recites her lines in earnest, with the diction of an English teacher; it is as though she is living each word. Irrespective of the film's low budget, her performance is rich with layers. It's not her fault that the movie failed, nor the fault of Robards or Burge. It was just a sign of the times.

Shakespeare classics on the big screen, along with religious epics, were a dying breed by the 1970s. Long gone were the days of Heston and his sensational portrayal of Moses in *The Ten Commandments* (1956). With the burgeoning miniseries format on television, the small screen was doing a more productive job of delivering media mosaics, including those airing on PBS: *I, Claudius*, starring Derek Jacobi, and the anthology series *Masterpiece Theatre*, hosted by Alistair Cooke. Other stellar vintage-geared small-screen sagas included NBC's all-star presentation of Franco Zeffirelli's acclaimed miniseries *Jesus of Nazareth* (1977, starring Robert Powell), in which Diana should have been cast but wasn't.

But at least by December 1971, she was back on the big screen in yet another uniquely gripping cinematic choice. This time, she portrayed Barbara Drummond, opposite George C. Scott, in Paddy Chayefsky's *The Hospital*, which was directed by Arthur Hiller. The film marked Chayefsky and Hiller's second collaboration (they previously partnered on 1964's *The Americanization of Emily*), while it presented a series of firsts in other ways. It was Chayefsky's first original screenplay, the first American picture for composer Morris Surdin, and the first production for Howard Gottfried, who went on the produce *Network* (1976), also written by Chayefsky, and *Body Double* (1984).

The Hospital also marked the screen debuts of Stockard Channing, Christopher Guest, and Dennis Dugan, and features future TV stars Katherine Helmond (*Soap, Who's the Boss?*), Nancy Marchand, and Robert Walden (both of *Lou Grant*, the former also from *The Sopranos*), and veteran actor Barnard Hughes (*Doc*). *The Hospital* opens with Chayefsky's uncredited narration describing the events that led up to Hughes's Dr. Schaefer indiscriminately utilizing the bed of his deceased patient for a tryst. The credits then begin, and though we never again hear Chayefsky's voice, the following statement appears in the final frames (which were shot at a New York hospital's then-new, and thus far unused, psychiatry wing): "We gratefully acknowledge the co-operation of the New York City Health and Hospitals Corporation and the Dept. of Public Works of the City of New York."

Diana's performance as Drummond earned her a Golden Globe nomination, while Chayefsky garnered the Writer's Guild of America Award for Best Comedy Screenplay and the Academy Award for Best Screenplay. Additionally, Chayefsky and Scott were nominated for Golden Globes and BAFTAs, with Chayefsky emerging victorious each time. Despite Scott's declining even an Oscar nomination for *The Hustler* in 1961, and his refusal of the Best Actor Oscar for *Patton* in 1971, he received the same nod for *The Hospital*.

According to what Chayefsky told the *New York Times* during the film's release, its core theme had to do with personal responsibility in an immoral society. One year later, in conversation with the *Los Angeles Herald Examiner*, he said that Scott's Dr. Herbert Bock's erectile dysfunctional represented "the impotence of the American middle class." He acknowledged his battles with Scott during filming, but in the end, he was satisfied with the actor's performance.

As to Diana's experience of Scott, in one interview, she described him as "a brilliant actor, undoubtedly, but he was very troubled." Apparently, for lengthy periods at a time, Scott made himself scarce on the set, which is when, as Rigg explained to Esler, "Paddy and I would hit the Scrabble board." But she was enticed by the actor's unpredictability. "You never knew what he was going to do ... there was this sort of power emanating from him. It was, like, reined in; you never knew when it would burst. I loved it. It was very exciting, and I think our scenes were quite good. So, I enjoyed the whole thing."[2]

As Rigg said in one interview, she enjoyed working with the film's director. "I loved Arthur Hiller. He was great. She called *The Hospital* "a very good movie," crediting Chayefsky for her casting. Upon catching her Broadway performance in *Abelard and Heloise*, "he fought for me to get the job," she said. "We adored each other." And as to those rounds of Scrabble they played, she added, "He'd put Yiddish words down on the board and I'd scream at him!"[3]

According to *Film Facts* magazine, Chayefsky had formed a production company in order to retain a measure of control over *The Hospital*. On January 3, 1972, he told the *New York Times*, "I was in on all basic decisions, including the final cut."[4]

Two years before, *Daily Variety* documented how Michael Ritchie had been the original choice to helm *The Hospital*. But due to "differences," he exited the film and was replaced by Hiller with an agreement that guaranteed a percentage of the profits. Diana, however, had no knowledge of any of those developments, but adamantly confirmed Hiller's firm creative grip. "Arthur was the director, definitely," she said.[5]

Several critics were not pleased with *The Hospital*'s ultimate reveal of a mad murderer and how that undercut Chayefsky's message of medical ineptitude. But, overall, the movie received favorable reviews, with many media outlets comparing it to *M*A*S*H*, Robert Altman's maudlin/merry Korean War medical romp from 1970.

In her recent assessment of the film, journalist/actress Andrea Whitcomb-May observed:

"There are three broken hearts in the 1971 comedy *The Hospital*, impeccably written by Paddy Chayefsky, who won an Oscar for his effort. The hospital itself is a character as well as the setting for the redemptive relationship between Barbara Drummond and Dr. Herbert Bock, roles driven full throttle by Dame Diana Rigg and George C. Scott.

"Dr. Bock is the Chief of Medicine at the chaotic Hospital. When commenting on a current administrative situation he observes, 'The incompetence here is radiant.' Bock could have easily been reflecting on his personal life. Both he and the hospital may soon crash and burn. Bock is recently separated, terrified of women, and contemplating suicide when along comes Barbara careening into his life at breakneck speed.

"At first it may seem that free-spirited Barbara will be taking the audience on a bumpy ride down back roads in a hippy VW bus; however, Rigg so deftly drives her performance that viewers sense a nimble course correction. There is a recklessness about Barbara's life, but with Rigg's masterful grip at the wheel, viewers are sped along her journey knowing there is a Ferrari engine purring underneath the hood. While using an American accent, Rigg's underlying Shakespearian talents turbocharge every scene with artful maneuvers. Only an actress of this magnitude could match Scott's raw power. They are superbly cast and shift gears smoothly through their scenes together.

"Barbara coolly comes on to Bock, sharing the tales of her sexual and suicidal journey. Rigg cruises through her "I had my breakdown" soliloquy with ease while revealing the depth of a character who suffered much and is now curiously content. Bock, meanwhile, weeps and rages about the wreck of his life and about life itself. He not only allows Barbara to see the cracks in his heart, but he also drives his vulnerability and desperation into her face.

"Barbara takes the lead and helps put Bock back on the road. Their passionate coming together is a collision of destiny releasing them and allowing them to love again.

"The broken-hearted hospital can mend too, now that Bock is again in the driver's seat. With the accelerating protests, incompetence, death, and murder, the aging hospital is tail-spinning into a fiery riot. Bock is tempted to abandon it and leave for Mexico with Barbara but, ironically, because she has put him on the track to recovery and redemption, he is able to stay behind and let her go—'Somebody has to be responsible, Barbara,' he tells her with rediscovered resolve. 'Everybody is hitting the road, running away. Somebody's got to be responsible.'"

Assuredly, off-screen, Diana was taking responsibility for her career and making movie headway by way of *The Hospital* in 1971. As she once explained, "Paddy went on to write *Network*, and wanted me to play Faye Dunaway's part. But I didn't get it. So, he called [the character she was to play] *Diana*."

Around this time, Rigg experimented with drugs. As she later recalled to reporter Laura Potter for *The Guardian*, "I tried cocaine and amyl nitrate. I can't take pot. I just go to sleep." She certainly had to remain alert in her career, because the offers kept coming. Though she had the luxury to pick and choose, as when in 1971, Rigg was invited to take the film lead in *Countess Dracula* but declined. Instead, Ingrid Pitt played the part of an elderly seventeenth- century Hungarian widow who maintains her misleading youth by bathing in the blood of virgins, regularly supplied to her by faithful servant Captain Dobi (Nigel Green).

The following year, Rigg received good notices for her performance as Dorothy Moore in the National Theatre's Company's premiere of Tom Stoppard's abstruse comedy *Jumpers* at the Old Vic.

On September 20, 1972, she joined actor Anthony Hopkins at the opening night premiere party for their run of Shakespeare's *Macbeth* at the National Theatre in London. She played Lady Macbeth opposite Hopkins's Macbeth in the classic tragedy, just as he was growing leery of live performing.

That same year, though previously rejecting *Countess Dracula*, Diana accepted a part in the comedy-horror film, *Theatre of Blood* (1973). Here, she portrayed Edwina Lionheart, a loyal daughter to a disgruntled Shakespearean British actor named Edward Lionheart, played by shock-master Vincent Price, who takes revenge against a band of critics.

Classically trained actor Damon Evans, who replaced Michael Evans (no relation) as Lionel Jefferson on TV's legendary sitcom *The Jeffersons*, always admired and eventually met Rigg. He shared his thoughts on *Blood*: "My very first indelible and fun memory of Diana was seeing her in *Theatre of Blood*. She played Edwina Lionheart with such cool crafted skill that I immediately fell in love with her, even though I knew she was an accomplice in Edwina's father's murders."

The working title for the film was "Much Ado About Murder," a play on words of the title of Shakespeare's *Much Ado About Nothing*. Its opening credits feature clips from silent film adaptations of plays by Shakespeare, including the 1922 German production of *Othello*, starring Emil Jannings and Lya de Putti, and unidentified productions of *Richard III* and *The Merchant of Venice*, all of which are referenced in *Theater of Blood*. The picture, shot in London, marked the final feature screen appearance of British long-time character actor Robert Coote.

The murders of the critics in *Theatre of Blood* each correspond to murders in famous plays by Shakespeare: George Maxwell (Michael Hordern) is stabbed to death on March 15 (the ides of March), mirroring the murder of the title character in *Julius Caesar*; Hector Snipe (Dennis Price) is run through with a spear, after which his body is tied to the tail of a horse and dragged, as is Hector in *Troilus and Cressida*; the head of Horace Sprout (Arthur Lowe) is cut off while in bed, as is Cloten in *Cymbeline*; Trevor

Dickman (Harry Andrews) has his heart cut out, completing the threat made but not acted upon by Shylock to Antonio in *The Merchant of Venice*; Oliver Larding (Robert Coote) is drowned in a vat of red wine, as is the king's brother Clarence in *Richard III*; Maisie Psaltery is smothered to death by her jealous husband, as is Desdemona in *Othello*; Chloe Moon (Coral Browne) is electrocuted, much as Joan of Arc is burned in *Henry VI*; and Meredith Merridew (Robert Morley) chokes to death while unwittingly consuming his pet dogs, similar to Tamora unknowingly eating a pie made of her sons in *Titus Andronicus*. In addition to these references, during the sword duel Edward Lionheart asks Peregrine Devlin (Ian Hendry) if he recalls the swordplay between Mercutio and Tybalt in *Romeo and Juliet*. The death of Edward Lionheart also mimics the conclusion of *King Lear*, as the king dies holding the dead body of his daughter Cordelia.

Diana considered *Blood* the favorite of her films, once defining it as "brilliant . . . so original. The characters are so wonderful. It has an implacability about it that everybody's going to get murdered at some time or another. It's a bit clunky in places but it's a wonderful idea."[6]

She had fun with all the disguises in the movie. "I adored it," she said, although she admitted, "I wasn't terribly good as the male policeman. It was awfully hard to be a fella . . . but . . . I loved working with all those folks, a great range of brilliant character actors in that film. Dennis Price [no relation to Vincent] was absolutely adorable. He, in his day, had been a huge heartthrob. Then there was Robert Morley, deeply eccentric, wonderful in the part, pink suit and all those poodles." As for Price himself, Diana loved him. He was, she said, "a master of the macabre" with "a wonderful sense of humor." Like Diana, the American-born Price reportedly favored *Blood* over all of his films, many of which were in the horror genre. Feeling stereotyped by his other work, *Blood* granted Price the chance to play Shakespeare on-screen (if in a play-within-a-movie premise). As Rigg once recalled, "I think Vincent Price gives a great performance, and proves that he could have been a great classical actor, had he wanted to."[7]

As the sole female critic subjected to Edward Lionheart's gruesome vengeance, Chloe Moon, played by Coral Browne, is a particular standout. Browne later recalled in the TV documentary *Caviar to the General* that she had little desire to make "one of those scary Vincent Price movies." But when the Chloe Moon role presented itself, she was persuaded by her friends Robert Morley and Michael Hordern to accept it.

After that, Rigg took the bull by the horns, and introduced Browne to Price, unaware that he was married. As Diana explained during her interview at Oxford, "Coral and Vincent were doing a sort of little pavane run around with each other and I knew something was going on. They were both well into their seventies [sixties, actually], so I thought, 'Aha.'"[8]

As Diana told Esler, Price had invited her to attend his performance in a charity presentation of the play *Cowardly Custard* at the Mermaid Theatre. "I went to the loo at the interval, Coral was in the next cubicle, she suddenly said [imitating Browne's nasal drawl], 'It's a long time since I've fancied a man of my own age, but I fancy Vincent.'"

Then, on their drive home, Price told Diana that he wasn't sure what to get Browne for her birthday, which was the following week. Aware of his somewhat careful sense with a dollar, Rigg told him, "Vincent, you have it on your person, and it won't cost you a penny."

From there, the *Blood* really began to boil, and Price eventually left his wife and wed Browne.

Meanwhile, the irony in Price feeling stereotyped in the horror genre is easily likened to Diana's similar struggles with her *avenging* experience in playing Emma Peel. Furthermore, her periodically feeling prejudiced against for her work on the stage, and/or being sometimes pigeonholed as a classically trained actress, found echoes in her part in the film.

Actor/director John Schuck is known for his likable performances on classic TV shows such as *McMillan & Wife*. He has also appeared in several live stage productions, including *Annie*, in which he played Daddy Warbucks. A respected professional within the film, TV, and theater communities, and across the board, Schuck offered this insightful commentary about Rigg:

"Diana paid the price for playing Emma Peel, because audiences and the industry, at times, were challenged to see her in any other role. Fortunately, she was an extremely talented, accomplished, and well-trained actor, at home on the stage and in a diversity of roles. Her stage work in particular, was a major accomplishment and she made the transition from sex symbol to character actor seem easy."

What wasn't so easy, however, was her marriage to Menachem Gueffen. On July 6, 1973, much to her own surprise and to the shock of others, Diana wed Gueffen, with whom unstill waters ran deep and troubled. Diana had claimed that she had "met her match" in Gueffen. They began their love affair following her disengagement from Philip Saville. But while courting, and with their twin artistic temperaments in check, she and Gueffen argued frequently. As she years later told reporter Rosanna Greenstreet of *The Guardian*, her "sudden and explosive temper" is the trait she most deplored in herself. "It takes a lot to light the blue touchpaper, but when I blow, duck."

As such, when it came to Gueffen, it was *duck, duck, goose*, so to speak—and he was *it*. Their battles became so intense during one vacation together that he tossed her luggage out a hotel window. Apparently, that erratic act was appealing, because she proposed to him on their flight home. But would this second major romance last, especially with her career on the upswing?

In an interview shortly following the ceremony, she professed her love for the artist, but quipped, "I give the marriage a year."

CHAPTER 9

WHEN DIANA MET *DIANA*

I like comedy best . . . because it is such a joyous thing.

—DIANA RIGG

IN THE EARLY 1970S, DIANA WAS A MEMBER OF THE NATIONAL THEATRE Company, which was then under the direction of Laurence Olivier. While at the Old Vic from 1972 to 1975, she accepted leading roles in premiere productions of two plays by Tom Stoppard. In 1972, she created the part of Dotty, the sensual diva and duplicitous spouse of George Moore (Michael Hordern) in the previously mentioned *Jumpers*.

By this time, too, Menachem Gueffen was exiting Diana's personal life. By 1974, the dueling duo agreed to a trial separation. In public, she blamed her "bloody awful independence." But some reports said the union formally ended only on December 3, 1976, only three years after it started—all because Gueffen was threatened by her brighter star, which continued to shine on stage.

She addressed the relationship in her conversation with Mary Parkinson in 1974. Before getting married, she was against the tradition. But then she wed Gueffen, and it was hardly a match made in heaven. "And because it all happened within a very short space of time, there was a great deal of pain involved," Diana admitted, and not just for her but also for her family. "My mother suffered a great deal, obviously. It is a very shaming thing. I feel deeply ashamed. I also feel bewildered because I have failed. And I failed on a level where it was inconceivable that I should fail. I suspect I failed because I was thirty-five and somewhat unbending and unchanging."[1]

It was that bloody awful independence thing again.

As such, a new love began to bloom, this time with Scottish laird and theater producer Archibald "Archie" Stirling, just as her career was beginning to blossom on Broadway. But she did not condone the mingling of personal and professional life, especially when it came to politics. As she told

Michael Parkinson in 1972, "I don't agree with it. I can perfectly see actors and actresses having strong political convictions. But I wonder whether it is slightly immoral to use your 'muscle' or your stardom, or what it is, to signing, doing, demonstrating . . . that kind of stuff. . . . I try to remain as apolitical as possible, and whatever I do is on a humanitarian level. It is usually for the minorities who are suffering. Whether it is for the Jews in Soviet Russia or autistic children or the blind or the deaf."[2]

However, such a stance might have been interpreted as a political activity, as was the case with the Panovs,[3] which became an issue for her "because of all the political associations. And the positions that I took in were signed by Jews and non-Jews alike. Thousands of people who just *had* to make a statement. And it was a passive statement. It was not demonstrative. It was simply on a piece of paper saying, 'Can something be done about these people?' I was asked to do this. And I did. It was a passive thing to do. I believe in those sorts of statements. Thereafter, the demonstrations that went on, I dissociate myself from completely because inside the theatre, I think it is ill-mannered, ill-judged, and altogether the wrong way to go about things."[4]

When asked if she thought that militancy or violence is ever justified, Rigg replied, "I think you get a different answer from different people. I am not at all interested in militancy. I prefer to give my time and my money to help when I can instead of waving a banner. I don't believe in that."[5]

In other words, she was not one for public displays of advocacy, handing out flyers and the like. She didn't go on marches. In short, Diana kept it all in check. She had long escaped what could have been the arrogance of her youth, and instead did what she could for charity, but discreetly. Though she was not one to toot her own horn for such work, the impact she made with her compassion was loud and clear. As she told Rosanna Greenstreet of *The Guardian*, one of those she most admired was "an old friend who has been living with AIDS for years and never complains or mentions it."

Another time, Rigg visited the Thiepval Memorial to the Missing of the Somme, a war memorial near the village of Thiepval, Picardy in France. Designed by Sir Edwin Lutyens, the center, which opened in 2004, pays tribute to 72,337 missing British and South African servicemen who died in the Battles of the Somme of the First World War between 1916 and 1918, with no known grave. Gavin Stamp, the author of *The Memorial to the Missing of the Somme*, described it as "the greatest executed British work of monumental architecture of the twentieth century." Diana said, "All those lost lives broke my heart."

As another example of her compassionate heart, she received an honorary doctorate from the University of Stirling in November 1988, and commenced a ten-year term as a chancellor there, albeit in a ceremonial rather than executive capacity. Rigg had long-standing connections with Stirling, having relocated to the area in the 1980s and, for several years, held the position of chair of the Macrobert Arts Centre Committee. She was an active member of the local community, serving as the chieftain of the Bridge of Allan Highland Games and holding the role of patron of the Stirling and District Association of Mental Health.

She was also a patron of International Care and Relief, and was for many years the public face of the charity's child-sponsorship program, which focused on international development, poverty, education, and gender equality.

Founded as a branch of International Christian Relief, the charity broke off from the American parent body and became independent under the name International Care and Relief, which enabled it to continue to use its recognized acronym, ICR. At the same time as becoming an independent organization, ICR moved away from aid relief, choosing instead to focus on long-term development operating specifically in East Africa.

Meanwhile, back in the States, amid the bright lights of the Big Apple's famed avenue, Rigg illuminated some of that big city's dimmest little corners with her charitable ways. She utilized her public persona in the most productive way; she'd periodically pay it forward with no Sunday visits to the park, but rather to a New York rehabilitation center whose residents struggled with substance abuse. But Diana didn't lecture against the perils of drug-taking. As she later explained to reporter Laura Potter and *The Guardian*, she'd offer them "drama therapy."

Such moments represented the perfect blend of her existence. She melded with grace her life and career which, for better and worse, was a comedy-drama of errors and triumphs. She knew one element did not exist without the other. Essentially, it was about balance, especially when it came to her work, which she took very seriously. On stage or before the cameras, she preferred to showcase the smiles as opposed to the tears. As she told Mary Parkinson in 1974, "Laughter is absolutely beautiful . . . it communicates itself everywhere. Also, it is possibly one of the most difficult things [to elicit]. I admire and respect comedians because all good comedy has a basis of truth . . . which is very difficult to define and find. And you have to keep that basis of truth and overlay it with comedy. There is a sort of fine line between drama and comedy. Drama is inward-looking. It is sort of flagellation. . . . But comedy is outward . . . manipulating an audience; making them laugh . . . always with that core of truth."[6]

However, such was not the case with her first, only, and short-lived American sitcom, *Diana*. That series made its inauspicious debut on NBC in the 1973-74 fall television season. The show was co-created/developed by Sam Bobrick (who had penned episodes of *The Andy Griffith Show*), Ron Clark (who wrote for *That Girl*), and Leonard Stern. The latter had recently completed a five-year hit run of NBC's *Get Smart*, which, in an irony, had spoofed *The Avengers*/James Bond spy genre.

Rigg began work on the series, which ran from September 10, 1973, to January 7, 1974, only two months after she had married Menachem Gueffen. In the sitcom, she played Diana Smythe, a recently divorced British fashion designer who relocates to New York City with aspirations of expanding her career. In the pilot, "The Lady Comes Across," written by Bobrick and Clark, she lands a high-profile position as a fashion coordinator at Buckley's Department Store. With her brother out of the country indefinitely, she moves into his apartment, which soon becomes invaded by several surprise visits from that brother's various girlfriends.

With each ensuing adventure, the TV version of Diana attempts to adjust to American life with a little help from neighbor Holly Green (Carole Androsky), copywriter Howard Tollbrook (Richard B. Shull), window decorator Marshall Tyler (Robert Moore), and new close friend Jeff Harmon (Richard Mulligan). All the while, she answered to her boss Norman Brodnik, played by David Sheiner, and his wife Norma, played by Barbara Barrie.

Prior to being picked up by NBC, *Diana* had been developed as *The Diana Rigg Show*, with Diana playing Elyse Smythe, and stage, film, and television favorite Nanette Fabray as Mrs. Brodnik. But following the show's title switch and other changes, Barrie replaced Fabray.

NBC held high expectations for the series, hoping to ride the skirttails of the women's liberation movement, and shows like *The Mary Tyler Moore Show*, That Girl, and *Private Secretary*. Through the decades, these shows, and a few chosen others, had blazed the trail for single, independent women in the workforce. But even with the initial assistance of Fabray, who had played Mary Richards's mother on her famed '70s sitcom, and director Jay Sandrich, who was directing the Moore show simultaneously, *Diana* never caught on. It didn't much help matters that the Stern-driven comedy aired opposite *Gunsmoke* on CBS and *The Rookies* on ABC Monday nights.

Rigg relayed how flattered she was to have been approached by Stern, whom she called as "a charming man." She labeled the experience as "extraordinary."

In an interview with *TV Week* magazine, dated October 7, 1973, Rigg explained the events that led up to her starring in her first weekly American-produced TV series. "I was always being offered formats [in England]. I was once offered six formats at one time, and each started off, 'Enter Diana Rigg, gun in hand . . .'"

This prompted the actress to write her own format. Though she nor viewers saw it come to fruition. "I always wanted to do a Western," she went on to tell *TV Week*, "because I was devoted to my father and he loved Westerns."

The format she wrote "was a gentle satire about an English woman coming into a Western town and it satirized the male-oriented society."

At which point, NBC executives explained to her that Westerns were out. Exhibit A: the network's once-huge Western hit, *Bonanza*. That series, which ran for thirteen seasons, lost ground when actor Dan Blocker, who played the hefty, lovable Hoss on the show, suddenly died. And *Bonanza* never recovered without Blocker's presence, while the genre seemed to die with him. Save for *Kung Fu*, the unique Eastern-style Western that ABC took a chance on that year (and won), the Western format went with the wind.

In stepped *Diana* creator/producer Leonard Stern, who came up with a format to Rigg's liking. In *Diana*, she would play a thirty-year-old carefree British divorcee seeking success in America, working in the advertising-merchandising division of the fictional Butley's Department Store.

At first, Rigg was enthusiastic about her new sitcom. "The thing about this series," she said to *TV Week*, "is it combines theatre and television. It's filmed before a live audience with three cameras and it's beautiful. In fact, it's like doing repertory. I know more about theatre than movies or television, so I feel more at home in it, more in control. With this series, it's so similar to theatre because of the interplay with the audience and with the other actors and actresses."

But even though it was a noble attempt, Diana simply could not get a leg up in the ratings; it didn't even have legs with its foundation. The premise was certainly unique and courageous for its time: at its center was a woman of divorce. But that character element did not even work for Mary Tyler Moore in the initial concept of her famed, self-titled CBS sitcom. With that show, the network requested producers to downgrade her TV Mary Richards's "divorce" to a *boyfriend-breakup* status.

In the end, Rigg, along with all of those involved with *Diana*, was disappointed with the show's failure. She remained oblivious to the fact that it was envisioned as "a carbon copy of *The Mary Tyler Moore Show*, only being English. So, it was doomed from the beginning," though she enjoyed working with the "great" Hughes and Shull, as well as Barrie, whom she described as an "adorable woman." "We had such fun, even though we were doomed. There's nothing like being doomed to pull people together."[7]

Like Mary Richards, as played by Moore on her groundbreaking series, Rigg's leading character on *Diana* was the moderate, calm voice surrounded by a group of over-the-top characters. "It was how it fell out," Rigg explained. "You don't have much say in the matter, frankly. I mean, I signed up for it and it was very good experience. God, learning sixty pages of dialogue a week then delivering it in front of a live audience. It was quite droll because, when I arrived, they sent the limo then when I left, they sent the studio station wagon. Just: get out of town."[8]

The *Diana* sitcom was indeed intended as NBC's answer to *The Mary Tyler Moore Show*, which had premiered on CBS just two years earlier to critical acclaim and high ratings. Where Moore's affable career-minded Mary Richards had moved to Minneapolis for a new life after the end of a lengthy romance, Rigg's Diana Smythe relocated from London to New York to make a new life following a divorce. In actuality, the divorce storyline had originally been part of Moore's show. But CBS thought viewers would assume Mary had divorced Dick Van Dyke, her TV husband on the network's long-running previous sitcom that bore that actor's name.

By the time Rigg debuted in *Diana*, the women's liberation movement was in full gear, the American female workforce was on the rise, along with the divorce rate (Rigg's own pending divorce notwithstanding). Besides that, Rigg was British; her previous series, *The Avengers*, was a one-hour action-adventure romp that, even though broadcast in America, was produced in the UK. In the eyes of not-always-bright network executives, all of that made a female divorcée-driven sitcom more palatable for the mainstream audience.

In her 1974 interview with Rigg, Mary Parkinson described the series as "a bit of a flop." To no one's surprise, Rigg corrected her with a smile, and said, "It was a *big* flop. The show didn't have a core of truth about it at all. We didn't capture [that]. I take just as much of the blame [as the production team]."[9]

• • •

Veteran actress Barbara Barrie played Diana's mother on the show. Barrie's résumé is impressive, encompassing numerous stage, film, and television credits. Her TV appearances include *Robert Montgomery Presents*, *Ben Casey*, *The Fugitive*, and the 1950s syndicated half-hour crime-drama *Decoy*. (The latter starred Beverly Garland as TV's first female police/detective, before *Honey West, Charlie's Angels*, and *Police Woman*. In a sense, Garland's character was a precursor to Rigg's Mrs. Peel on *The Avengers*.) Barrie also starred in the first few seasons of ABC's long-running 1970s–80s police sitcom *Barney Miller*, in which she played opposite the show's star, Hal Linden. Barrie was familiar with portraying strong-willed female characters and playing opposite other women who appeared in such roles, including Rigg.

In reflecting on her costarring days with Diana on *Diana*, Barrie described the series as "a domestic comedy, more or less. It was something Diana had never done before. But she just plunged in and did it. She was very brave."

With regard to the Rigg series essentially being a British version of *The Mary Tyler Moore Show*, on which Barrie had made a guest appearance, the actress commented:

"I had never seen *Mary Tyler Moore* when I did that show. I didn't even know what *Mary Tyler Moore* was like. Somebody said during the shooting [that] we were supposed to be doing a knockoff. I was like, 'I have never seen the show, and I am not even sure that Diana has seen the show.'

"We were doing original material," Barrie continued. "We were not constricted by having to be like anything else. I mean, when I first went to do *The Mary Tyler Moore Show*, they asked about experience. And I had never seen it. Not everybody was aware of it all the time. We were just doing a sitcom [with *Diana*]. We were a lot of good actors."

The production team was also top-notch, led by the esteemed producer Leonard Stern. "Oh, well, he was very full of himself," Barrie said. "But very charming. He was really a good person. I don't think I can describe it. He was very theatrical. He was the perfect type for a television producer."

Although Barrie could not recall exactly how she was cast in the series, it may have had something to do with being a friend of Leonard's sister-in-law. "We were very close," she intoned. "Maybe that was it." One thing is certain: she did not formally audition for the show. "They just called me and said, 'Come and do it.'"

Once cast, Barrie was impressed with Rigg on the set. "She was a very fun-loving woman. She would bring these huge baskets of candy bars, all different kinds . . . and they were placed on the table during our table reads [of the script]. And everybody would eat them in the middle of the afternoon."

Barrie also remembered when Diana discovered Frederick's of Hollywood. "At the time, it was a store which catered to sexual appetites, with all kinds of lingerie and, I guess, vibrators. Diana just took an instant delight in it. And they had, in the store, rubber bosoms. Naked bosoms that you wound up at the bottom and they walked around surfaces. And they were hilarious. And she got six or eight or ten of them. I can't remember. And when things would get boring around the table, she would get out those rubber bosoms and they would start walking all over the table. It was hilarious! We just loved it. Then we'd eat our candy bars, and she would put the bosoms away. But she loved that store. It was a very sexy thing. She was really out for everything.

"And the bosoms were naked, of course," Barrie clarified. "They had lace around the bottom and a bra. And they would just travel all over the table. She brought them into the studio."

From one perspective, that fascinating development somewhat ties in with *The Avengers*, and the measure of appeal she brought to the screen by way of Emma Peel. But Barrie did not recall Rigg discussing Emma or her catsuits from the '60s show. "She may have. But we talked about a lot of other stuff."

That included Rigg's unsuccessful marriage to Menachem Gueffen, with whom she had just tied the knot. At the time, Barrie was wed to Jay Harnick (a marriage that lasted from 1964 until his death in 2007). She and Harnick had two children, and as Barrie revealed of her conversations with Diana, "We spent a lot of time in her dressing room talking about marriage. She eventually divorced [Menachem], who was Israeli. She was very upset. She would go home after shooting and he would leave dirty dishes and was running around the pool. She was just miserable. And she asked me what I would do. It wasn't that he was a bad guy. It was just a mismatch, you know. She would try to solve the problem. And she couldn't solve the problem.

"She became very friendly with Archie after they divorced," Barrie said. "And we went to London one time, and they had a townhouse—in the middle of London—with a swimming pool in the back."

As it turned out, Barrie had attended one of Rigg's last birthday parties in New York. "She was just lovely . . . utterly charming," Barrie recalled. "And so was her father."

Archie Stirling had his charms as well, but as Barrie observed, his marriage with Diana simply did not work out, whether or not he felt intimidated by her career. "I only know that they just could not get along very well. That's all I know."

Fellow actress Juliet Mills, Rigg's live-theater acting colleague from years before, had just finished her run in TV's *Nanny and the Professor* right about the time the *Diana* show debuted. And she had worked for Stirling in his production of *The Heiress* on stage.

Off-stage and off-screen, Mills has been happily wed to actor Maxwell Caufield, who is some twenty years her senior, for over four decades. And she offered some pertinent insight into what helps to make a celebrity marriage, or one such union between actors, work. "One doesn't know other people's predicaments . . . or relationships or challenges. I think when two people are very busy . . . in the same business . . . but in different areas, different locations . . . or different countries, I think it's harder to maintain a relationship. Maxwell and I have been lucky. We've both been unselfish when it comes to working. If he's working, I don't want to be working. If he's touring [in a play] I want to be touring with him . . . and I want to be not working and enjoying myself and sharing the travel and tour and the people we meet. I don't have to be working with him or be on the tour. I get as much pleasure out of Maxwell working as I get out of myself working. And that is the honest truth. And I don't think that all that many couples in our business could probably say that."

And while probably not many couples in any business could say that, Mills also credited her wedded bliss to observing the same in her parents. Born to celebrated actors, Sir John Mills and Mary Hayley Bell, Mills is also the older sister of actress Hayley Mills. While her sibling may not have been as successful in marriage as she, both have maintained a down-to-earth personality; not an easy feat in the world of the Hollywood spotlight. But once again Juliet credits her mother and father with contributing to her quality of life. "I have loved a lot and was taught a lot [about life] from the beginning. I was brought up by two people who were madly in love all my life and all of their lives. So, I had that role model. That's what I know and knew a relationship can be. If it really works and both people are trusting and generous and loving and there's a great deal of laughter, then you have a foundation for a successful marriage. That's how my parents raised me. I mean, I recall when they were celebrating their fiftieth and sixtieth wedding anniversaries. Before he'd go to London to work . . . he'd leave her a little love note on the kitchen table. And that was very impressive to me and that's what I wanted."

And that's what Mills found when marrying Caufield. As she continued to explain, "He said, 'I'll love you forever.' And I believed him. I knew that he would and that he was my soulmate, and age, culture, or nationality, or any of that, didn't matter. It was just him . . . he and I connected on a spiritual basis as well as in every other way. That's all that mattered and still does. And that doesn't mean that we don't argue . . . every healthy couple does that. But overall, we have the best time together . . . we share everything we have. We have so much in common, and we're very grateful."

Sadly, such was not the case with Diana and Archie. What's more, Mills never felt rattled by being known mostly for *Nanny and the Professor* whereas Rigg's frequent recognition for *The Avengers* at times proved burdensome for her. "I am known for *Nanny* even now," Mills said. "It's amazing, all these decades after the show ended. And I'm known for that series more than anything, really. And people are so nice about it. And it doesn't bother me in the least, and I don't feel stereotyped or confined by that. I can still go back to the theater and play any character and be happy with and knowing that.

"In playing Nanny," Mills concluded, "I always felt the audience liked her and I took that as a compliment. Because if they liked her, that means they liked me. I didn't feel so very far away from myself in playing the role and I was just always glad that people remember the show in such a happy way . . . as part of a happy time in their life. It's a gift to be able to do that or be a part of that."

Whether the cancellation of the *Diana* sitcom was due directly to Rigg's too-close affiliation with *The Avengers*, or was somehow affected her failed marriage to Archie Stirling, are debatable questions for the ages. As Barbara Barrie put it, "All I know is that we had a very nice show, a great cast, and a good director. When it was canceled, we were all pretty disappointed. But it never really took off, so we weren't surprised."

The series might not have even made it today, even with its core theme of female empowerment. "Television is not very powerful anymore," Barrie noted. "It was really powerful when I was a young woman, because in those days you did those shows and had unlimited exposure on what was then only three networks. Now, you have so many different networks on cable, satellite, streaming . . . producing thousands of shows. It's all different today. It's just the way it is. Everything changes in life. We're not going to change television. It will change by itself. I'm not going to judge it. It's just the way it is."

Although Diana was an outspoken trailblazer for equal pay for women, Barrie acknowledged, "I think we're all still lagging behind on that. It's not solved yet. But Diana wasn't afraid of anything. She was a grabber of life. She just did everything. *That's* how I remember her.[10]

• • •

The *Diana* sitcom also starred actor Bernie Kopell, a semi-regular on classic TV sitcoms like *Get Smart* and *That Girl*. The former, produced by Leonard Stern, is a spoof of the James Bond movies and *The Avengers* TV show, both of which featured Rigg. The latter was somewhat of a precursor to

The Mary Tyler Moore Show and subsequently the *Diana* show, which, like the *Moore* series, featured episodes directed by Jay Sandrich. A few years before Kopell found super fame as Doc on *The Love Boat*, he had appeared in the *Diana* pilot. "Diana Rigg was a wonderful person," he said, "and a wonderful actress . . . with long, lovely legs.

"And she loved other actors," he added, "and was very supportive of them. She had no ego whatsoever when it came to sharing or giving the spotlight to other performers or scene-stealers. She was a team player in the best definition of that term."

One of Kopell's scenes with Diana proved particularly memorable. As he recalled, "I was to be in bed, and I ad-libbed [*singing*] 'Born Free.' But one of the producers said, '*Cut!* We can't have you do that because it'll cost $214 [for musical licensing fees].' But Leonard Stern said, 'Keep it in, it's funny.' And Diana certainly had no issue with it. And so, we kept it in, and they paid the enormous $214, which allowed me to sing the song, and the scene played beautifully."[11]

As was the case with Barbara Barrie, Kopell enjoyed working on the show but still had misgivings. "The pilot was terrific, but unfortunately the rest of the series was not. And Diana was so disappointed that it didn't continue. But she was a sweetheart. We went to lunch every day to Musso and Frank's in Hollywood."

During Kopell's off-screen conversations with Rigg, she shared with him her feelings about other projects she had been involved with—namely, her most famous performance, and her second-most famous performance. Kopell revealed, "Diana never had an issue with being known for *The Avengers*. She loved working on the series, and was open to talking about it. Though her experience of [acting in] *On Her Majesty's Secret Service* was not a pleasant one."

• • •

Rupert Macnee also shared his thoughts on the *Diana* TV show, if from a very different perspective. His father Patrick Macnee, Diana's *Avengers* costar, made a special guest appearance on the series. The title of the episode, which originally aired November 12, 1973, is "You Can't Go Back," an obvious wink and nod to *The Avengers*. And as Rupert recalled, his father enjoyed his on-screen reunion with Rigg. "Oh, he loved it! Doing television was his thing. I'm sure they had dinner and stuff during that time, as is the case many times when a given actor makes a guest appearance on any show.

The senior Macnee's appearance on the *Diana* sitcom resulted by way of request from Rigg and the show's producers. "It was a combination of both," Rupert acknowledged. "I don't think it was something they planned from the beginning, as if to say, 'OK, let's create a role for Patrick.' But it was something they knew the audience would love.

"It was a good experience," Rupert said of his father's guest appearance on *Diana*, which only took two or three days to complete. "And their reprised time together on-screen was something that neither of them regretted."[12]

CHAPTER 10

HER CRAFT, UNSTONED

I think the fact that I refuse to keep just marching on the spot
has kept my career going.

—DIANA RIGG

IN THE FALL OF 1974, FOLLOWING THE DEMISE OF THE *DIANA* SITCOM, RIGG portrayed Eliza Doolittle in director John Dexter's British West End stage production of George Bernard Shaw's *Pygmalion*. It was that 1913 work that inspired the musical *My Fair Lady*, in a later production in which Diana would play Mrs. Higgins on Broadway. But before that transpired, Dexter, a blatant bully, thought her rendition of Eliza lacked vulnerability.

In her interview with Rosanna Greenstreet of *The Guardian*, Rigg recalled something Dexter said. In fact, it was one of the most unkind things she had ever heard: "John . . . told me I was getting hard. It knocked me back and I've acted on it ever since."

As she expressed in another interview, Dexter "was a demanding man, very demanding. His career was quite extraordinary. . . . John was very honest. I remember he could be very cruel, a fact that I didn't like, obviously but he had an overall view.

"The thing I absolutely hate," she continued, "is when directors don't know what they want, but then ask you to do it this way, then maybe that way, because they haven't made up their minds what they want. So, you're running around in circles trying to give them what they want. For me, it's really bad news, because I get bored with listening to myself and I get tetchy with them for not knowing."

However, despite Dexter's rude, ultimately misogynistic behavior, Rigg respected his passion for the theater. "I loved him dearly," she later told *The Telegraph*, "and was very sad when he died."

Around the time of her performance in *Pygmalion*, Diana also appeared in episodes of ITV's *Sunday Night Theatre* and *Affairs of the Heart*.

That same year, Rigg returned to the New York stage as Célimène in a modernized version of Molière's *The Misanthrope*, for which she received her second Tony nomination. Clive Barnes, of the *New York Times*, praised the onstage pairing of Diana and Alec McCowen: "The result is more a sonata of four hands than the double concerto the play can be, but what a sonata! Miss Rigg can make the artificial genuine and return retroussé noses to style; she has a voice as dry as a vermouth-less martini and is as sweetly cutting as a dewy-eyed malice. Her gossip has the music of laughter about it. Her youthfulness is spirited, vital and all-consuming."[1]

Diana was nothing if not persistent in her quest for quality entertainment. Despite the failure of her sitcom, she agreed to being cast in very different roles, among them Philippa in the 1975 CBS TV movie, *In This House of Brede*, earning an Emmy nomination in the process. Directed by the distinguished George Schaefer, and filmed in Ireland and England, *Brede* allowed Rigg a dynamic opportunity: to play a successful London businesswoman who leaves her comfortable life (and the man who loves her) to become a cloistered Benedictine nun.

Rigg had worked hard for the praise that she garnered from critics and fans from productions like *Brede*, but she didn't seek out those accolades. Yet, too, Diana had received her share of bumpy notices along the way, although these did not seem to dampen her enthusiasm for her craft.

"Critics have to sit through an awful lot of rubbish," she once observed. "In fact, I've been in a play where I felt sorry for the critics."

That unnamed play was assuredly not Ronald Miller's *Abelard and Heloise*, which marked her return to the London stage in the early 1970s. Presented at the West End's Wyndham Theatre, *Abelard* also starred Keith Michell, an Australian actor who moved to the United Kingdom, where he enjoyed a long career on stage and screen. The two actors got along famously, on-stage and off-. They once even rode side-by-side in an 1880 Starley Meteor Sociable, also known as the "honeymoon" bike.

According to a report by *Hollywood Studio Magazine* in 1971, the American premiere of *Abelard and Heloise*, presented by the Center Theatre Group at the Ahmanson in New York, was followed by a black-tie reception at the Founders Circle. There, "200 gathered to congratulate Diana and Keith as well as the Ahmanson's artistic director and producer of *Abelard and Heloise*, Elliot Martin with his pretty blonde wife, Marjorie."

"The elite of the industry turned out and stayed late enjoying the drinks, stroganoff, music, and each other," *Hollywood Studio* continued to chronicle. "For example, the Kirk Douglases, Gregory Pecks, Charleton Hestons, Billy Wilders, and Walter Pidgeons."

Diana most likely would have objected to then such "all-inclusive" yet now-deemed-offensive descriptions for leaving out the wives' names, as if they weren't important enough to mention. But needless to say, other Hollywood notables representative of the era attended the gathering, including esteemed actors Jean Simmons (*Planet of the Apes*), Agnes Moorehead (*Bewitched*), Cesar Romero (by then best known as the Joker on TV's *Batman*), and former *Peter Gunn* spy-series star Craig Stevens.

One year later, Rigg's sympathy for critics was rattled by a harsh review of her New York reprise of *Abelard*. The performance marked her Broadway debut, for which she earned the first of three Tony nominations. But American theater critic John Simon unfairly described her feminine physique, which she exposed in a nude scene with Michell. Michell appeared in the buff from one side of the stage, and Diana from the other. In brief, Simon said she was "built like a brick basilica [mausoleum] with insufficient flying buttresses."[2] And while Diana once noted how there is a general tendency to overlook how "many people are indirectly affected by thoughtless and cruel journalism," her direct response to Simon was marked with triumphant calm: "He should have seen me after the menopause. There was no shortfall then!"

Though, too, in her BBC-TV interview with Michael Parkinson, Diana did acknowledge some discomfort with being naked on stage. "I come from Yorkshire. Nobody takes their clothes off in Yorkshire . . . except on a Friday night."[3] And as she relayed to Gavin Esler of Kent University, *Abelard* was "the daftest thing I ever did." She was told the questionable scenes were necessary for the play, in order for the characters to discover their sensuality. And while she had to convince herself to bare it all, Diana didn't see the point of addressing the issue in public, mostly because newspapers at the time had a limited amount of space to cover stories. She figured, "We all have breasts and . . . penises and . . . bodies in common. [But] . . . the most precious thing that we possess are our personalities and our spirits. . . . From the Victorian Era onwards too much emphasis has been placed on covering your body. . . . To trust . . . and love each other sufficiently to show our spirits is infinitely more important."[4]

But when a certain men's magazine later requested that she pose in her birthday suit, Rigg declined. "I don't want a navel stapled and, also, nipples always tend to be slightly purple in *Playboy*." She remained equally unimpressed by images of male nudes, images that were then appearing in magazines like *Cosmopolitan*, which featured a centerfield of actor Burt Reynolds. "Nudes don't turn me on. I don't turn myself on, nude, and I very much hope that I didn't turn other people on, nude."

While performing Abelard in the city of Newcastle, England, Rigg was amused by a telegram she received from a male postal clerk. "I don't know why you bother," he wrote. "My girlfriend's tits are much larger than yours." Meanwhile, when Rupert Macnee was in his mid-twenties, he had attended Rigg's Los Angeles performance of *Abelard*, and some twenty years later, for her appearance in *Medea*. At the former, he interviewed her backstage, and recalled a "very funny and quite disarming" woman. Of Rigg's *exposed* performance, he recalled her walk upstage as "definitely not full-frontal nudity. But more of just a sense of it."[5]

Rupert also remembered a conversation he had with his father about Rigg and the British periodical, *Tit-Bits*, which was published from 1881 to 1984. The magazine/newspaper's title was "literally what it means," he said. "*Little gossip*. And I don't know why Daddy and I thought it was funny, but Diana told us, 'I was in *Tit-Bits* magazine.'

"Both she and Daddy were well-trained and well-educated," Rupert revealed. "They had a love of words, and the meanings of words. The day he died, and not long before, we were still cracking endless jokes. Because we both have that same kind of humor. They are sort of puns, but different. My mother was like that, too, with imaginary words, and so was Diana."[6]

It was indeed Diana's love for words that inspired her to have the last laugh on John Simon's review. Proving her wit to be mightier than any sword, she published her worst reviews in the book, *No Turn Unstoned: The Worst Ever Theatrical Reviews in History*. With an acerbic tone, and her tongue-in-cheek and in-check, the slim but fiery tome, which she wrote in one year's time, became the ideal representation of Rigg's ever-burgeoning life and career.

As Jay Sharbutt observed for the Associated Press, *No Turn Unstoned* was "a collection of nasty but funny reviews of actors singled out for pummeling by critics. She said the title comes from George Bernard Shaw's observation that 'a critic is a man who leaves no turn unstoned.' Most of the reviews were sent in by British players, famed and otherwise, after Miss Rigg wrote them and asked for sample nasties."

One critic cruelly observed, "Sir John Gielgud has the most meaningless legs imaginable." According to Sharbutt, "a top English actress, one of [Diana's] closest friends," dispatched this lulu: "Glenda Jackson has a face to launch a thousand dredges."

It was all such sweet revenge for the notation made by John Simon, the acerbic *New York* critic, on her brief nude appearance in *Abelard and Heloise*.

But Diana just laughed it off, saying few American actors she asked sent her their awful notices. "I only got them from people with secure stage backgrounds, people like Katharine Hepburn, Jean Stapleton, Stacy Keach," she told Sharbutt. "The others, their secretaries wrote and said, 'X is too busy on meaningful projects.' Or whatever."

"Failure discomfort" is the reason she noted for the low percentage of responses from many American actors who, she reckoned, found "discomfiting to discuss failure. This [American] society, I think, is for the most part hugely optimistic and wishes to remain so . . . they have no philosophy for failure."

Conversely, the British see failure "as an experience we've all had—some of us more often than others—on the way to success." They believe, and she concurred, that "when you can freely quote a bad notice and it is funny, then it's an exorcism. It proves you're above it. You are no longer influenced by it. You're no longer nurturing the hurt."

Irrespective of that philosophy and the various characters Rigg portrayed, she nurtured to maturity accolades with razor-sharp, epigrammatic remarks. She continually rose to the occasion no matter the platform and despite the situation. In the process, she contributed to her craft and talent as an actress.

Case in point: a relatable encounter she once had with playwright Arthur Miller. As she explained to veteran Denver journalist Norvel Rose, the conversation with Miller took place in Boston, where he received a literary honor. Both arrived early at the event, and Diana suggested they go for a drink. As she told Rose, "It was a wonderful opportunity to be able to speak to this god."[7]

The evening progressed, and due to Miller's vast body of work, theatrical insight, and expertise, Diana decided to pick his brain. In attending various premieres over the years, he said that he enjoyed seeing many of the same plays with different productions. Diana was eager to hear his thoughts on the dichotomy between each presentation and performance of the various actors, decades apart. According to Diana, Miller replied, ruefully with one word: "Personality."

"That says it all, doesn't it?" she said. "People choose to bring their personality to a part, instead of serving that part."[8]

But is there value in having even a famous actor or actress bring their offstage personality to a character they portray? Does it relinquish or diminish some portion of the actor's true self? Rigg thought the opposite: an actor's fame does not automatically allow them to manipulate or distort whatever character they're playing to suit their artistic needs or comfort level. "For the most part," she said, actors "tend to serve the part." There are watchable, mesmeric performers who choose not to alter the roles they have given to portray. "It's the distortion that authors resent," she clarified. "If I were an author, I'd resent [the intrusion]."

Rigg was referring to an author of fiction, as opposed to her nonfiction work, *No Turn Unstoned*. But she still thought it absurd that an actor would consider their artistic input superior to a given fiction author's creative vision for a character. She felt actors should only interpret the writer's words, not expand on them. She believed it was the actor's obligation (a "must") to "subsume" their personality into a role. She found Miller's theory "absolutely fascinating," believing it the actor's job to fully disengage their personality when interpreting a role. "It's what you've got to do in order to serve the play," she said. "To do justice to a play also makes you a more empathetic person."[9]

According to Rigg, it was legendary actress Sarah Bernhardt who said, "I put a part in front of me and see if it is 'in nature,' and if it is, then I know it can be played." For Diana, that was another "fascinating truism," one that authenticated how an actor is to properly measure and fill the gap between themselves and the character they're portraying. "As a result," she said, "you've got to know a great deal about yourself. . . . Most actors and actresses have a profound sense . . . of themselves. . . . If they don't, then they're lost."[10]

Rigg's various acting ideologies begged deeper exploration, especially in view of her outspoken personality and nature, and how those qualities affected her career. As she explained to Gavin Esler, one director had a few personal issues with her: "Peter Hall said I was the rudest walk-on he'd ever come across because I couldn't do sycophancy. I simply couldn't."[11] In her discussion at Oxford, she addressed the challenges facing female performers, in particular those who may reject the opportunity for mainstream fame to pursue the more theatrical path that she followed. In doing so, Diana was allowed more time to learn, develop, and hone her craft. But would that work for everyone?

Such a career path would require an actor's individual strength of character to maintain and keep in sight their career goals. Otherwise, as Rigg said, the performer "would be sidetracked." For her, an actor's end product should not be fame, but to better understand themselves as human beings and to "know how far you have to develop, how much of yourself should be developed."[12]

Rigg cited the development of her vocal cords while performing Euripides's *Medea* onstage. She found the play "very testing," due to its lengthy arias, monologues, and speeches, one after the other, page after page. But in the process, she discovered and refined a certain timber in her voice.

"Somebody said it was in its *spoken range*," she recalled, "almost as big as a singing voice." She was intrigued by what she heard. "The vocal cords respond to your thought," she discovered. "You think of a note, and the cords accommodate it. That's what singing is about."[13]

Rigg believed the same thing transpires when an actor recites a monologue. "The cords have to be trained, and in order to sustain the cords you need [to have] breath control. And that in itself is an art. . . . In the old days, a lot of the actors could do a sonnet . . . fourteen lines in one breath. Yes. That was the test."[14]

Diana found it similarly challenging when performing the play *Phaedra*, based on Racine's 1677 tragedy *Phaedra Britannica*. She had to recite five consecutive speeches. "It demanded the most astonishing breath control," she said, "and the range of your voice had to be huge."[15] (Four lines are to be recited, almost without taking a breath.)

In Racine's original version, Phaedra, wife to the long-absent monarch Theseus, falls in unrequited love with her stepson, Hippolytus, whose heart belongs to Aricia, a captive princess. Upon his return, Theseus learns that Hippolytus has been falsely accused of seducing Phaedra and summons the god Neptune to kill him. Mortified and ridden with guilt, Phaedra commits suicide.

Rigg appeared in several renditions of *Phaedra*. One, produced in London, circa 1975, was translated and adapted by Tony Harrison for director John Dexter at the National Theatre (where they had previously partnered with Diana for a production of *The Misanthrope*). The other, also in London, was adapted two decades later by Britain's poet laureate Ted Hughes at Almeida Theatre for director Jonathan Kent (with whom Diana had previously collaborated on successful productions of *Medea* and *Mother Courage*). A third adaptation, produced at the Brooklyn Arts Center, was directed by Ted Hughes.

According to what Rigg later said at Oxford, the Hughes adaptation, which also featured classical actress Barbara Jefford (as the nurse), was "wonderful." And Diana conquered those breathy passages. "Bit by bit," she became "closer and closer until suddenly one night: *Bingo!* I'd got it."[16] She delivered the lines without pausing once, and exited the stage with Jefford, who turned to her and said, "Well done."

Jefford empathized with Diana about a role they had both played. Rigg said, "We had that sort of wonderful tacit understanding of an older generation recognizing what the younger generation was trying to do in order to serve that character. It was great."[17]

For the Dexter/National Theatre production, Richard Ellman, of the *New York Times*, agreed.

Diana Rigg, as Phaedra, shows herself once more to be an excellent actress. Her slender frame is weighted down with a good deal of heavy, untropical clothing to fill out her majesty. That mortal illness which is her love has stained her cheeks with tears. The pain of speech contends in her with the pain of keeping silent, and once, on learning that her stepson, Thomas, loves another, tormented laughter breaks from her. Her declaration to Thomas of her own love, at first ambiguous, then abject and self-loathing, is very well done, and the scenes of her confession and suicide by poison shake the audience. Sarah Bernhardt is said to have exploited these two scenes and disregarded everything else in the play. Miss Rigg does not soar so high or so fitfully; she has thought through the whole performance and works in every line. As yet it must be admitted she is not grand: she is a person and not a Bernhardtian presence.[18]

Meanwhile, Rigg faced challenges beyond breath control during the 1975 production, in which Jefford, the senior female thespian in the troupe, portrayed her maid. "There was a sort of tension on stage . . . between us," Rigg said. "Of course, there was. You know it always happens."[19]

During Rigg's interview at Oxford, a young female audience member said she had attended a discussion that was led by actor Mark Williams, best known as Arthur Weasley in the *Harry Potter* film series. Unlike Diana, Williams apparently believed actors should bring part of their own personality to the roles they play, lest they fade into the distance. If so, that seems contrary to Diana's philosophy about remaining true to the words of the playwright or screenwriter. Would the actor become, as the audience member suggested, "a slave to the text"? Is it incorrigible for performers to draw upon their own interpretations of character, potentially transforming a book, a script, or text—as with a production like *Medea*—and making it applicable for the Modern Age?

As stated earlier, Diana believed that to "*serve* the text" was a better choice of words. Specifically, to "the point at which you learn how far you have to travel, knowing yourself and understanding the character that you're playing. . . . And knowing how far you have to travel to subsume yourself into that part."[20]

Rigg worshipped good writing, saying, "Where would we be without it in our theater? We wouldn't exist. We wouldn't have careers. We'd have no means of earning a living without good writing." She worked with *bad writing*, and did what she could to transform it into *good writing*, but that didn't always work. In fact, "it seldom works," she said. Whereas "really good writing" is "such a gift!"[21] She didn't feel or understand the need to distort the material to serve the actor's purpose.

All things considered, Diana in several ways allowed her authentic self to seep into every role she played. Irrespective of the character, she believed it was the actor's voice, brain, body, and wit that contributed to the interpretation of a role. At the same time, she believed none of those elements needed to contribute to the detriment of the text or the character the actor is playing. As a theatergoer herself, she enjoyed her share of performances over the years. Some she deemed riveting, with certain actors "doing their thing," and others being "absolutely brilliant." But if the actors were not serving the playwrights? "Sorry, darling. No. Not so brilliant." As she told Esler, "Words . . . deal with texts. . . . I've been so lucky with the playwrights and directors that I've worked with. But it always comes down to what's on the page . . . always."

Rigg was protective of esteemed colleagues who created and guided those words, including playwrights Tom Stoppard and David Hare, and directors like Jonathan Kent. As Kent would later exclaim in a statement to the press, Diana's "combination of force of personality, beauty, courage and sheer emotional power, made her a great classical actress—one of an astonishing generation of British stage performers."

Rigg proved as much in November of 1995, in Yorkshire, when she played Anna Fierling, aka Mother Courage, for Kent in the Royal National Theatre production of *Mother Courage and Her Children*, Hare's reimagining of Bertolt Brecht's 1939 epic. Matt Wolfe, of *Variety*, observed that Hare's "urgency refashions a potentially tiresome dramatist-as-ideologue for our own warring age." With the play, Wolfe claimed that Rigg reinvented herself as an actress "so that not only does her cart-pulling Courage avoid cliché, but the performance itself reveals a theatrical courage not seen from Rigg before. Throw in the work of a remarkable composer, Jonathan Dove, and the National continues what is by anyone's reckoning an extraordinary year—Brecht hasn't been this bracing for some time."[22]

It was yet another young female member in the audience at Rigg's Oxford discussion who deemed herself "one of the lucky ones." During a trip to London, she had been mesmerized by Diana's "magnificent" performance in *Medea*. Impressed by her powerful voice, and in just the way she walked on stage, the young woman wondered how Diana "cut off" from her character when not performing the part. Was it a challenge "to be Diana Rigg again" after delivering such a strong performance?

Not in the least, she asserted. Whereas other actors might literally carry home a part of their character, Diana didn't see the point, saying, "For me, I pour . . . everything into that time when I am at the theater." She enjoyed the preparation, such as the moment before the curtain rises. In general, she would arrive backstage an hour prior to the performance. Not so much for "getting into character," but rather for "the preparation of being by yourself," applying the required makeup, or adorning the costume. "And then," she said, "I love the walk to the stage . . . and then stepping on stage . . . that moment when you encounter the audience. You think you're into that scene, but at the same time there's a consciousness about, 'What kind of an audience is it tonight? What do they like tonight?'

"In a very instinctive way," she continued, "you're sort of putting out feelers [to the audience, and wondering], *Are they with you? Are you going to have to win them over? Are they sitting back, folding their arms, saying 'Show me'? Or are they longing for you to succeed?* That's what I love about it. It might sound pompous, and I do hope it doesn't, but it is a communion. The audience, when you think about it, they come to *believe*, so it *is* a communion. And it is our responsibility to meet that belief with all the powers, and art, of our profession."[23]

If only by the laws of statistics, periodically, there is still the opposite effect. For one reason or another, the play or the actor's performance does not connect with the audience on any level. Diana described that as being akin to "*misery*. You just want to go home and climb under the duvet."[24]

Fortunately, there will always be the next performance. And for Diana, "That's the point. There's always another audience." And she was often asked how she managed to perform, night after night, day after day, sometimes twice a day on the weekends, and even during weekdays. She said it just depends on the actor—and the audience. "You pull something out of us, each night, which we might not know was there. And you can be sort of like this, you know, 'Show me!' And that's a challenge too.

"It can be really, really cold when you first step out on stage and the audience isn't with you. Something might have happened. They might have had to, I don't know, wait in the queue to get their tickets, wait in the rain for a bus. You know, audiences do change . . . and it's lovely when we've won you round."[25]

In the process, she surprised herself at times when feedback from the audience, combined with the sense of the occasion, made her feel she had delivered a stronger performance than she had imagined for a particular night. "Oh, yes," she said. The audience periodically "pulls something out of you." And she viewed that extraordinary experience with humility. "You must never mistake the reasons why it exists, because it's that communion. I swear it's that communion."[26]

CHAPTER 11

A LITTLE NIGHT MUSIC WITH A THREE-PIECE SUITE, AND MORE

I'm a practicing Christian,
so maybe that's why I understand evil so well.
It's a starting point, isn't it?

—DIANA RIGG

ON DECEMBER 3, 1976, RIGG'S DIVORCE FROM MENACHEM GUEFFEN WAS finalized. Through the highs and lows, Diana was not one to flinch in the face of challenge and viewed life's conflicts and victories as character-building. This only added to her unbreakable luster as a veteran actress of grace and gravel.

Diana soon began a romance with Scottish laird and theatrical producer Archibald Stirling. On May 30, 1977, their daughter, Rachael, was born. Diana called that day as the happiest in her life. As she later told reporter Rosanna Greenstreet of *The Guardian*, "I fell asleep entirely happy."

Conversely, she later told Laura Potter, also of *The Guardian*, that she had taken antidepressants after having Rachael. "Yes, I had the baby blues very, very badly. Here I was with a beautiful healthy baby and a husband who adored me, and I was in a terrible pit of depression. The only effect the antidepressant had was I was crying faster than I used to, so I stopped and eventually came out of it. I do, on reflection, see that my body was mourning. I had nurtured this other being which had left my body and my mind was reflecting that."

Motherhood, however, did not prevent the thirty-eight-year-old Diana from accepting a part in the motion picture adaptation of Stephen Sondheim's 1973 Broadway show *A Little Night Music*. The film, an American-West German-Australian production, was directed by Harold Prince.

As drama writer Jay Sharbutt noted for the Associated Press, the film adaptation of *Night Music* granted Diana her first chance to sing on-screen. The movie, as Sharbutt noted, "fizzled," while Diana said that it "wasn't an auspicious beginning in the musical world, for me."

The story involves one Frederick Egerman (Len Cariou), an older man who marries a seventeen-year-old virgin named Anne (Lesley-Anne Down). Eleven months later, she is still a virgin, and Frederick is beginning to get restless. He decides to visit an old flame, a famous actress known as Desiree Armfeldt (Elizabeth Taylor). Desiree has grown tired of her life and decides it's time to settle down. Although she already has a married lover, Count Carl-Magnus Mittelheim (Laurence Guittard), she sets her sights on Frederick. She prevails upon her mother to invite the Egermans to her country estate for the weekend. But when Carl-Magnus and his wife, Charlotte (Diana), show up as well, things begin to get farcical (represented with the show's signature song, "Send in the Clowns," sung weakly by Taylor). In the end, all the lovers are reunited.

Elizabeth Taylor received most of the press on that film. Having recently turned forty, the former ingénue continued to fascinate her public well into middle age. This was in large part due to her personal life, with her many illnesses and many marriages, particularly her on-again, off-again relationship with Welsh actor Richard Burton. When the two showed up in the same film, like *The Sandpiper* or *Who's Afraid of Virginia Woolf?*, there were reams of publicity, lines at the box office, and accompanying accolades. Burton, who had been classically trained in the theater, was by far the better actor of the two, but when both he and Taylor were nominated for their performances in *Virginia Woolf*, it was Taylor who walked away with the Oscar. This understandably galled Burton, causing another of the intense fights for which the couple was notorious.

Taylor also made a strong impression on Diana, but it was a mixed one at best.

"Do you know, she was the most beautiful thing you have ever seen?" she said. "Quite ravishing. I mean, deeply spoiled, but not unpleasant. She didn't know that other people existed, that's all." Despite this, Diana managed to find within herself some empathy for Taylor's cosseted life and indulgences. As she explained, "I'd be up at six o'clock, and I'd be sitting in corset and costume, fully made-up, with an Edwardian hat on my head that had a dead bird on the front and feeling deeply uncomfortable. And she'd come up with a glass of what looked like orange juice, and she'd say, in this very amiable way, 'Good mooorning!' And of course, you'd want to kill her."[1]

Although the critics were gentle with Diana, the film was justifiably panned, with much criticism directed at Taylor's performance, and ending up bombing at the box office.

Diana must surely have gotten more satisfaction from a six-week TV variety series on the BBC, called *Three Piece Suite*. The show includes widely diverse sketches penned by such top British writers as Roy Clarke, Dick Clement, Terrence Brady, and Charlotte Bingham. Diana showed off not only her versatility in playing three separate characters in each episode; she showed off her sense of humor as well.

Paul Mavis, of DVDTalk.com, writes appreciatively of this little-remembered show, particularly when it came to Diana's involvement.

In her 2011 interview included as a bonus on this disc, Diana Rigg remembered [how unkind the critics were to *Three Piece Suite*] with her citing the prejudice critics held back then concerning women in sketch comedy. Of course, I've seen the ultra-cool, ultra-smooth Rigg half-smirk her way through every one of her spoofy *Avengers* episodes, but I don't think I had ever seen her "go broad" as she does so often here. Well, simply put: she pulls it off. Comedy may be hard, as the saying goes, but the results are easily determined—it's funny, or it's not. And Rigg *is* quite funny as she swings from Benny Hill–type slapstick to her more familiar sly spoofing, to some rather funny/sad offerings in *Three Piece Suite*. Obviously trying to stretch her imposing, glam image by appearing in a variety of guises, from frump to nearly nude (John Simon had *no* idea what he was talking about there . . . but then again, he never did), Rigg clearly seems to enjoy going off the wall, and her energy is infectious (I love how at the end of each episode, she reads all the credits for us, giving us that much more time to drink her all in).

The first episode in particular illustrates her considerable range, from the frumpy lonely hearts in *Hearts & Flowers*, looking through the newspaper personals (she's still too beautiful to *completely* pull off such a nudge), to a brassy American "starlet" in *Screen Night* (her accent is good and her nude body is even better, and there's an amusing *cinema verité* take-off that's quite good), to a paralyzingly funny spoof of David Lean's *Brief Encounter*, shot in black and white with a masterful Peter Barkworth lending support (catching up on old times, the once-successful Barkworth states, "I'm more like a window cleaner," to which Rigg deadpans, "How horrible for you."). Gawn Grainger is a funny little snot in *Little Things . . . Parking*, providing an amusing, bickering couple premise that might have expanded nicely into a regular series with Rigg (these characters show up again in *Little Things ... That Go Bump in the Night*, which is just as funny). *Wonder Woman*'s take-off *Wonderful Woman* is painfully unfunny (what is Bob Hoskins doing there?), but *Public Lives*, a double spoof on Coward's *Private Lives* and the ongoing romantic saga of Liz Taylor and Dick Burton, is an absolute scream, with Tony Britton doing a very funny take-off on Burton (I love it when possessed by his own ridiculous love and his far too many riches, he desperately offers to buy her a zoo or a submarine). *Miss* is a beautifully snarky, sad take on a *Miss Jean Brodie* type, disillusioned by having to return to teaching after a failed love affair (Rigg is truly skilled here in a difficult role), while *This Situation* features one of my favorite British supporting players, Freddie Jones, in a hysterical performance as a German shrink ("If I was mad at you, I'd break your arm."). And of course, the mythic pairing of two TV icons—Rigg and Monty Python's John Cleese—in *Every Day in Every Way* is inspired, by Cleese stealing the show as an obsessed, phobic neurotic. All in all, an entertaining romp for the multi-talented Rigg (too bad this didn't go for another "series/season").

In 1980, Rigg returned to more urbane comedy by starring in a TV production of a 1927 Noël Coward play. Set in eighteenth-century France, *The Marquise* concerns the rather tortured romantic lives of two generations in a family of aristocrats. Count Raoul De Vriac (Richard Johnson) and Duke Esteban (James Villiers) are lifelong friends who feel it would be most advantageous if their offspring were to wed one another. However, the offspring in question, Adrienne (Mary Chilton) and Miguel (Daniel Chatto), do not share in the enthusiasm for this idea; for one thing, each is already in love with someone else. Just as the situation seems hopeless, into the story walks the charismatic Marquise Eloise (Diana, of course). Before the third act curtain, she has resolved the situation in a manner that satisfies all concerned.

Also, by 1980, Rigg had been nominated by *Time* magazine as Britain's best actress. As Michael Billington of the *Winnipeg Free Press* observed, she had "proved herself in both modern work and the classics as well as in all the media. But her particular forte is a combination of sharp, ironic intelligence with a hint of vulnerability. She looks good, speaks well and can move like a swan on water. What, however, makes her the ideal modern actress is her rare blend of challenging wit and real heart.

"She has most recently displayed those qualities," Billington continued, "in Tom Stoppard's *Night and Day* in which she played Ruth Carson, the wife of a mining engineer caught up in an African civil war. It was fascinating to see how Rigg caught both sides of the character. On the one hand, she displayed a cool, insolent mockery towards an Australian reporter who embodied all her fears about the foot-in-the-door tactics of the press.

"On the other hand," Billington added, "she was all yielding warmth when pole-axed by a handsome young journalist. Despite a pinched sciatic nerve, she played the role for most of the first six months of the run and showed how comedy and true feeling can be artfully combined.

"But in Shakespeare, Shaw and Stoppard," Billington concluded, "she has demonstrated that she is temperamentally more at ease in comedy where her unique combination of irony and vulnerability makes her capable of switching easily between the roles of aggressor and victim. She always reminds me of those lines in T. S. Eliot about lovely woman stooping to folly and pacing about her room again alone . . . she smooths her hair with an automatic hand and puts a record on the gramophone. She is the very incarnation of modern woman—independent, assertive but also glad now and again to compromise her ideals for the sake of a long-term relationship."

At point, Rigg took on Noël Coward and his 1981 TV movie adaptations of Ibsen's *Hedda Gabler*. We hear again from journalist/actress Andrea Whitcomb-May who, in her own career, once played the lead in Gabler for a stage production in the 1980s:

"Henrik Ibsen's tragedy *Hedda Gabler* is often referred to as a female *Hamlet*, and Dame Diana Rigg's performance certainly lives up to such a lofty comparison. Rigg inhabits the title role of *Hedda Gabler* with subtle elegance and powerful yet understated craft. Having just returned from her honeymoon with her new husband George Tesman, Rigg's Hedda makes her entrance as a statuesque beauty throwing ice all over the warm and jovial family reunion between her new husband and his affable Aunt Julle.

"Out of loftiness, frustration, and boredom, Hedda has developed a knack for mischief, and she delights in cunningly toying with others. Rigg artfully maneuvers through scenes as her manipulative Hedda teases, mocks, entices, consoles, reveals, and hides her desires. The other characters are often her prey, and she alters her personality in accordance with the target presently before her. While simmering underneath with frustration and fury, Hedda delights in bossing the servants, haughtily feigning compassion towards her new aunt-in-law, and tormenting an old schoolmate. Rigg deftly allows the audience quick peeks into Hedda's own torment, which she politely explains away as mere boredom.

"Hints are dropped that Hedda is with child, to which she impatiently reacts with thinly veiled disgust and desperation. It is clear that pregnancy will suffocate her in the loveless marriage. Tesman is a respected scholar and seems amiable enough, but they are a mismatched pair. He seems to desire a domesticated wife, while Hedda is anything but 'domestic.' Rather, she craves an active social life that they cannot afford, and his wit is no match for Hedda's. He adores her beauty but doesn't take the time to get to know her. He seems oblivious to her intelligence. Hedda may have resigned herself to marriage due in part to social pressure, but she adamantly refuses to cave into its new set of social demands.

"Hedda's sense of desperation isn't revealed in her words, as 19th-century European societal demands precluded such openness. A little flirtation here and there might be fine, but not the plain truth about the unhappiness of a stifling marriage. Rigg gives insights into Hedda's growing despair with nuanced sighs, inflections, glances, and movement. All of her pent-up emotion culminates in a shocking finale that none of the characters are able to grasp, leaving the audience with the judge's words, 'People don't do such things.'"

• • •

Following her performance in *Hedda Gabler*, Diana found herself in the distinguished company of Kermit the Frog, Fozzie Bear, the Great Gonzo, and Miss Piggy. Marking the directorial debut of Muppet creator Jim Henson, *The Great Muppet Caper* was budgeted at $16 million, although it ended up costing closer to $20 million. Principal photography began on September 8, 1980, and included the following landmarks: Holland Park, St. Paul's Cathedral, Piccadilly Circus, Trafalgar Square, and Battersea Park. After three weeks on location, the production moved to EMI Elstree Studios, in Hertfordshire, for four months. The family-friendly comedy was released by Universal Pictures in early 1981. Expectations were high. Its predecessor, *The Muppet Movie*, had been one of the biggest hits of 1979. But on its opening weekend, *The Great Muppet Caper* grossed much less in 680 theaters in North America, than the reported $32 million earned by *The Muppet Movie*. The failure to repeat the success was partly due to oversaturation. *The Muppet Show* was still airing on syndicated television, and *Caper* was released soon after the original film was pulled from theaters.

It's safe to say that none of the above minutia would have interested Diana. She only took on the project because of her five-year-old daughter, Rachael.

"She was passionately in love with Miss Piggy," she explained. Diana even accompanied Rachael and a group of her friends to the Elstree studios to meet their porcine idol. No sooner did the girl lay eyes on the Muppet diva than she burst into tears. "She was more frightened than anything because Miss Piggy was huge. They had several Miss Piggys. The people were lovely, Frank Oz and Jim Henson, absolutely charming, lovely people, and I'd adored [The Muppet Show] on the telly. I was a fan.'"²

Diana recalled one behind-the-scenes anecdote involving her costar, Charles Grodin. "I don't know what was going on—something technical. Charles and I were in the scene with Miss Piggy when we had to do take after take after take. Finally, Charles said to me, under his breath, 'Bet you never thought you'd be doing fifteen takes for a fucking puppet!'"

• • •

In March of 1982, five years into her relationship with the debonair Archie Hugh Stirling, the nephew of Colonel Sir David Stirling, founder of the Special Air Service (SAS), Diana decided to make it legal. The two were married in a civil ceremony at the Municipal Building in lower Manhattan. Officiating was David N. Dinkins, the future mayor of New York City, then in the less prestigious position of city clerk.

If there was a common theme to Diana's career at the time it would be Agatha Christie. She appeared on stage in a new production of the British mystery writer's Witness for the Prosecution, as well as a big screen adaptation (by Anthony Shaffer) of the novel Evil Under the Sun. The latter had a lot going for it: a $10 million budget, a score consisting of music by the late Cole Porter, and a lush shooting location, and that included Mallorca, Spain, home to the film's director, Guy Hamilton (who makes a cameo as a pedestrian passing the offices of the insurance company, and who directed four James Bond films).

Producer Richard Goodwin wanted to provide, as he put it, "terrific escapist entertainment that you can take the kids to and make it look beautiful at the same time." And, for the most part, he succeeded. Like many of Christie's stories, a large group of people (usually members of the idle rich) gather in one exotic location. Before long, one of these insufferable individuals is murdered, and one (or more) of the survivors is the culprit. Fortunately (or unfortunately, if one happens to be the killer), the world's greatest detective, Hercule Poirot (or his female counterpart, Miss Jane Marple), just so happens to be there as a fellow vacationer.

Of course, to film buffs, who did it is not as important as who's in it. Like the then-recent Christie-inspired blockbusters (Murder on the Orient Express,

The Mirror Crack'd, and *Death on the Nile*), the producers did not scrimp when it came to hiring some of the stage and screen's greatest character actors to bring the story to life. Capably in the lead is Peter Ustinov (in his second film with Rigg) as Poirot (his second such portrayal, the first being in 1978's *Nile*), who makes it his solemn duty to flush out the guilty party (or parties). Is it Daphne Castle (Maggie Smith), a former actress who now runs the spa? Perhaps it's that rich old couple who produce Broadway shows, Mr. and Mrs. Odell Gardener (James Mason and Sylvia Miles). Then again, it *could* be that argumentative young couple, Christine Redfern (Jane Birkin) and her husband, Patrick (Nicholas Clay). No? How about that vengeful, backstabbing gossip columnist Rex Brewster (Roddy McDowall)? Still, no? Then it *must* be Sir Horace Blatt (Colin Blakely), who had given a real diamond to his mistress, the conniving Arlene Stuart Marshall (Diana), who, in turn, returned a fake version following the end of their affair!

Everyone is clearly having a good time with their over-the-top characterizations. In his review in the *New York Times*, Vincent Canby takes especial pleasure in an "extremely promising sequence in which Miss Rigg graciously entertains the guests in the drawing room after dinner by singing 'You're the Top,' when Miss Smith attempts to upstage her with unwelcome harmony. When these two actresses are on the screen, you can believe the hotel's register lists as recent guests Ivor Novello, [siblings] Fred and Adele [Astaire], and even Cole Porter."[3]

As it turned out, Rigg and Maggie Smith had children who performed together in another production based on an Agatha Christie novel. In 1989, Rachael Stirling and Toby Stephens (Smith's son) appeared in the ninth season premiere episode of *Poirot*, titled "Five Little Pigs" (which was Poirot's follow-up book to *Evil Under the Sun*).

Chosen for the 1982 Royal Film Performance, *Evil Under the Sun* was screened on March 22 at London's Odeon Theatre, Leicester Square, in the presence of Queen Elizabeth II with proceeds from the premiere going to the Cinema and Television Benevolent Fund. But the film's actual world premiere occurred one month earlier, in February 1982, in Australia, where EMI's *Can't Stop the Music* (released in 1980 and starring the Village People!) had had its best box-office returns.

That clarified, Roger Ebert offered his insightful assessment of the murder-mystery genre itself, with the following review in the *Chicago Sun Times*:

I can observe, however, that one of the delights of the movies made from Agatha Christie novels is their almost complete lack of passion:

They substitute wit and style. Nobody really cares who gets bumped off, and nobody really misses the departed. What's important is that all the right clues be distributed, so that Poirot and the audience can pick them up, mull them over, and discover the culprit. Perhaps, then, one of the reasons I liked "Evil Under the Sun" was that this time, when Ustinov paused in his summation (after verbally convicting everyone in the room), and it was clear he was about to finger the real killer, I guessed the killer's identity, and I was right. Well, half right. That's better than I usually do.[4]

In July of 1982, Diana re-teamed with Anthony Hopkins for a production of Ibsen's *Little Eyolf*, which was featured in the BBC television anthology series *Play of the Month*. It was adapted by Michael Meyer and directed by Michael Darlow. The cast also included Peggy Ashcroft, Emma Piper, Timothy Stark, and Charles Dance. In the story, Rigg plays Rita, a wealthy woman married to Hopkins's Alfred, a writer who feels trapped by their loveless, unfulfilling marriage. The death of their disabled son wreaks havoc on their relationship as they struggle to find redemption for their personal failures.

Critic Paul Mavis, of DVDTalk.com, was unimpressed with the play, the playwright, and the show's vaunted leads. Hopkins fares better of the two, Mavis writes, calling his performance "stagey, showy, and enjoyable." Rigg, he avers, is "not at her best here, shoehorned into a role that emphasizes her sometimes too-stately, slightly starchy disposition (in the bonus interview included here, she talks of dreading delivering the line about little Eyolf's crutch found floating in the water. She was right to worry . . .)[5]

• • •

Despite the unavoidable flops and the occasional bad review, Diana tried to remain optimistic when taking on each new project. But when she was offered the chance to make her long-awaited Broadway debut in a new show about the celebrated French writer—and famed cat fancier—Sidonie Gabrielle Colette (1873–1954), she was plagued with doubt. The play came with some impressive credentials; the book and lyrics were by Tom Jones and Harvey Schmidt, whose play *The Fantasticks* holds the record as the world's longest running musical in theatrical history.

Colette was originally to star Debbie Reynolds, the former MGM star who had recently scored a hit in the 1973 Broadway revival of the musical *Irene*. When it came time to commit to *Colette*, Reynolds chose instead to star in what would be a failed spinoff of Aaron Spelling's ABC series *The Love Boat*.

There had been a trial run in Seattle, after which changes were made, and more were needed. One journalist who viewed the play during another tryout, this one in Denver, described it as "a musical in its infancy; a production in evolution on its way to Broadway. The play opened in Seattle where changes were made. . . . In the role of the famous French writer, Colette, is Diana Rigg, playing her first musical and for a first timer her performance is good." Or as Rose put it, "Diana shared her enjoyment of living, of being part of a creative projects development, and the value of teachable moments on and off stage."[6]

Diana, whose only other experience with musicals was the unsuccessful screen version of *A Little Night Music*, was not convinced. Without false modesty, she had hoped to introduce a role that, fifteen years hence, would prove a major success for somebody else.

Colette became Diana's initial attempt at a stage musical. As she mused to journalist Jay Sharbutt of the Associated Press, "I took it probably because I'm quite perverse, always tackling new things—which this certainly is for me."

But as Sharbutt observed, "It's difficult to believe the classically trained Miss Rigg has been tackling new and old things for 24 years now, doing what the English call 'the lot.' Shakespeare. The Greek classics. French farces. *Hedda Gabler*. Tom Stoppard whizbangs. James Bond (OK, just one of those). *The Great Muppet Caper*."

The latter, Rigg told Shabutt, received fine notices from her daughter Rachael, who was then only five years old. Apparently, Rigg said even Rachael's father Archie had enjoyed the film.

One lyric from the show that resonated with the positive-thinking Diana was: "To know is joy, to feel it is joy, to experience it all is joy, the good and the bad, the living and the dying."

She was also a realist, however, and she could tell that instead of improving, the show was moving steadily away from the authors' original vision. This recalled a belief that she had repeatedly stated in her years in the theater, that actors and directors are there to serve the text.

Finally, a decision was made to close the show before its final stop on Broadway. As director Frank Dunlap sadly commented to the press: "It just didn't work out."

• • •

Nothing good, it should be said, ever comes easily in the theater. Even the greatest playwrights and the most revered thespians experience failure; they are, after all, only human. When a name like Laurence Olivier is mentioned today, one thinks only of the legend. Behind that veil, however, was a fallible man, one susceptible to the ravages of time. Diana worked with Lord Olivier in a 1983 TV production of *King Lear*, in which the seventy-six-year-old actor was cast in the lead.

"We were all there to pay homage to him," Diana recalled. "He'd never done it, and he was ill. I was a replacement for Faye Dunaway [in the role of Regan]. She'd worked with the director Michael Elliott, a lot before then; suddenly, I don't know how, I was asked to do it. Michael was tetchy with me for some reason I simply couldn't understand. I think he'd worked so closely with Faye Dunaway, having this image of exactly how he wanted Regan to be played.

"It was about the third day into rehearsal," she continued, "when he was on me again."

Olivier stepped up and told Elliott, "Leave her alone. She knows what she's doing."

Apparently, Olivier wanted to do every lengthy speech in one take because, as Rigg explained it, "He wished to approximate what would happen on stage, but he couldn't do it. It was agony, *agony* watching him force himself. He never got through any of the speeches. They had to be cut together."[7]

Rigg then followed her performance in *Lear* with other small-screen productions like Dickens's *Bleak House*, as Lady Dedlock, in 1985. That same year, she appeared in a live stage production of *Antony and Cleopatra*, with Denis Quilley at the Chichester Festival Theatre in West Sussex.

And, once again, failure was in the air.

"First of all," she explained, "the set was a bugger. It was grey. It had to double for Rome and Egypt, with the bias in Rome. Those huge grey columns were just not Egyptian at all. No sense of sunlight, heat, luxury, and Cleopatra. I'm not blaming the set. I'm saying it was part of the reason that the thing didn't work. Obviously, performances are the main reasons. I just wasn't happy, and I just didn't find her."[8]

By this, she meant that, try as she might, she could not find the character, which she still considered the best of Shakespeare's female characters to portray.

Two projects that represented far less of a challenge to Diana would at least appeal to her daughter Rachael and her little friends. The first was a fantasy-comedy film called *The Worst Witch*, released in 1986; the second was a turn as the Evil Queen in a direct-to-video live-action version of *Snow White*, from 1987.

The Worst Witch was directed by Robert Young (not the actor from *TV's Father Knows Best*, but the helmer of movies like *The Haunting* and *Splitting Heirs*), and costarred Charlotte Rae (aka Mrs. Garrett from TV's *The Facts of Life*) and Tim Curry (*The Rocky Horror Picture Show*). Based on Jill Murphy's *The Worst Witch* eight-book series of children's books (1974–2018), the story covers four years in the life of protagonist Mildred Hubble. With shades of *Harry Potter*, the film's core setting is a school of magic, Miss Cackle's Academy, which has elements of Murphy's experiences as a student of the Ursuline High School, Wimbledon (a Roman Catholic secondary school for girls ages eleven through nineteen).

Were such films beneath Diana Rigg by association? Not according to her.

"Oh, absolutely don't look down on anything," she told an audience of aspiring actors. "It may be rubbish, but you could, you might, learn from it. You might learn something from other actors. And you're out in front of an audience. I mean, always remember what's the point of staying at home waiting for the part. The best thing you can do is to go out and practice and perform in front of an audience or a television camera or a film camera.

"I was immensely lucky that I'd been five years at Stratford," she reflected. "I mean, I'd been a year in rep, and then I went to Stratford, and I was there for five years, and then I got this television job, and then I went back to Stratford. And some then I was off and running because *The Avengers* had catapulted me into sort of, I was famous, which it would have taken me twenty years on the stage to reach that degree of fame, if that. So, television is incredibly powerful, incredibly important. But let's not forget it's sort of restricted as well. And you've got to keep your options open. And, my belief is, for longevity, you have to go back to the theater, because theater audiences are the most faithful audiences of all."[9]

The host of the question-and-answer format asked his distinguished guest if, after starring in *The Avengers*, and then moving in with James Bond, whether she feared being typecast.

"Well, not *The Avengers*," she answered confidently. "Yes, I could have been, but then I went back to the theater. And I did a couple of television [programs] and then I did the James Bond [film] and I mean, if everybody asks about it, I knew exactly why I'd been cast. I was *there*. George Lazenby had no experience acting; I think he'd just done an advertisement. And I was there as a professional to sort of guide him through, which I was very happy to do, up to a point. It didn't end entirely happily, as you probably know. Although the film itself is much loved, and George was pretty good [in it], he was just extraordinarily difficult. And so . . . they didn't ask him back. And he, I think he must, deeply regret it."[10]

As Damon Evans recalled, the year Diana appeared in a live production of *Snow White* was the first time he saw her perform live on-stage: in Stephen Sondheim's *Follies* in 1987 at the Shaftesbury Theater in London. "She played the role of Phyllis originated on Broadway by Alexis Smith," Evans said. "She simply blew my mind. I knew Ms. Rigg as a versatile theater and television actress, not a Musical Theater performer. Yet, there she was singing the most difficult Sondheim music and handling it with the aplomb of a song-and-dance veteran. I thought that she was absolutely amazing."

Sondheim, meanwhile, had composed a song for Rigg, titled "Ah, But Underneath." As she once explained, "It was an accolade . . . and he got his ginger on my character. To further elaborate, the lyrics went like this: 'In the depths of her interior, were fears she was inferior. And something even eerier, but no one dared to query her superior exterior.'"[11]

• • •

In addition to *Follies* and *Snow White*, both from 1987, Diana also appeared that year in *A Hazard of Hearts*, the first of two little-known screen dramas that could easily run back-to-back today on the Lifetime Channel for Mother's Day.

A Hazard of Hearts is a particularly effective adaptation of Barbara Cartland's novel, starring Helena Bonham Carter, Marcus Gilbert, Edward Fox, Fiona Fullerton, Christopher Plummer, and Stewart Granger. The gothic tale centers on an innocent young woman (Carter) who falls under the spell of a marquis (Gilbert) and his scheming mother, played with relish by Diana.

In 1989, Rigg performed in *Mother Love*, her second low-profile film from the era. In brief, *Mother* is a nightmarish tale of a young married couple whose life is muddied by the presence of the husband's disturbed mother (Diana). Her conniving, vengeful ways lead to all kinds of trouble, from disharmony in her son's marriage to out-and-out murder. (*Mother Love*, incidentally, costars David McCallum, whose superspy series *The Man from U.N.C.L.E.* found popularity at the same time as *The Avengers*.)

Also in 1989, Diana was offered an interesting television drama script titled *Unexplained Laughter*. Based on a novel by Alice Thomas Ellis, the drama was adapted by Alun Owen and directed by Gareth Davies. In what is essentially a character study, one with very little plot or action, Diana plays Lydia, a London-based freelance writer whose boyfriend leaves her for another woman. To avoid the many painful reminders of her former relationship, she and her friend Betty (Elaine Paige) take a spontaneous trip to Wales. Lydia and Betty seem to be complete opposites; nevertheless, they exude a strong sense of mutual respect, bringing credibility to the pairing.

The trip, however, manages merely to complicate matters, as Betty must now deal with her own unrequited relationship, one involving a man solely devoted to the Almighty. Love, for everyone else anyway, is all around them. There's a lady having an affair with the local physician; there's a bleeding-heart naturist who can't see the forest for the trees; there's even a narcissist in love with *himself*. The only one *not* pining for someone is Lydia. She has gathered her wits about her, and does not hold back on her waspish observations. Rigg and Page are so adept at the brittle dialogue, in fact, that they could easily pass as a British comedy team of the drawing room school. Because she perceives herself now as being above the fray, Lydia seemingly throws caution to the wind and believably threatens to seduce two brothers just for the fun and torment of it all. There's another provocative sequence, in which she arranges a little picnic, right by some pornography-painted rocks, just to stir things up with the locals. In the end, she comes to view her ex (Jon Finch) for the self-involved loser he is.

The scant few who recall seeing the film when it was first shown on British TV's *The Play on One* series in 1989 praised it for its intelligent script and darkly comic dialogue. The film itself remained in obscurity until it turned up on DVD in the *Diana Rigg at the BBC* collection. It currently awaits reappraisal.

Having long ago abandoned roles requiring a sex symbol, the aging actress seemed quite comfortable playing troubled or outwardly villainous characters, a trend that would later culminate with her stage triumph in *Medea*. It was a fascinating evolution to observe, particularly to those devoted followers who saw in her a vast potential for playing darker roles. Diana enjoyed playing "bad" or "evil" characters like Tyrell, calling them "so much more interesting than good. There are some actors who don't like to play bad; they like to be liked. I love [my characters] to be disliked."[12] She pondered the point even further: "I'm good at evil. Some actresses exude innate sweetness and goodness—I don't. I've got a darker side that I can call upon; and I understand the damage that some people do, wanting power and control over others, which is truly frightening."[13]

Someone who must surely have approved of Diana Rigg taking this new, more sinister path was Vincent Price. Diana had worked so well with Price in *Theatre of Blood*. One of the things that makes Price so beloved by his fans is the fact that this patrician gentleman, who so exquisitely frightened

generations of moviegoers, was in fact such a gentle soul in real life. With
his classic features and erudite manner, Price was the ideal host on the
PBS program *Mystery!*, beginning in 1981. Sadly, as with Olivier a few years
earlier, illness took a savage toll on Vincent Price's body and talent. Parkinson's disease gradually robbed him of his beautiful voice and his perfect diction. When he retired from his hosting duties in 1989 at the age of
seventy-eight, he must have been heartened that, if he *had* to be replaced,
it was at least by someone who truly loved and admired him. Diana would
serve as the show's new dignified host for the next fifteen years.

   Mystery! began as an anthology series produced by WGBH in Boston.
The show was created as a mystery, police, and crime drama spinoff from
Masterpiece Theatre (which was hosted by Alistair Cooke from 1971 to 1992).
From 1980 to 2006, *Mystery!* featured mostly British crime dramas pur-
chased from, or co-produced with, the BBC or ITV and adapted from works
of British mystery fiction. The initial host of *Mystery!* was film critic Gene
Shalit. Then came Price, who was followed by Diana. She had the chance
to introduce and star in two shows under the *Mystery!* umbrella: *Mother
Love* (in which she would costar with David McCallum from October to
November of 1989) and *The Mrs. Bradley Mysteries* (in which she would
costar with Neil Dudgeon from 1998 to 1999). Diana had previously won
a BAFTA Award in 1985 for her work on *Masterpiece Theater*'s adaptation
of *Bleak House*, and she would exit *Mystery!* in 2003. The following year,
Mystery! aired without a host. In 2008, the show was rebranded under
the *Masterpiece* umbrella and brought in Alan Cumming as the host.

CHAPTER 12

THE BRADLEY BUNCH

I'm not just an actress. I am a person of very
diverse tastes and needs.
And I need to be the person I am. I need to feed it.
Does that make sense?

—DIANA RIGG

BY THE END OF THE EIGHTIES, DIANA'S SECOND MARRIAGE WAS IN TROUBLE.
Deep trouble. Her career, too, seemed to stall, causing her to resort to the
lecture circuit to pay the bills. What was happening? Although she would
not give specifics, she at least alluded to this difficult period when she said,
in conversation with Louis Wise, "The shit hits the fan from time to time,
and it was time it hit the fan for me. It was the same time my husband
left me, and that was it! You can't argue. I'd kind of swanned through life
before, and I learnt a few hard lessons."[1]

She was now past fifty, a tough time for any working actress. Is that why
the offers for parts stopped coming in, or at least diminished?

"I suppose so," she said at first. She thought about it for the moment
before she added, "But no. I proved them wrong subsequently."[2]

That she did. Her career, at least on the stage, was about to enter a
golden era, one in which she would win plaudits and standing ovations for
her riveting portrayals of Medea, Mother Courage, and Phaedra. She even
undertook the challenge of French dramatic tragedy in five acts, written
in alexandrine verse by Jean Racine. That wonderful confidence she had
exuded as a child could not be suppressed any longer.

"And I mean, I looked good," she told Wise. "In fact, I looked *über*-good,
because I'd lost so much weight," a side effect from the divorce, a classic
response, she suggested, to such a life-altering experience. As to those who
gain weight following such a traumatic event, Rigg smiled gently and said,
"I would advise *my* route."[3]

Regarding the stage production of *Phaedra*, Diana spoke affectionately of Ted Hughes, the English poet who had adapted it, even though she was not personally fond of him. She was called to his farmhouse in Devo and read the text with him one morning.

"That wonderful voice," she beamed. "Just down to his boots, then beyond."

Following that, and a bite to eat, Hughes took her fishing, which she fully embraced. "We didn't catch anything," she recalled. "I didn't take my rod, and it's a bit personal, that—because you like to use your own rod. It's rather like a fountain pen; you're used to it." She continued: "Anyway, I was *horrified* by his fishing box! *Slovenly* is the only word for it. Mine is so precise and anally tidy, and his was . . . it was a bordello!"[4]

Ted Hughes died, aged sixty-eight, in 1998.

As much as she loved the theater, she relied on the higher salaries paid in network television. Two TV movies she made, broadcast respectively in 1992 and 1993, are *Mrs. 'Arris Goes to Paris* and *Running Delilah*.

Mrs. 'Arris is based on the 1958 novella by Paul Gallico. It tells the delightful story of a spunky London charwoman, Ada Harris (Angela Lansbury), who becomes fixated on the idea of owning a gown designed by Christian Dior. Ada and her friend and fellow char, Vi Butterfield (Lila Kaye), must scrimp and save to travel to Paris, where Ada plans to personally visit the House of Dior to make her purchase. To provide the story with its requisite element of conflict, and to prevent the script to devolving into treacle, there is the unsympathetic character of Claudine Colbert, played with brisk efficiency by Diana. While there are those egalitarians who applaud Ada's lofty ambition, Madam Colbert frankly resents the intrusion of this common person and her presumptuous attempts at entering the exclusive world of *haute couture*. Of course, as this is essentially a modern-day fairy tale, everyone—even the stodgy Madam Colbert—ultimately succumbs to Ada Harris's ingratiating ways.

In 1982, Rigg had headlined in the short-lived stage musical *Colette*, in which she played la romancière Collette (with what she termed, "my British voice"). But in the end, her performance as Colbert in *'Arris* became the first of three times that she played a Frenchwoman on-screen. Subsequently, she would do so with costarring roles in *The Last King* (2003), as the historical Queen Henrietta Maria, and *The American* (1998), as Mme de Bellegarde.

Either way, it was nothing less than terrific to see Diana perform with the equally esteemed and accomplished actress Angela Lansbury in *Mrs. 'Arris Goes to Paris*.

Diana's TV movie from 1992, *Running Delilah*, was written by Ron Koslow and Robert J. Avrech, directed by Richard Franklin, and aired on ABC. Originally intended as a television series, it was released on video in Japan, Sweden, and the UK the following year, and was finally run as a one-off on American television in 1994. To capitalize on Quentin Tarantino's then-current success, the video box cover has an unmistakably *Pulp Fiction* look to it, with a black-haired, black-outfitted Kim Cattrall pointing a long silver gun (or phallus) straight up. As the eponymous Delilah, she is a top female agent who dies while on a risky mission to stop a weapons dealer. She is somehow revived and given all new artificial body parts, making her invincible. (Did I mention this was science fiction?) There is an especially concise review of *Running Delilah* on Amazon.com, credited to a Canadian writer whose pseudonym is "Mister Blue":

This is your basic love story. Boy meets girl, girl gets into an accident and becomes a cyborg. Featuring a young Billy Zane when he had hair; it also has Diana Rigg. That pretty well covers it.

Genghis Cohn, based on a novel by Romain Gary and adapted by Stanley Price, was originally an episode of the British television series *Screen Two* in 1993, the same year that Steven Spielberg's highly affecting *Schindler's List* was released. Like Spielberg's acclaimed film, *Genghis Cohn* is also about the horrors of the Holocaust, but this film is a *comedy*. And apparently, the talents behind the project managed to pull it off. Paul Mavis, the critic who has written about this and other offerings in the *Diana Rigg at the BBC* collection, certainly thinks so. He states that *Genghis Cohn* is "simply brilliant."

In the story, music hall comedian Genghis Cohn (Antony Sher) is killed by a brutal Nazi officer, Otto Schatz (Robert Lindsay), during World War II.

Many years later, Otto has become a highly respected police commissioner, investigating a series of murders. But when his foundation is shaken to the core when he encounters the taunting ghost of Cohn, Schatz is slowly driven mad.

Diana's role, that of Rita von Stangel, an SS officer's imperious widow, is a relatively minor one, although she makes the most of it. Her regular sexual encounters with Schatz are predicated on his wearing her late husband's military uniform during intercourse. The primary source of humor found in *Genghis Cohn*, however, derives from *schadenfreude* concerning the heinous Schatz. We see him devolve from a cocky, racist killer to a haunted, terrified shadow of his former self. Before the story's end, he has lost his standing in the community, his position--everything, in fact, that he holds dear. Our last view of him is that of a broken shell of a man, running a small delicatessen.

• • •

It was in London, circa 1991, when actor Damon Evans finally met Diana "face to face." As he recalled, "It was a small event with a select number of invited guests that was held in a private residence, which I believe had been arranged by either our director, Simon Callow, or our producer, Howard Panter. The event was to welcome the headlining cast of *Carmen Jones*, composed of a number of Americans, that was slated to open at the Old Vic Theater. We had just begun rehearsals.

"The cast," Evans continued, "was led by opera singer Wilhelmina Fernandez, who had made a splash in the French film *Diva*. They were all excited to meet Diana because she had become a television icon because of Emma Peel and *The Avengers*.

"Of course, I was in as much awe as everyone else. On the other hand, I was also aware that she had extensive stage training and theater experience performing the classics as well. That impressed me much more than her television stardom because I wasn't a particular fan of the series, having never really watched it."

Evans "deeply" regretted that he didn't see her in such stage productions as *Medea*, *Mother Courage*, as Violet Venable in *Suddenly Last Summer*, or as Martha in *Who's Afraid of Virginia Woolf?* "I'm sure in each case she was quite remarkable," he said.

In first meeting Diana, Evans mostly remembered her resistance to "the sex-symbol label and persona that had been thrust upon her as a result of her television celebrity. And that she demanded equal pay along with her male costar Patrick Macnee. That was unheard of in the 1960s. I respected that very much indeed, even though I had yet to fully comprehend all of the ramifications of taking such a stance and the professional consequences that can result in being labeled 'difficult.'

"When we met," Evans continued, "she came across as a rather down-to-earth lady who was dressed in what the Brits would call a casual chic outfit. She roamed around the buffet table talking randomly nonstop about various things. The one thing that stood out the most was her reference to her daughter as being at the age when she was becoming more and more interesting and evolving into her own right as a separate and unique human being.

"There was a remove and distance about her that led me to assume she could be a rather elusive individual and hard to get to know," he added.

"That said, there was nothing cold about her whatsoever. Actually, I felt that she had a sly sense of humor and a wit that could be quite engaging. I guess I would sum her up as a cordial yet private person who had certain boundaries which she'd expect you to respect. In-kind, she'd reciprocate with as warm an amiable relationship as possible for her.

"I've always loved the type of versatility which she embodied as an actress," Evans concluded. "This is something that the Brits do so well. Shakespeare one day, Stoppard the next, a TV series this season, a musical on the West End the next, and a film, and on and on and on. Ms. Rigg did all of these things with what came across to her public as being *seemingly effortless*."

• • •

In 1994, a few years after Damon Evans met Diana, she spoke of her "appetite now for really good work in the final third of my life." She went on to describe the theater as her "home . . . I don't belong anywhere else." As journalist Paul Bond wrote on the World Socialist Web Site, wsws.org, "The outstanding achievement of Diana Rigg's life was to demonstrate that a great theatre actor can move to other media without losing the qualities that made them great in the first place."

But Diana did not exactly prove that in 1994 with her choice of *A Good Man in Africa* as her latest project. The film's director, Bruce Beresford, admitted that it in no way measured up to his Oscar-winning successes *Driving Miss Daisy* or *Tender Mercies*. He was hardly alone in this assessment. Only in retrospect did Beresford realize what made *A Good Man in Africa* fail so spectacularly. "I realized that although the novel that it's based on is terribly funny, it was very anecdotal," he explained. "It had no narrative. On about the second day I realized it was never going to work, because the scenes don't link. I thought, 'I'm sunk! I'm never gonna get out.'"[5]

The presence of such cast stalwarts as Diana Rigg, Sean Connery, John Lithgow, and Louis Gossett Jr. led to Beresford feeling an ongoing sense of regret concerning this film. Each of these seasoned actors had worked hard and uncomplainingly for him, but Beresford was so displeased by the results that he worried he had unwittingly contributed to the end of their respective careers. In fact, he told this author that he wished they had questioned their involvement in such a botched affair.

Although Connery and Rigg did not share any scenes together, which was a missed opportunity on several levels, four years after this movie, he would star as a villain in the big-screen adaptation of Rigg's TV hit *The Avengers*, starring Ralph Fiennes and Uma Thurman as Steed and Peel.

And while that 1998 box-office dud had issues of its own, the deck was still stacked against *A Good Man in Africa*.

Janet Maslin, of the *New York Times*, writes:

A good book is the basis for *A Good Man in Africa*, but its mordant humor has curdled badly on the screen. Although William Boyd, the author of these gimlet-eyed observations of colonial antics in Africa, adapted his own novel and also served as one of the film's producers, *A Good Man in Africa* now has none of the cunning that it had on the page. . . . It is directed in woefully unfunny fashion by Bruce Beresford . . . whose talents ordinarily take a more quietly dramatic turn. Here, lumbering through the machinations of a frenzied farce, he displays a comic touch that is unfailingly mirthless, and a penchant for offending his audience in needless, obvious ways.[6]

• • •

In 1993, Diana was involved in the resurrection of a play that had seen its first production in 431 BC.

"*Medea* started very small with Jonathan Kent, directing at the Almeida [in London], and it was [sold] out, but no West End producer picked up on it," Diana explained. She passionately believed that Euripides's tale, based on the myth of Jason and Medea, was still relevant, that "there was more life in this play. It wasn't dead. It had further to go." She approached Bill Penwright and beseeched him to "please, resurrect it. Trust me, it will work." Upon reading Penwright's revised edition, she knew her instincts had been correct.

"We toured all round England," she said. "And each place we toured at there was, oh, absolutely very little advanced publicity, very little word of mouth, but we played a week in each place.

"And gradually, gradually we built 'til, by the end, we were playing to a full house in each place we went to. And then we went to London, to Wyndham's Theatre, where we were selling out and then a Broadway producer picked up on it. And we went to Broadway, and we became [sold out] for a two-thousand-year-old play—absolutely fantastic. And I begged the producers to put Euripides's name up in lights. I thought two thousand years afterwards, wonderful! Let's put him up there. And they said, 'No, no, no, it'll put the people off,' and I said, 'Well, *I'll* pay for it" No! [they said] And they refused to do it. But there we were. On Broadway, a sellout, and it was the same company all the time . . . all the way through, we'd stayed together. That, to me, is the perfect experience to have with a play. That you start so modestly and without any true thought that it would ever, ever, take the journey that it did. But it did. And it was a miracle and I look back on it with such pleasure. Just, yes!"[7]

Diana was in the midst of what she would later refer to as the happiest time of her career. Her fans remained loyal and cordial to her, and she always gracious in return. A lovely illustration of this can be found in some letters to the editor of the *New York Times*, which appeared in September 1994. Janice M. Cauwels, of Maywood, New Jersey, was so inspired by Diana's performance that she wrote a letter to the editor. A longtime admirer of Diana, Cauwels was raised during the original run of *The Avengers*. She felt that both Ms. Rigg and Mrs. Peel were everything she was not: "independent, brave, and beloved." As she told a friend, "Diana Rigg is not only beautiful but also someone who makes *me* feel beautiful as well."[8] Diana replied in kind to the *Times*, and Cauwels, whose words, the actress claimed, were perhaps the nicest compliment she had ever received. Another compliment, this one from the American Theatre Wing, came in the form of a Tony Award for Best Actress of the Year in *Medea*. To top off this extraordinary time in her career, the former Yorkshire girl was awarded the title Dame Commander of the Order of the British Empire by Queen Elizabeth II.

Let's face it: fan letters and awards are great, but there is nothing like a dame. And when CBS News journalist Anthony Mason asked Diana if awards meant anything to her, she said, "Of course, they do. And anybody who says they don't is talking rubbish."

• • •

Diana continued to perform on the London stage throughout the 1990s in productions like *Night and Day, Colette, Mother Courage*, Sondheim's *Follies, Suddenly, Last Summer*, and *All About My Mother*. She also made TV appearances in BBC productions of Danielle Steel's *Zoya* (1995). Directed by Richard Colla, *Zoya* is a typically lush Steel saga that encompasses fifty-three years of tumult, tragedy, and romance in the life of a dispossessed Russian countess (Melissa Gilbert). Also in the cast were Bruce Boxleitner, Philip Casnoff, David Warner, and Diana.

Other TV guest-shots included *The Haunting of Helen Walker* (1995), *Samson and Delilah*, and *The Fortunes and Misfortunes of Moll Flanders*, both from 1996. In the latter, Diana played Mrs. Golightly, and had another brush with James Bond, though she nor anyone else knew it at the time: the *Flanders* cast included actor Daniel Craig, who would go on to play 007 in a successful series of Bond films, beginning with *Casino Royale* in 2006 and ending with *No Time to Die* in 2021.

Meanwhile, *Samson and Delilah*, directed by Nicolas Roeg, is the biblical saga of the braided Israelite strongman (this time played by Eric Thal) and his Philistine temptress (Elizabeth Hurley). Besides Diana, other supporting actors in the film include the ever-prolific Dennis Hopper, Michael Gambon, Daniel Massey, Paul Ferguson, Ben Becker, and Jale Arıkan.

As reviewer Robert Hayes of letterbox.com succinctly observed, "For all the talent involved, one would think the result would be better." As with Cecil B. DeMille's 1949 film adaption starring Hedy Lamarr and Victor Mature, "the actor playing Samson [Mature] has a limited range, and Delilah is there as eye candy. Some nice Nic Roeg touches, though."

Vastly more memorable than these assorted projects is *Masterpiece Theatre*'s 1997 retelling of Daphne du Maurier's 1938 novel, *Rebecca*. The story centers on a mousy girl whose name is never known to the reader. She has been hired as a traveling companion to a dreadful old woman who berates her for the slightest infraction. While on a particularly unhappy vacation with this over-privileged tyrant in Monte Carlo, the girl meets the enigmatic Maxim De Winter, a wealthy widower and the lord of England's Manderley estate. Taking pity on the unhappy youth, De Winter suddenly (and unromantically) proposes. The girl thinks this handsome sophisticate is merely toying with her, and she tells him so. He insists that his proposal is genuine and encourages her to leave with him for Manderley immediately. And just like that, this veritable child is thrust into the position of being the lady of a vast estate, with a team of servants at her disposal. The most intimidating member of the staff is the general factotum, Mrs. Danvers. Although she is starchily civil to the awkward young lady, her resentment is palpable. The reader soon learns the reason behind Mrs. Danvers's thinly veiled hostility: she was, and still is, deeply devoted to Maxim's late wife, the elegant Rebecca De Winter. Maxim is made aware of the unhealthy dynamic, but he is dismissive of his timid bride's concerns. His inaction will ultimately lead to the revelation of dark secrets, and the fiery destruction of his beloved Manderley.

Rebecca, of course, had been filmed once before, in 1940. That now-classic black-and-white psychological thriller was produced by David O. Selznick and directed by Alfred Hitchcock (in what was his first American production). The leading cast members, each of whom earned Academy Award nominations for their work in the film, were Laurence Olivier as Maxim, Joan Fontaine as the second Mrs. De Winter, and Judith Anderson as Mrs. Danvers. Remaking so famous a picture may seem like an exercise in cinematic futility, but the 1997 color remake is well done and beautifully acted. Charles Dance and Emilia Fox are adequate as the leads, but it is Diana's textured performance as Mrs. Danvers that remains lodged in the memory—not only the viewer's but Diana's as well.

During her question-and-answer session at the Oxford Union, an admitted fan of Rigg's interpretation asked the actress if she had enjoyed the experience of making the film.

"I loved doing it," Diana said with conviction. "Judith Anderson, a very great [Australian] actress, had done it before me, and I think won loads of awards for it. So, it was a bit of a challenge because you know that a predecessor sort of very much made it her own. When I was at school, I, we had a *pash*—it was called a passion, on older girls at school, not necessarily carnal. I mean, it wasn't. That you, just you, and I remembered that. And I thought, there's something about Mrs. Danvers loving Rebecca as she does, and being obsessed by Rebecca as she [is], and there's something of the schoolgirl passion for Rebecca. So, I had a wig, and it was pulled across, and I had a kirby grip [*indicating her hair clip*] in it, to sort of just be that schoolgirl person. . . . Sometimes, the impulse has gone bad, but the initial impulse was love. She *loved* this woman. But this love turned to obsession, and the obsession turned into evil. And . . . it developed. And I, again, thoroughly enjoyed it because it's a wonderful adaptation. And again, it's a wonderful book."[9]

• • •

After impressing viewers as Mrs. Danvers on *Masterpiece*, Diana transitioned seamlessly into Mrs. Bradley on *Mystery*. There is just something about a mature woman who dabbles in sleuthing that brings an especial comfort to dedicated readers of mystery novels. Agatha Christie had Miss Jane Marple and the lesser-known Ariadne Oliver. Angela Lansbury, who had found her niche on Broadway, gained a massive new following on CBS's *Murder, She Wrote* as Jessica Fletcher, a writer of fiction who solves real-life murder mysteries between cranking out manually typed manuscripts. Now, Diana was taking her turn at the amateur detective subgenre. Drawing on her ability to connect with a live audience, Diana occasionally breaks the fourth wall and speaks directly to the viewer. Her character, the creation of prolific novelist Gladys Mitchell, is Adela Bradley, a jaded divorcée and psychologist who solves crimes in the posher homes of 1920s-era Britain. Adela has a valuable assistant in her chauffeur, George Moody (Neil Dudgeon), with whom she also shares an unmistakable sexual tension. Reminiscent of her portrayal of Mrs. Peel,

Diana brought strength, adventure, intelligence, dry wit, style, and flare
to Mrs. Adela Bradley.[10]

The ninety-minute pilot, "The Speedy Death," was shown in 1999. Four
new episodes, filmed in 2000, aired in 2003: "Death at the Opera," "Rising of the Moon," "Laurels are Poison," and "The Worsted Viper." Diana
Rigg, performing double duty as the show's host and leading player, deftly
handled the introductions, including the first one:

> Adela Bradley doesn't mince words. And why should she? They are
> her greatest weapon against fools, cads, criminals ... and ex-lovers.
> Words also came easily to Adela's creator, Gladys Mitchell, who
> published nearly eighty novels in her long lifetime. Gladys introduced
> Mrs. Bradley in 1929 in the book, *Speedy Death*. She endowed her
> breezy heroine with attributes she herself possessed, including an
> interest in Freud and a passion for all things British: Morris dancing,
> mayday rituals, and the Loch Ness Monster. Over the course of some
> sixty-six mysteries, Adela Bradley married and divorced three hus-
> bands, was made a dame of the British Empire, and was a consultant
> to the British Home Office. She also developed prodigious abilities
> at pub darts, snooker, billiards, and knife-throwing. One thing she
> cannot do is knit.[11]

That knowledgeable critic of all things Rigg, Paul Mavis, had this to say
about the short-lived series.

> Apparently, this particular series didn't go over well with critics
> and audiences in England when it first appeared, and that may
> explain why it only ran one "series" ("season" in Brit-TV talk). I
> have to confess I've never read any of the Mrs. Bradley mysteries,
> so I can't speak to the fidelity of these adaptations; however, from
> what I've read, these handsome pieces played fast and loose with
> the plotlines and with the central character itself, ticking off the
> novels' devoted fans. Having never read them, I'm not beholden
> to any preconceived notions, so I took these five little movies as
> they came. That being said, I enjoyed them well enough. Certainly,
> they're not the equal of a good [David] Suchet Poirot or a [Joan]
> Hickson Marple, but *Rigg* certainly is the equal to those perform-
> ers, and she's a stitch as the waspish Mrs. Bradley. The mysteries
> by and large were forgettable, with one or two twists that I didn't
> see coming. But again, nothing remarkably original or new. And

curiously, there was a faintly lugubrious tone to the movies that I found inexplicable. These are, after all, supposed to be taking place during the jazz era—why the curiously leaden approach? The lines are funny enough (I love Mrs. Bradley dismissively noting, "It was a country sort of place, where birds and animals wander around uncooked") and Neil Dudgeon, now of *Midsomer Murders* fame, has an amused, cocky air to him that I liked. If all the pieces were in place, then . . . why the murky, muted tone? Still, it's great to see Rigg glancing sideways off to us and letting off a snarky comment or two (her son says, "There are worse crimes than being dull," to which Rigg dismissively replies, "*Really?*"); she's the whole show here, and that's enough, in the end.[12]

• • •

According to stir.ac.uk, the official website of the University of Stirling, in October 1998, Diana was installed as the university's fourth chancellor, thereby becoming the first woman to hold the position. During the installation at Stirling's Church of the Holy Rude, she told the 300 assembled guests: "The academic world is a far cry from that of a thespian, although both have a lot of learning to do. I hope to be a credible chancellor to Stirling University and to enjoy and learn about this new world."

In a media interview to mark her appointment, and as further documented on the university's website, Diana said she would "rather be proactive than just a figurehead." She added: "I think it will be fascinating. It's an honor, but it's an honor you have to meet. I intend to do it to the best of my ability. I think it's very nice that a woman who is not an academic and comes from an acting background is given this opportunity. I think it shows a lot of imagination and I am very grateful for that."

As chancellor, Dame Diana conferred the degrees of thousands of Stirling students and also several honorary graduates. Additionally, she officially opened the Macrobert Arts Centre in 2002, after spearheading the fundraising campaign to turn it into Scotland's first dedicated theater for children.

That same year, Diana, along with fellow British actors Derek Jacobi, Ian Richardson, and Donald Sinden, traveled to Sydney, Australia, for an historic gathering of talent for the acclaimed Royal Shakespeare Company production of *The Hollywood Crown*. As the *Sydney Morning Herald* suggested, the casting troupe was a "triumph, complete with one dame, two knights and one Commander of the British Empire." Ian Richardson, however, was quick to clarify that there was no "tub-thumping, flag-waving promotion of the seriously listing *House of Windsor*."[13]

All worked well in unison with "Riggers," as Diana was affectionately known to her thespian peers. As the Scottish newspaper *The Herald* pointed out, she was "the undisputed center of attention."[14]

Also in 2002, Diana had enough when she successfully sued the *Daily Mail* over a dastardly report that suggested she was a retired recluse and bitter over the collapse of her second marriage to Archie Stirling after his affair with Joely Richardson. They photographed Diana close by to her French home clutching a baguette and printed it with the caption: "Shopping for one."

Retired? Hardly. Recluse? Not in the least. As reporter Stuart Jeffries later assessed, "After two marriages, Rigg had not had a live-in lover for many years, but that's not the same thing."

But it was the *Mail*'s false claim that Rigg was embittered about her marriage ending years earlier that hurt. As she later expressed to Jeffries, "I had never said those words. I had sworn not to talk about my marriage breakup. But those words had a terrible effect on me. I read them, sobbing, thinking about my marriage."

As to any possibility of another marriage, Rigg said, "I'm very good at living with somebody. I think my ex-husband would accede to this because I tend to please. I come from a generation where, when my dad arrived and parked the car, [my mother] would rush upstairs and put some lipstick on, which I think is so charming. I'm wasted living by myself in a sense. But don't anybody, please, take that as an invitation to step forward."

As many celebrities will attest, being the undisputed center of attention clearly has its downside. As Diana stated further about being that unwitting target of the *Daily Mail*, "They just wrote rubbish. . . . And I felt I *had* to [do something about it]. And I was advised not to. And everybody said . . . 'It's tomorrow's fish and chips' wrapping.' Well, it isn't. It just isn't. Because they said, I had a house in France. I *have* a house in France. Somehow, they found out where I was. They sent a photographer out there. They photographed me with a huge baguette saying, "Shopping for one." They then said I was in retreat. I had retired. And, was living as a recluse in France. Now this is pretty damaging [to my career]. And it's also pretty undermining. It's almost like you are going to retire, that they are dictating your life. So, I had to fight back, and it was a torturous process. I wouldn't advise it to anybody because they fight dirty. Of course, they do. I was absolutely fascinated by the ladies that they had on retainer. And there they were with their power suits, and beautifully groomed. They were all on retainer. And there they were, lying, manipulating the law, in order to prove a point, which was a lie. So, I *had* to fight it. And I *did* and we *won*, thank goodness. And the editor of the *Daily Telegraph* said, would I like to write an article about it? So, I did. And the response I got from the general public, from people who'd been in similar cases [was heartening]. I remember a father whose daughter's reputation had been trashed by the *Daily Mail*. And, she'd had no redress at all. I am anti- the press of this kind, that like to throw mud at helpless people. I just disagree [with this approach]. And I will *fight*, if ever it happens again."[15]

With regard to the Levinson Inquiry (the judicial public inquiry into the culture, practices and ethics of the British press),[16] the situation with the press had improved. "Well, I think they know that there is a point at which the law will step in, that much they have, they have to recognize. Whereas before there was, I mean, this was patently . . . a complete lie. And they actually retired me, and this was thirty years ago. To be *retired*? And, interestingly enough, for months later, people said, 'Oh, I thought you were gonna live in France.' I mean, the power of these newspapers is huge. Never, never underestimate them."[17]

• • •

By 2005, Diana found herself once more on the big screen, this time in *Heidi*, an adaptation of the classic children's 1881 novel by Johanna Spyri. The story is a young orphan girl, played by Emma Bolger, her crusty grandfather (Max von Sydow), and their life in the mountains. Diana played the young girl's grandmother in what one film critic described as a "handsome production" directed by Paul Marcus, which also starred Geraldine Chaplin.

There is much to appreciate in this version of *Heidi*, or as a review on commonsensemedia.org put it, "There's very little content of concern." (The review goes on to note frightening or otherwise objectionable scenes, which are minimal.)

The same year of *Heidi*'s release, actor Samuel West worked alongside Rigg for a charity show. Due to his parents' friendship with Rigg, he had known of her work "all of my life." While he had never seen Diana perform live on stage when he was younger, West would later team with her in what turned out to be one of her last performances, as Mrs. Pumphrey, in the PBS series *All Creatures Great and Small*.

But he had been familiar with her early work from afar with the Royal Shakespeare Company. Then in 2005, he worked with her, albeit fleetingly, for a recital to support the Oxford Playhouse. As West explained, "I was at the University of Oxford and connected with the Oxford Playhouse, which is the . . . theatre in Oxford. And we did an evening there of fundraising, which Diana was a part of. I had known Rachael [Stirling], her daughter, for a very long time. It was the first time I had ever worked with Diana. And we were just doing the normal sort of fundraising where you would do a reading. Some people sang songs, and others read extracts from Shakespeare."

West recalled visiting Diana in her dressing room, where she offered him a glass of wine. He was in between appearances on stage, and "wasn't in the habit of having a glass of champagne in the interval. But Diana offered me one. And she said, 'I find the second half always goes a little better.' So, I said yes to that, and, as far as I remember, the second [performance] did go rather well. She was right!"

With extensive insight into an actor's life, West discussed Rigg's work ethic and that of British thespians in general: British actors love to act, even if they have a small part in a little play. As West explained, "I am the fourth generation of acting in my family and I was always brought up with that belief . . . that if something appeals to you, you should do it. And I think that Diana believed that, as does her daughter Rachael."

As West observed, "One of the conversations I remember having with my father was when I was rather busy and I was offered a one-day radio play. It was going to be quite hard to fit in. And I told him, 'I don't know what I am going to do about this. It's tight. The part is nice.'"

His father then asked him, "Are you good casting?"

West replied, "Yeah. Yeah."

"Well, then," his father continued to wonder, "is it going to be better because you're in it?"

And without blowing his own trumpet, West replied, "I think it might be."

To which his father then concluded, "Then you have to do it."

"So, I did," West recalled. "And it turned out to be the only time I worked with that writer, who died soon afterwards. I was really grateful, because it was an interesting job. But my father took the point that it was the sort of thing that one should do. I think most English actors are freed by that ideal. It is a small country. So, nobody just does theater. Nobody just does film. Also, we don't necessarily need to do things where are likable. And Diana had benefitted from playing people that aren't necessarily liked very much."

West added, "The performance is separate from the character. As it should be. And whether Diana was playing likable or unlikable characters, she obviously was not those characters in real life. No actor is, of course." With a smile, West clarified, "Although, we do have certain problems with soaps in Britain where, if you play a nasty character, you do tend to be attacked in supermarkets."

It's not the actors who are being attacked, but the characters they play; there are those who, at times, unfortunately, are perceived to be in real life who they play on-screen. In such cases, the given audience member cannot separate fantasy from reality. But that's not the actor's problem, and as West observed, "I think Diana very much took that attitude toward her work. She did [a role] because it interested her and because she thought she would have something to say about it."

Rigg had been trained in acting since she was a child, and her skill remained with her to the day she left this world. And it was a varied skill, which she proved time and time again, whether she was playing melodramatic Shakespeare or in light TV comedic performance like that in the BBC's *Three Piece Suit* (which she did in the 1970s). In all such cases, Diana proved her chops as an actor beyond *The Avengers*.

As West observed, "I'm sure that is true. She had the disadvantage to be extremely beautiful and look iconically fabulous."

West's mother, he said, "had it in a different direction when she played Sybil in *Fawlty Towers*" [from 1975 to 1979]. "She was very funny in it and it was a great creation and the show was very successful. As a result, for the rest of her life she hasn't been offered very much Shakespeare."

On the other hand, "Diana didn't quite have that problem," West stated, "because she did play some great parts on stage [early in her career and toward the end of her life]. But I think for a long time, and also, when she died, she was Emma Peel. It's great to have a part like that . . . that pays your bills for so long and that people remember you by."

Assuredly, small- and big-screen audiences remembered many of Rigg's other performances, including those in films as late as 2006's *The Painted Veil* (a remake of the original 1934 movie adaptation starring Greta Garbo). According to journalist Benjamin Hathaway, writing in screenrant.com, "*The Painted Veil* featured Edward Norton as a bacteriologist studying infectious diseases in Shanghai. Norton's Walter Fane must contend with both a loveless marriage to Kitty Garstin Fane (Naomi Watts) and the rapidly spreading cholera epidemic.

"Rigg enters the narrative once the Fanes' marriage has been put on rocky terrain," Hathaway continued. "When Kitty begins to put her hard-partying lifestyle behind her, she volunteers at an orphanage. The orphanage is run by French nuns [with the leader, Mother Superior, played by Diana]. Rigg's character has a substantial impact on the narrative, as she informs Kitty that Walter has a paternal instinct. This sets Kitty and Walter on a path toward reconciliation."

Also in 2006, Diana would be featured in TV episodes of *Avonlea, Murder in Mind*, and *Victoria and Albert*, the latter of which earned her yet another Emmy nomination.

In 2008, she performed in Chichester with a production of *The Cherry Orchard*, which was not the success she had hoped for.

By this time, performing off-stage in more intimate circles, like the bedroom, was becoming less a priority for Diana. In fact, in 2009, she told Laura Potter of *The Guardian*, that sex wasn't important to her at all. "Not anymore," she said. "I'm all for people of my age having a continued sex life, but although I had a wonderful sex life I'm perfectly reconciled and happy not to go there again."

She may have quite productively offered "drama therapy" years before to those struggling with substance abuse at that New York drug rehabilitation center. But when she sought professional therapy for any personal issues she may have had, Diana "found it totally pointless." As she continued to tell Potter, "When my marriage broke up I went to three separate therapists and each was worse than the last. I can only speak for myself. There are other people it's been incredibly useful for, but not me."

Other than that, at this point in her life, Diana was healthy. "For my age, I'm quite good," she told Potter.

In 2011, she made a triumphant return to the theater with a new production of *Pygmalion*. Diana had an interesting history with Bernard Shaw's famous 1913 play. In 1974, she played an especially gritty Eliza Doolittle in *Pygmalion* at London's Albery Theatre.[18] Thirty-seven years later, she played Mrs. Higgins in a West End revival of the play, then nearly a century old.

In 2018, Diana made her triumphant return to Broadway at New York's Lincoln Center as Mrs. Higgins in a revival of *My Fair Lady*, the musical based on *Pygmalion*. A reporter for CBS News interviewed Rigg at the time, calling the show "a rousing revival." But the production, at least behind the scenes, was not without its controversies. At one point during the run, Lauren Ambrose, the young actress playing Eliza, decided that, henceforth, she would not perform the Sunday matinees. Known for her role in HBO's *Six Feet Under*, she simply wasn't used to the grueling demands of an eight-show week, although she had performed two non-singing roles on Broadway. She also said that she needed to spend more time with her husband and two children.

In a statement released to the press by Lincoln Center Theater, artistic director Andre Bishop wrote:

The decision for Lauren to perform seven performances a week was made due to the intense demands of this enormous, taxing role. Eliza requires a singing actress who can belt and sing in a high, operatic range as well. Julie Andrews often said and wrote that there were performances of *My Fair Lady* when she wasn't sure she could make it to the end of the show. The most important thing is that Lauren protect her stamina to continue to deliver beautiful shows to our audiences.

Her veteran costar, however, was not pleased—no, not pleased at all. She promptly fired off the following email to the show's producers.

I learnt, courtesy of a newspaper, that our leading lady will not be appearing in future Sunday matinees. Now, call me old-fashioned, which I unashamedly am, but I don't think this development is fair to audiences. They booked their seats in advance, paying an exorbitant price for them to see what they have been led to believe is the original cast. The very least we can do as actors is to acknowledge their presence as a privilege and take care never to abuse it. It's time managements put their audiences first and insist on the old adage, slightly adapted by me, "The show must go on—with ALL principals."[19]

That email was somehow obtained by, and reprinted in, the *New York Post*. As Rachael Stirling later explained, her mother suddenly became "persona non grata backstage." Diana remained steadfast, or as Rachael said, "She didn't give a hoot." The veteran actress's strong belief was that, if your name is on the billboard, you show up for every show. Period. And to be fair, she practiced what she preached. During her Tony Award–winning run in *Medea* in 1994, Diana ruptured a vocal cord in rehearsals. "They put a camera down my throat, and I could see the tear," she recalled. "There was a note in the spectrum of my voice that I could not hit. No sound would come out. So, I had to re-orchestrate all those speeches and arias to avoid that note. It was a fascinating exercise in learning how to keep going."[20]

Did she ever think of taking a few days off?

"Never."

Following up on the story, *Post* reporter Michael Riedel phoned Diana, who was now the soul of diplomacy, possibly as a means of keeping the show's investors calm. She made it clear that she had nothing but praise for Ambrose's interpretation of Eliza, which was, she said, a "definitive performance." She even acknowledged that Ambrose's decision to spend more time with her family is "perfectly understandable." Finally, she opined that the Eliza understudy, Kerstin Anderson, was "spectacularly good."

Privately, however, Diana simply could not accept the work ethic of this new generation of performers. "I'm flying the old flag for a generation of actors who performed even when they were at the death's door," she said. She then added, sadly, "But I suppose it's a tradition that has been lost. It's the norm these days, so I guess I should just shut up."[21]

Diana earned a Tony nomination for her performance in *My Fair Lady*. So did Lauren Ambrose (Eliza), Harry Hadden-Paton (Professor Henry Higgins), and Norbert Leo Butz (Alfred P. Doolittle), among others. Tony winners Bartlett Sher and Christopher Gattelli served as director and choreographer, respectively, for the production, which had previewed at the Lincoln Center Theatre on March 15. In all, there were thirty-nine previews and 509 performances. The show opened on April 19, 2018, and closed on September 9, 2018.

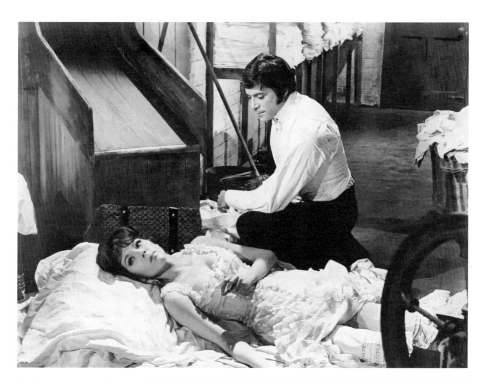

On March 23, 1969, Diana makes her big-screen debut in *The Assassination Bureau*, which costars Oliver Reed. Courtesy Classic TV Preservation Society (CTVPS).

Diana takes charge and makes history (again) as
Contessa Teresa "Tracy" di Vicenzo, the first Mrs.
James Bond in *On Her Majesty's Secret Service*, released
on December 19, 1969. Courtesy mptvimages.com.

Diana and George Lazenby were all
smiles as Mr. and Mrs. Bond for their
on-screen wedding in *On Her Majesty's
Secret Service*, but not so much when it
came to their reception of one another
off-screen. Trinity Mirror / Mirrorpix /
Alamy Stock Photo.

Front and Center: In 1970, Diana brings her classic stage training to the big screen as Portia in *Julius Caesar,* Stuart Barge's film adaptation of William Shakespeare's legendary play of the same name. An independent production of Common Wealth United Entertainment, shot in England and Spain (and the first movie edition of the play to be produced in color), *Julius Caesar* also stars Charlton Heston as Mark Antony (bottom center), Jason Robards as Brutus (bottom right), Richard Chamberlain as Octavius (bottom left), Richard Johnson as Cassius (middle left), Jill Bennett as Calpurnia (middle right), Robert Vaughn as Casca (second top), and John Gielgud as Caesar (top). Courtesy Classic TV Preservation Society (CTVPS).

On the release date of December 14, 1971, Diana checks into *The Hospital* with George C. Scott. Courtesy Classic TV Preservation Society (CTVPS).

Diana stars with Vincent Price (among others) in *Theatre of Blood*, her favorite film, released on April 5, 1973. From the author's collection.

Diana with first husband, artist Menachem Gueffen, at Heathrow Airport as they prepare to fly to Los Angeles for their honeymoon in 1973 (they would divorce in 1976). Trinity Mirror / Mirrorpix / Alamy Stock Photo.

Diana returns to American TV on a weekly basis with *Diana* (above), a sitcom that airs on NBC from September 10, 1973, to January 7, 1974. To everyone's surprise, Patrick Macnee, her former fellow *Avenger*, makes a guest appearance (bottom). Courtesy Classic TV Preservation Society (CTVPS).

Barbara Barrie (later of *Barney Miller*) plays her mother (above). (Below) Bernie Kopell (later Doc on *The Love Boat*) guest-stars in the *Diana* pilot. Courtesy Classic TV Preservation Society (CTVPS).

PLAYBILL

ST. JAMES THEATRE

The Misanthrope

Diana performed *The Misanthrope* with Alec McCowen at the St. James Theatre on Broadway in 1975. Courtesy Classic TV Preservation Society (CTVPS).

The Diversity of Diana: on February 17, 1975, Diana stars in *In This House of Brede* (top), playing a London woman who foregoes romance and a career to be a Benedictine nun. Two years later, Diana dazzles more loosely in *Three Piece Suite* (bottom). Courtesy Classic TV Preservation Society (CTVPS).

Diana stars with Charles Grodin and Jim Henson's creations in *The Great Muppet Caper* in 1981. Courtesy Classic TV Preservation Society (CTVPS)

Diana with Maggie Smith (her future *Game of Thrones* costar) in *Evil Under the Sun* in 1982. Courtesy Classic TV Preservation Society (CTVPS)

In 1982, Diana stars on stage in *Colette* (above), and marries Archie Stirling in real life (bottom). Courtesy Photofest and Classic TV Preservation Society (CTVPS).

Diana returns to *King Lear* on stage, this time as Regan, opposite Laurence Olivier's valedictory lead role in 1984 (top), plays the Evil Queen in *Snow White* in 1987 (bottom left), takes the winning lead in *Medea* by Euripides in Jonathan Kent's 1992 production at the Almeida Theatre, London transferring to Wyndham's Theatre in 1993 (bottom right). Courtesy Classic TV Preservation Society (CTVPS).

One of the Many Spies Who Loved Her (One Way or the Other): In 1994, Diana had a splendid time filming *A Good Man in Africa* with fellow former screen spy Sean Connery, who opted out of 1969's *On Her Majesty's Secret Service*, starring George Lazenby, with whom she married on-screen but got along with less famously off-screen. Connery, meanwhile, appeared in the big-screen adaptation of *The Avengers*, from which Diana felt compelled to distance herself. Though she had better "love" on the small screen in 1982 when she performed in PBS's *Mother Love* with yet another fellow former screen spy, David McCallum (from TV's *The Man from U.N.C.L.E.*, which also starred Robert Vaughn—Diana's costar from the 1970 film adaptation of *Julius Caesar*). Courtesy Classic TV Preservation Society (CTVPS).

From 1989 to 2003, Diana hosted the *Mystery!* TV anthology series. Courtesy Classic TV Preservation Society (CTVPS).

Diana had previously won a BAFTA Award in 1985 for her work in *Bleak House* (top left), a TV adaptation presented by *Masterpiece Theatre* (*Mystery's* mother series). Courtesy Classic TV Preservation Society (CTVPS).

Diana starred in two shows under the *Mystery!* umbrella: *Mother Love* (in October/November 1989, with David McCallum, top) and *The Mrs. Bradley Mysteries* (from 1998 to 1999, with Neil Dudgeon, bottom).

Diana delivers an Emmy-winning performance as Mrs. Danvers, in the 1997 PBS *Masterpiece* presentation of *Rebecca*, also starring Charles Dance and Emilia Fox. Courtesy Classic TV Preservation Society (CTVPS).

PART FOUR

FOREVER
AFTER

The elegance continues. Courtesy Classic
TV Preservation Society (CTVPS).

CHAPTER 13

THE QUEEN OF THRONES AND THORNES

I loved the idea of playing this naughty old bag,
offering her own explanation. It's my idea of heaven.
—DIANA RIGG

APPARENTLY, ONE RULE OF THUMB IN THE THEATER IS: THE MORE FUN YOU
have making it the less good it's going to be. "I think what they're talking
about is if you're wallowing in drama and enjoying it," Diana explained.
She recalled hearing a recording of Sarah Bernhardt, performing in *Phaedra*.
"It was very French, and very, sort of, *floriate*. All that was going on. She
was really enjoying it, and you just *knew* that the audience was probably
fast asleep."[1]

However, when doing comedy, that rule, Diana said, "doesn't apply."

Diana always enjoyed performing comedy. One project to which she
was drawn instantly was an episode of *Extras*, British comedian Ricky
Gervais's HBO series. Diana was impressed with the script, which she
described as "beautifully written, very concise." Her role, that of herself,
was one she could all but play in her sleep. Her costar in the episode, *Harry
Potter*'s Daniel Radcliffe, would be playing himself as well. The two actors,
separated by two generations, got on marvelously well together. Diana
added: "In fact, it took forever to film because we were laughing so much."[2]

According to David Naylor, Diana's cameo as herself on *Extras* was "an
absolute gem. 'Have you still got that catsuit from *The Avengers*?' . . . 'Go
away, Daniel.' Brilliant casting, and an unforgettable moment."

As Benjamin Hathaway of screenrant.com noted, "Rigg isn't in much of
her episode of *Extras*, but it's an appearance memorable if only for its shock
value and hilarious comedy. Playing herself, Rigg stars opposite Daniel
Radcliffe, who is also playing a variation of himself. . . . In the episode,

Radcliffe is portrayed as somewhat of a self-proclaimed lady's man with little fear. It's a surprising performance from the (at the time) fairly young *Harry Potter* star that culminates at the moment when he accidentally flicks a prophylactic onto Rigg's head."

A similar pattern of hilarity emerged when Diana appeared on television with her daughter, Rachael. The two were cast together in "The Crimson Horror," a 2013 episode of the long-running BBC television science-fiction series *Dr. Who*. Diana acknowledged that it was difficult for the two actresses to complete a scene without one or the other, or both, started laughing. "It's known as *corpsing* on stage," she said. "I don't quite know why . . . laughter died or something like that. But anyway, I'm a great corpse, and I can go off at the drop of anything. And so, with Rachie [Rachael], together, we do tend to corpse."[3]

As journalist Dalton Norman, observed on screenrant.com, "By 2013, Rigg was one of Great Britain's grand dames of the screen, and her appearance in *Doctor Who*'s season 7 was a big get for the series. Although the episode she appeared in was Doctor and companion-lite-story, it was appropriately grand for the 100th installment of the new *Doctor Who* series, and Rigg alone elevated it with her presence. Rigg also appeared alongside her daughter Rachael Stirling in the episode, and in an interview from *The Andrew Marr Show*, it was revealed that the parts were specifically crafted with them in mind. Plenty of established stars graced the *Doctor Who* universe over the years, but Rigg was one of the brightest."

According to Norman, "*Doctor Who*, season 7, episode 11, 'The Crimson Horror' saw the Doctor and Clara travel to the Victorian era as they teamed up with Madame Vastra to solve a grisly murder mystery. Rigg appeared as the evil Mrs. Gillyflower, who conspired to infect the world with poison (except for a select few people she considered worthy). It was a unique part for Rigg in that it was distinctly villainous compared to her usual parts. In Rigg's best movies and TV shows, she was often a hero, and 'The Crimson Horror' was even a direct role reversal of her iconic part, Emma Peel, in *The Avengers*.

"Although it was one episode," Norman continued, "Rigg was an excellent antagonist to the Eleventh Doctor and Clara, and her plan was super-villain-like (which was certainly a nod to the sorts of stories on *The Avengers*). While it ultimately had no bigger impact on the ongoing continuity of *Doctor Who*, "The Crimson Horror" was received positively by critics and Rigg was especially applauded for her turn as Mrs. Gillyflower. Even with a sillier premise, Rigg put her heart and soul into the part she stole nearly every scene she was in.

"In the same *Andrew Marr Show* interview, in which she revealed that the parts were written specifically for herself and her daughter, Rigg also expounded upon her time working on *Doctor Who*. Despite acting alongside one of the weirdest aliens in *New Doctor Who*, Mister Sweet, Rigg was highly entertaining and thoroughly enjoyed working on the show. Although she had already established herself as a legend, she wasn't above making a mark on the iconic sci-fi franchise. Considering Rigg's own important legacy in the history of British television, she came full circle when she played Mrs. Gillyflower in *Doctor Who*," Norman concluded.

Actor/writer Mark Gatiss deserves the credit (or blame, as the case may be) for casting the celebrated Dame Diana Rigg as Mrs. Gillyflower, a part he wrote especially for her, on *Doctor Who*. He later said how much he enjoyed seeing Rigg "flit effortlessly between serious drama and outrageous camp" over the years. Gatiss retained fond memories of their first encounter. "What first met you was the presence," he said. "Diana sailed into a room like a galleon, draped in a stylish shawl, the blond bob framing those famous cheekbones. We were performing together at the Old Vic in Samuel Adamson's version of *All About My Mother*, she as the actor Huma Rojo and I as her dresser, Agrado. It was a glorious, naughty time. She would eat a pork pie before every show and sit on the stairs, smoking furiously."[4]

Rigg and Gatiss occupied their own mutual admiration society. Diana was exceedingly fond of the actor/writer, whose credits included penning several episodes of the *Sherlock* series. Like Gatiss, she treasured their time together on stage at the Old Vic. He played a transsexual, and she played a lesbian, and the two got on well. Gatiss had also worked, and as Rigg said, "became friendly" with Rachael in *The Recruiting Officer*. It was then that he had the inspired idea of casting both Diana and Rachael on *Doctor Who*.

Diana may have been enjoying her immersion in the shallow end of the entertainment pool, but not everyone was impressed. In a conversation with the author, Ray Austin acknowledged that Rigg was a great actress, but that he was saddened when her career seemed to come full circle. As he explained, "She started off coming into *The Avengers*, and knowing what it's all about, television, and talking with Roger Moore, and not wanting [to do] television anymore and to go into the theater, and become the dame of theater, which she did, and now she's slipping [back] into television. *Dr. Who*? *Hello*? Where did *that* come from?"[5]

Austin did, however, approve of his colleague's participation in HBO's acclaimed series *Game of Thrones* (2011–2019). This, after all, was a dramatic series, and "she was a dramatic actress. She was of Royal Shakespearean blood. And that's where she wanted to go, and she got there."[6] It also introduced her to an entire new generation of fans, those who were too young to remember *The Avengers.*

Or as David Naylor put it, "Almost half a century after Emma Peel revolutionized TV, Diana was back portraying another confident character that radiated class, wit, beauty, and intelligence—Lady Olenna Tyrell on *Game of Thrones.*

"Her exceptionally savage lines ('Put the pen down, dear. We both know you're not writing anything,' 'I wonder if you're the worst person I've ever met?') were the stuff of legend, and made her a fan favorite for the four years she was on the show.

"As 'The Queen of Thorns' Diana was masterful at delivering shade aimed mainly at men, but saved her best for Cersei . . . 'Tell Cersei . . . I want her to know it was me.' Mic drop!

"It was great to see her back [on TV in a weekly capacity]," Naylor continued, "not only because older women are rarely afforded screen time, let alone characterized as clever badasses in the manner of Lady Tyrell . . . but also because once again, she stole every scene she was in and garnered four more Emmy nominations in the process.

"One of the best characters in the series," Naylor concluded, "Olenna wielded her power in a manner quite different to Cersei or Daenerys: soft power and strategic thinking—at its best. She was a smart badass with a sharp tongue who was one of the most dangerous women of Westeros. And she did it all without ever having to touch a sword!"

• • •

Before landing the role of Olenna Tyrell, Diana had never watched the series, nor had she read the books upon which it was based, so she was surprised at how popular the show became. So popular, in fact, that fans would beg Diana to provide them with so-called "spoilers," to see which direction the show would take next. The actress had a pat answer for that: "No, no, they, they make you sign a confidentiality agreement. And all that. We get something called sides every day when you go to the studio. And that scene that you're about to play in, and your name is stamped on it. You sign for it when they hand it over to you. And you have to hand it back at the end of the day, in case you sell it to somebody."[7]

Confidential agreement or not, Diana did not feel qualified to discuss the show's twists and turns in any detail. "I don't know enough about that sort of entertainment," she said. "I really don't."[8]

Perhaps not, but Diana understood her character. When she was asked how she could play such an evil person, she would usually answer by talking about the pleasure she took in exploring her dark side. "Playing a baddie is much more interesting than playing a goodie. I mean, they're *boring*. But a baddie has an infinite capacity for evil, and [therefore], drama. Yeah, so, I didn't prepare. It's all on the page. You know, you learn it and you know within the human condition, which we all have within us, all the recipes. And there is a degree of evil. I recognize it. I mean, *I* couldn't kill. But I recognize the motive *behind* killing. Jealousy, for example. If you felt that wiggly germ of evil [in real life], then you can expand on it, in any direction you want. That's why I find playing baddies so absolutely wonderful. And then I come out of it. And I'm a saint."[9]

That closing line never failed to elicit a laugh from her listeners.

Diana once compared her audition for Tyrell to that of Emma Peel. In each case, the producers at hand contacted her agent, and that was that. She had never seen an episode of *Avengers* or *Thrones* and was oblivious to their popularity. She considered each as just another job, for which she was sent a script and thought, *I can do this.*

But when it came to first playing Tyrell on *Thrones*, there was a slight challenge. One scene was especially long and wordy. Diana suspected that the show's young producers were testing an old actress to see if she was still capable of memorizing long speeches. To call their bluff, Diana was determined to do the scene in one take, which she did.

Otherwise, playing Olena was an effortless assignment due to the contributions of David Benioff and D. R. Weiss. These two writers "had my number," as Diana liked to say. In other words, they knew how to write for her *and* her character, providing her with "really lovely, meaty, meaty scenes."[10] One line that stands out comes when Olenna tells Daenerys Targaryen (Emilia Clarke), "I've known a great many clever men. I've outlived them all. You know why? I *ignored* them. The Lords of Westeros are sheep. Are *you* a sheep? No. *You're* a *dragon*."

Diana also enjoyed performing with Julian Glover and Charles Dance, both of whom she had worked with before. "On these sets you hook up with people you haven't seen for a thousand years, and it's lovely," she said. As for Dance, she said with a twinkle, "He's a wonderful old actor laddy, isn't he? It was great playing with him. And I'm very fond of him." Feeling the apparent need for clarification, she added: "Non-carnal."[11]

In addition to the old-timers on set were a host of young actors and actresses. Diana was once asked if she took on something of a mentor role with these less-experienced performers. Her answer? "Only if they ask." In a way, the grand dame of the theater pitied her young costars. As she explained, "An awful lot of those kids haven't done the training. And I grieve for that. Because they have reached a sort of status, and how, and where, are they going to go from there? Unless they've done some *training*."[12]

At times, Rigg did feel the show's producers could have been a little more lenient with her due to her age. It made her wonder what time Maggie Smith was called to the set for *Downton Abbey*. "It would be nice if they didn't wake me get up at five a.m. and work a twelve-hour day," she said, "and my caravan is never big enough to have a doze. I'm always knackered when I get home. I think they deliberately have lots of British actors in the cast because, like me, they're grateful and don't demand a sixty-foot Winnebago, their own chef, physiotherapist, secretary, and PA [production assistant]."[13]

Diana's most taxing task on *Thrones* involved the number of takes she was required to shoot. As she explained in one interview, "Because it is video, you are doing maybe twenty-six takes for a two-hander . . . which should only require six. They don't care. They've got so much money it doesn't matter. Depressing. I'm ready to run a hot bath and get the razor out after take three. Because I bore myself."[14]

Then in her late seventies, Diana never considered retiring, even if learning lines had become more of a hurdle. As she acknowledged to *Digital Spy* in 2015, "I get tetchy with myself when I forget. . . . I've heard Maggie Smith gets tetchy for the same reason."

Rigg had recalled "a wonderful story" about Smith, when a second assistant director had approached her on the set of *Downton Abbey* and asked, "Dame Maggie, can I get you anything?" To which Smith replied, "Yes—a death scene."

Death scenes, both real and replicated, are to be expected when actors approach their eighties. In December of 2017, Diana stopped smoking after the diagnosis two months before of a serious illness, a cardiac ablation, which led to heart surgery the following year. During the procedure, the actress's heart stopped beating. For how long? She didn't ask. But it was clear that time was running out.

Although she considered herself relatively religious, Diana did not experience any sort of spiritual or ethereal event while under the knife. But had there been the proverbial journey through the "tunnel of light" that has been documented by so many in recent years, Rigg may not have been aware of it, because her vision and understanding of God was unclear. "I'm sort of halfway to being a Buddhist as well," she told UK's the *Times*. "I'm a—what do they call it in parliament? A crossbencher. That's what I am in religion."[15]

• • •

A remarkable aspect to this late stage of Diana's career is that, even after being reestablished in a major series, she still accepted other, less popular vehicles. In 2015, for instance, she served as narrator for *The Honourable Rebel*. As Peter Bradshaw of *The Guardian* noted, "Hammy acting and direction hinder this docu-drama about the Hon Elizabeth Montagu—film industry fixer, loyal sister and spy. . . . Diana Rigg narrates from Montagu's own memoirs, and there are sporadic on-camera interviews with friends and family, and black-and-white portraits of the real-life principals flashed up on screen. But then there is the laborious drama, with its sometimes-toe-curling dialogue."

Also in 2015, Diana appeared in the TV movie *Professor Branestawn Returns*, which was followed in 2016 by the miniseries *You, Me and the Apocalypse*. The latter is a dystopian dramedy that charts humanity's final days as a comet soars toward earth. Diana's character was that of the demented yet elegant millionairess Dorothea Sutton, whom the actress described as "the mum from hell . . . wonderful . . . indomitable . . . utterly selfish. Nothing would stop her." Dorothea's favorite line was, "Gerbils eat their babies," a trait she obviously admired. The role provided Diana with yet another bizarre creature to add to her credits. And why not? As she said, "I *am* bizarre, aren't I?" Though she clearly enjoyed playing such over-the-top characters, she also embraced Dorothea's more refined side. "I didn't know whether I had to be glamorous," Diana explained, "but they decided to make me glamorous. That's wonderful because I so rarely get the chance! I'm an old bag for the most part on *Game of Thrones*, so it's lovely to be glamorous . . . as glamorous as you can be at my age."[16]

Perhaps it was the humorous premise of the 2017 TV movie *A Christmas Carol Goes Wrong* that encouraged her to accept her off-screen role as Aunt Diana, the narrator. The Cornley Polytechnic Drama Society has been blacklisted by the BBC after ruining their teleplay of Sir J. M. Barrie's *Peter Pan*. Refusing to take their ban lying down, the infamous group forces its way back on the telly by hijacking the jewel of the Christmas schedule, a live production of *A Christmas Carol*, staged by a professional acting troupe, headed by Derek Jacobi as Scrooge.

That same year, Rigg surfaced in the second season of ITV's *Victoria* series. The sophomore session of that Daisy Goodwin–produced show featured Jenna Coleman as Victoria and Tom Hughes as Prince Albert. ITV had aspired to make good on the first year's triumph when the show bested BBC One's *Poldark* in the Sunday-night drama ratings.

Set in the 1840s, *Victoria* features Sir Robert Peel on Downing Street and Victoria coping with the competing demands of being a mother and a queen. Diana plays the Duchess of Buccleuch, the queen's advisor and mistress of the robes, accented with what would become a brazen trademark of Diana's dialogue:

"You're not the only one who's felt in low spirits after the birth of a child," the duchess tells the young queen.

"But I am not a woman," Victoria responds. "I am a queen."

According to Benjamin Hathaway, and his observations on screenrant. com, "Rigg's character, the Duchess of Buccleuch, is somewhat of a mild antagonist to the titular character in the series' second season. While the Duchess was a mild-mannered woman in her 30s in real life, the series thankfully took some creative liberties and brought on Rigg as an altered version of the real-life figure."

Whereas Diana told Valentine Low of *The Times*, the show and its producer had granted her the opportunity to portray "a really terrific character that personifies all the prejudices and the snobbisms of the Victorian era. Complete un-PC. She saw *Othello* and it shocked her sensibilities and she didn't think Shakespeare should be performed in polite society. Hates the French, all the food is covered in sauce, and you don't know what's underneath. Not very keen on the Germans. They're boring. And the Irish are feckless. She's fun to play. I don't go along with what she represents, but she is fun. She has got some great one-liners."[17]

In episode two of the second season of *Victoria*, Rigg's duchess makes a grander-than-usual entrance. Accompanied by her niece, Wilhelmina Coke, the new mistress of the robes is introduced to Queen Victoria and Prince Albert. As journalist Bill Young of tellyspotting.com put it, "In one priceless scene-stealing moment," the duchess "waltzes into the room and greets them with a rather flamboyant curtsy."[18]

But as Valentine Low pointed out, the leading role in Victoria had little do to with the real Duchess of Buccleuch. That would be Charlotte Ann Montagu Douglas Scott, Duchess of Buccleuch and Queensberry, who served as mistress of the robes from 1841 to 1846. Victoria was said to have described her as "an agreeable, sensible clever little person," one who was later deemed a godmother to the duchess's daughter. The real duchess, at twenty-six, remained close friends with Victoria, and was only eight years older than the queen when Victoria ascended to the throne. Diana, meanwhile, was *forty-eight years* older than the thirty-one-year-old Coleman.

"Well, they have made a change there, haven't they?" she mused, adding, "I hate people being coy about my age. I'm not coy about *my* age."

Rigg did not observe any other similarities between she and the character. "Absolutely not. I'm not little, for a kick-off. I'm considerably taller than Victoria." But she did consider herself "sensible. I'm down to earth and practical."

The *Times* interview took place in Rigg's trailer near Ripon Cathedral, one of *Victoria*'s locations, and the actress was disturbed by lorry noises. As Low noted, "with all the imperious *hauteur* available to a dame of the British Empire," she barreled, "Excuse me! How long is this going on for?"

"There may be lorry drivers out there who would stand up to an actress trying to boss them around," Low said, "but not many, and they weren't working that day. The driver quickly found someone else to annoy."

Low suggested this was just the sort of power that arose from being a dame. Rigg laughed and replied, "Absolutely nothing to do with damehood. It's simply to do with my manner, which is, 'Don't brook any argument. Very good for the duchess!'"

Another dose of Rigg's dame-denial demeanor was evident when a public relations representative interrupted Low's interview with Rigg and decided it was over. But Dame Diana was having none of it. "Excuse me, why?" she asked. "If the gentleman is finished, *then* we are finished."

Low was not finished and preferred more time. "To be honest," he thought, "I am getting the impression that, if ever there are differences of opinion on set, I would definitely prefer to be on Rigg's side."[19]

On set, behind the scenes, on camera or in live theater, Rigg left an impression.

• • •

Diana was seen briefly in the feature film, *Breathe* (2017), directed by Andy Serkis, and starring Andrew Garfield, Claire Foy, and Tom Hollander. According to Brian Tallerico, editor of rogerebert.com: "This is a deeply sentimental version of a story that demanded more honesty and depth. And the final act feels purposefully manipulative, trying to pull the heartstrings in a way that the true story merits but the film hasn't really earned. The characters here are too flat and one can't shake the feeling that it's betraying the truth of their story to tell it with such a gauzy, TV movie sheen on top of it."[20]

As *Game of Thrones* took its final season bow in 2019, Rigg reflected on her tenure as Olena Tyrell, the thrice-Emmy-nominated role she had played on the series since 2013, two years after the show debuted. After finally winning the Emmy (among other accolades) for her work on the series, Diana accepted a special award at the Cannes series TV festival in France. At the podium, she described Olena's moment of demise, which involved drinking poison. She called it "just wonderful," and later told UK's

The Telegraph that Tyrell died "with dignity and wit, and wit is not often in final death scenes."

Her involvement in this popular series did something for Diana Rigg that few successful performers ever experience: she equaled, and some would even say surpassed, the cult status she had attained with her early star-making appearance, as Emma Peel on *The Avengers*.

• • •

In 2019, the actress held a press conference in London to promote her one-woman show, *An Evening with Dame Diana Rigg*. In this production, she promised to cover her decades of performing, which had begun exactly sixty years earlier. It was a life that allowed her, for one, the luxury of own-ing a chateau in the south of France. She referred to it as a manor house with one tower, whereas "really self-respecting chateaux have two." Rigg purchased the property from a British "gruesome threesome. Very grue-some." Allegedly, the locals referred to it as Chateau James en Air, which translated, means "legs in the air." She thought of having a little shield or a plaque with her "coat of arms being some legs apart, with fetching red stilettos on the end. Don't you think?"[21]

• • •

After remaining single for over two decades, Diana was done with men. She was content, minus the pangs, sorrows, and joys romance tends to bring. Much to her chagrin, however, she was still being propositioned, once in a great while perhaps, and likely by some aging Baby Boomer who still imagined this elderly woman as the catsuit-wearing Emma Peel. But Diana wasn't buying it. As she told a reporter for the *Daily Mail*, "I didn't know what to do with it. I mean *them*. I mean *him*."[22]

Diana was simply having too much fun to worry about such things.

"I would advise anybody coming up, to constantly, constantly chal-lenge yourself. I mean, I think it's the same in any profession. You can't just *not* want to know. I mean, for example, I have a life, a wonderful life outside the theater. I read prodigiously. For ten years I was chancellor of Stirling University. I was chancellor of the university. I've been on count-less boards. I travel the wide world [and do not necessarily receive four-star treatment]. I have been to countries like the Galapagos and Bhutan, because it's there. And I long to see, and, and learn and absorb. I was, not long ago, in Burma."[23]

For her eightieth birthday, on July 20, 2018, Diana hosted a massive, music-scored, dance-filled *soiree* at a bookstore in Lower Manhattan. There, her nearest and dearest gathered, including her daughter Rachael, her son-in-law Guy Garvey, and as she recalled, even "my ex . . . the one I talk about," meaning Rachael's father, Archie. A disc jockey spun records at the party at which, according to what Rachael later told *The Guardian*, her mother "boogied 'til dawn with all the hot young dancers." Also, that night, a new cocktail, "Dame Diana's Dynamite," was apparently invented.

Apparently, even at eighty, there was still some life in the old dame yet.

CHAPTER 14

FINAL BOWS

All these old images of me floating across the screen; the
terrible charms of what you were and what you are. I know
who I am, but these people who see as I was then, don't.

—DIANA RIGG

DIANA PERIODICALLY RECONFIRMED THAT SHE "NEVER RELIED ON MY
beauty for anything," much less her career, which was more than evi-
dently based on her enormous talent. But when her looks went, "it was
inevitable," she said. "You have to be philosophical about it. I don't mind
getting old except for the pain. I have two new knees. So, going downstairs
is not perfect. Nobody tells you about the pain."[1]

Though constricted in physical movement, she also felt somewhat confined in aesthetic measurement to her contemporaries. "I have no way of
comparing myself to other people my age. I can't compare myself with
Jane Fonda, can I? I haven't had the work done. I admire the discipline of
someone who maintains that degree of beauty, but I'm not prepared to
do it. I just want to put my arms around them and give them a cuddle and
say, 'Just forget it. Don't put yourself through it. There is life after being at
the pinnacle of your beauty.'"[2]

As recorded by IMDb, Diana once revealed, "I had an eye job in my
early forties. Someone took a photograph of me in a play, after I'd lost a
lot of weight, and I did look like Miss Havisham. I thought, 'I have to do
something—I'm too young to look like this.' So, I went and had an eyelift
once the play was finished, and the doctor said that it would last only
about eight years. I imagined after that it would all cave in with a terrible
groaning sound, like scaffolding, but it didn't, and I haven't had anything
done since. I look at women who are my age who look absolutely ravishing
and I know they have had something done.

"Well, why not?" she suggested. "If I meet a woman who is immaculately groomed, I really admire her discipline. I grew up admiring out-of-this-world screen goddesses, such as Ava Gardner and Rita Hayworth, but I have to acknowledge that I haven't the patience for getting dressed up very often—at my age, you think: 'Why bother?' Now that I'm older, I don't go to premieres or first-night parties, not even my own.

"The older you get," Rigg continued, "I have to say, the funnier you find life. That's the only way to go. If you get serious about yourself as you get old, you are pathetic."

During a 2014 interview in London with Stuart Jeffries of *The Guardian*, Diana attempted to cross Fulham Road. As he helped her along the path, Jeffries noticed her frail but vibrant appearance. "Elegant from two-tone shoes to circular, tinted glasses, she is thwarted by the traffic," he recalled.

"It's my damned tin knees," she told him as they linked arms and walked across the street. Diana had just an operation on one of her knees, which Jeffries assumed she might have damaged with lengthy tap-dancing routines in the 1987 West End production of Sondheim's *Follies*.

But such was not the case.

"It's genetic," Rigg told him, like her brother, then eighty, who struggled with the same issue.

However, she acknowledged, "The older you get I have to say, the funnier you find life. That's the only way to go. If you get serious about yourself as you get old, you are pathetic."

She and Jeffries soon settled in the garden of a French café. As he further observed, Rigg would have sought out the garden to indulge her twenty-a-day habit, but she had given up smoking a few years before, so she now makes use of the garden, as Jeffries put it, to "catch the early spring rays and feed crumbs to the birds."

"I found myself talking aloud to the pigeons in the park the other day," she told him. "The male pigeons were busily pursuing the female pigeons. I said: 'You silly farts. Can't you see they're not interested?' And then I realized there were people listening to me."

Diana then compared it all the senior community of human beings. "I think women of my age are still attractive. Men of my age aren't. . . . They've got their *cojones* halfway to their knees. They have the same descent as tits."

This lively conversation was taking place because Diana would soon be seen in the fourth season of *Game of Thrones*, reprising her performance as what Jeffries termed "the irascible, be-wimpled" Lady Olenna Tyrell, for which she had by then received her sixth Emmy nomination.

In Rigg's "The Crimson, Horror" episode of *Doctor Who*, her Winifred Gillyflower character had blinded her daughter (Rachael Stirling) and was sent to destroy all life on Earth using prehistoric venom from a red reptile secreted in her bosom. "Now Mr. Sweet," she said before attempting to unleash Armageddon on Victorian Bradford, "let the whole world taste your lethal kiss!"

Both Gillyflower and Olenna "supported the idea that Rigg is austere, abrasive, tough as old boots," Jeffries noted.

But Diana rejected that assessment. "They always write about me that way ever since I made a bit of a ruckus about getting paid less than the cameraman on *The Avengers*," she told Jeffries. "I'm portrayed as this tough broad, but I'm not.

"I don't know how your *Guardian* readers are going to take this," she continued, "but I've had a housekeeper for twenty-four years. So, I'm well looked after. I'm a deeply spoiled woman. I make no apologies about it at all. I think they think: 'Oh, poor woman, she's living on her own.' Not a bit of it. My bed is turned down every night."

With regard to her personal life, she was open to the possibility of remarriage in her senior years. As to her professional life, she decided, "I don't want to retire. I never want to retire. What's the point of it?"

In her interview with Rosanna Greenstreet of *The Guardian*, Rigg admitted how unfond she was of her "sagging chin line." But she would have rather been "clever and ugly" than otherwise. "If you're clever you can always make people think you're attractive."

As such, while she may have never deemed herself undemanding amid her colleagues, Dame Diana remained in demand, certainly when it came to her acting skills. Her physical body may have been faltering, and her face may not have been cosmetically altered to showcase a fabricated fountain of youth. But she could not possibly have cared less, nor did anyone else, including her peers and fans. Her creative body of work, the only aspect of her career and life that mattered, continued to expand in remarkable and all-encompassing ways.

• • •

All Creatures Great and Small was the first in a wonderful series of nonfiction books by James Herriot. According to what journalist Bridie Pearson-Jones documented on mailonline.com, Herriot's collected works have sold 60 million copies internationally and have never been out of print.

Herriot, whose real name was James Alfred Wright had been a veterinarian in the bucolic Yorkshire Dales beginning in 1937, working in a veterinary clinic owned and operated by the slightly eccentric Siegfried Farnon and his roguish younger brother, Tristan. James, a serious but pleasant young married man, works closely with an array of colorful locals and their animals, developing many close relationships along the way. A well-received British television series, based on the Herriot books and consisting of ninety episodes, aired originally from 1978 and 1990. Thirty years later, a new version of the show, produced by Playground Entertainment and shot on location in Yorkshire, made its broadcast premiere on the UK's Channel 5 in September 2020; its American debut followed in January 2021, on PBS.

As Pearson-Jones chronicled, *All Creatures Great and Small* premiered in the UK with an audience of 3.3 million viewers, making it the most viewed show to air on Channel 5 in five years. "The reboot of the 1980s hit," Pearson-Jones continued to note, arrived "amid a huge surge in popularity of shows about rural life, with *Our Yorkshire Farm*, following the real-life dramas of a shepherdess and her nine children, emerging as the surprise hit of the summer. Its most famous adaptation originally ran on the BBC from 1978 to 1990 with Christopher Timothy as the Dales vet and Robert Hardy as his boss, Siegfried Farnon."

The show screened after *The Yorkshire Vet*, a reality show about the Skeldale Veterinary Centre in Thirsk, North Yorkshire (the former the practice of James Alfred Wight). Meanwhile, *The Yorkshire Vet* is narrated by Christopher Timothy, who played Herriot in the original series of *All Creatures Great and Small* that aired three decades before.

In the first season of *Creatures*, Diana had the scene-stealing recurring role in the show as Mrs. Pumphrey, a fussy old lady who lovingly dotes over her beloved Pekinese, Tricky-Woo.

Actor Nicholas Ralph, who played James Herriot in *Creatures*, described Diana as "brilliant" in the role. "Any anxiety you may have had before meeting her was completely washed away as soon as you did, because she was so lovely and easy to chat to. She had a twinkle in her eye, still had a wicked sense of humor, and she kept everyone on their toes."

As Ralph observed, "What I took away from working with her—and it's something that, certainly with the more experienced actors, I was always aware of—was her approach to [the] text, and then her approach to every take. So, paying attention to each take, when some things are slightly different and some things remain the same as the shots come in, from light to close, how does the performance change? A lot of things like that. Also, if you want to have a dramatic pause, it *has* to be earned. So, if there was ever any gap in any scene where it wasn't warranted, Dame Diana would be like [*snaps his fingers*], 'Come on, are we going? Let's go.'

"For this one scene, it was actually just me and Cal [Woodhouse], and we were entering this massive estate, this big country house. So, it was a long walk for us from the hall to where Dame Diana was sitting; it took a little while. And so, we heard, 'Can we not have the boys walk from a bit closer? And if you can you bring the camera [closer]? My soul is on the floor.' That's what she said. It was just brilliant. She was, at that point in her career, so experienced, she knew it inside and out, she knew what she was doing, so yeah: she knew that they didn't need this long walk, and it could've been shortened, so that her soul didn't have to be on the floor. Yeah, that was really funny. I just loved that."[3]

Callum Woodhouse (Tristan) had this to say about Diana: "It was a real honor and a privilege to have gotten to work with her. It was one of her final jobs, and she did such amazing work on it. She makes her first appearance in episode two, but it's not until episode four that you really get to see her shine. It was amazing getting to share the screen with her, a real honor. It was amazing, because she'd come from such a different time, and just through the way that she spoke on set, you could see how she'd grown up. On set, we'd finish a scene, and then she'd just turn around and shout, 'Cut! Print!' Like when it all used to be on film reels. She just wanted to do the one take, and if it was fine, she'd be like, 'Well, we don't need to go again, do we?' And most of the time, she got her own way. And it was great, because we always got an early finish, so we were in the pub by seven!"[4]

Samuel West (Siegfried) smilingly recalled: "Obviously, we know Diana as Emma Peel, and we know her as a film and television star for many, many years, and I also was lucky enough to see her on stage a number of times, particularly as Medea. But she was first working at the Royal Shakespeare Company in the 1950s. So, it was something very touching for me (whose parents are both actors with similarly long careers, about the same generation, and were very fond of Diana and worked with her many times) to watch Nick [Ralph], who cut his teeth in the theater, but whose first job this was, as it were, sharing the baton with somebody whose classical career went back to Viola in the 1950s, with the new Royal Shakespeare Company. I just felt that that was a sharing of the profession—a sort of a continuation of the profession, which I know Nick would understand and respect, because he's a theater boy, as well. That's something that not many people talked about: that she was a great stage actress. It was really nice just to see. That's one for Nick, to tell his grandchildren or great-grandchildren, that he worked with somebody who started their career, I don't know, forty years before he was born."[5]

West also shared some personal observations about Diana on the *All Creatures* set: "She made a beeline for the most attractive men on set, which doesn't include me! She took a shine to Paresh, our runner, almost immediately, and he had to follow her around all day. She's also quite easily bored—which I always admire in an actor—such that she would sometimes walk away from a set, from a scene. Sometimes in the dance scene where I was arm-and-arm with her, she walked, and as soon as she got out of shot, she would say, 'Well, I think that was rather good, don't you?' I'd say, 'Um, I think we're still rolling, Diana.' We had to keep it down a bit.

"I also think it's an extremely good performance. It's hard, doing any guest-starring role, because you haven't got long to make an impression. And these are all parts that people talk about, 'Who's playing Mrs. Pumphrey?' 'Who's playing Tricky?' Or, when you say you're playing Siegfried Farnon, people go, 'Oh, don't [mess] it up,' or, 'You won't be as good as Robert Hardy [the late British actor who had played Siegfried in the earlier series],' or, 'Oh good, that's a really good idea.' But there is immediate name recognition, so that's really hard. Also, you're working with a dog! Nobody wants to work with a Pekingese, particularly one who is such a—I was going to say, 'scene stealer,' but 'scene grand larcenist' would be closer to the mark—as Derek, who just has to sort of waddle along, and nobody's watching anything else. You might as well give up!"[6]

CHAPTER 15

ENCORE

I want to stay alive . . . forever. My ambition? Don't croak.

—DIANA RIGG

DIANA WAS SEEMINGLY NEVER WITHOUT SOME SORT OF PROJECT. ONE unrealized project was a history she was to write of American theater and its criticism. But there were many others, both big and small.

In 2019, for instance, she lent her prodigious narration skills to *The Snail and the Whale*, a twenty-five-minute animated short film, directed by Max Lang and Daniel Snaddon, and based on Julia Donaldson's acclaimed children's book. In the story, a little snail (voiced by Sally Hawkins) dreams of adventure and seeing the world. One day, she meets a friendly humpback whale (voiced by Rob Brydon), who agrees to take his tiny new friend on a journey around the globe. However, when the whale becomes beached, it's up to the snail to save him. The message of the story is that, no matter how small one may be, individual can always make a difference.

In 2020, Rigg delivered what would be her final TV appearance as Mother Dorothea in an adaptation of *Black Narcissus*. Based on the 1939 novel by Rumer Godden (previously adapted as an acclaimed British film in 1947), the story tells of a group of young nuns who attempt to establish a mission at a remote cliff-top palace in the Himalayas, once known as the House of Women. But its haunting mysteries awaken forbidden desires that seem destined to repeat a tragedy.

Diana's final feature film—although she didn't realize that at the time— was *Last Night in Soho*, which was released in 2021. Helmed by the New Zealand–born Edgar Wright from a screenplay he penned with Krysty Wilson-Cairns, *Soho* is a horror-thriller set in the mid-1960s in London. Diana plays a kindly landlady who rents a room to Eloise (Thomasin McKenzie), who has come to London from rural Cornwall to study fashion. There is a downside to that room, however: it may be haunted by a previous occupant, Sandie (Anya Taylor-Joy), a singer who, in 1965, aimed to become the next Cilla Black, the performer who ran with the Beatles and recorded a string of chart-topping hits. Something is transporting Eloise back to Swinging London, where she is at first enthralled to see the bright lights of the big city through Sandie's eyes and then horrified to witness Sandie's ruin at the hands of her manipulative lover, Jack (Matt Smith).

Following its premiere in Venice, reviews of *Last Night in Soho* were mixed. In *Variety*, Guy Lodge found it to be "a surprising misfire, all the more disappointing for being made with such palpable care and conviction. Wright's particular affections for B-movies, British Invasion pop and a fast-fading pocket of urban London may be written all over the film, but they aren't compellingly written into it, ultimately swamping the thin supernatural sleuth story at its heart."[1]

Others were far more receptive to the director's efforts. Mark Hanson, of *Slant*, wrote, "In everything from its use of color, POV shots, and images that play with perspective and reality, *Last Night in Soho* draws much inspiration from the giallo's constellation of tropes to conjure a suspenseful fever dream."[2] *Little White Lies'* David Jenkins notes that Wright "flexes his considerable technical muscles by having Eloise and Sandie constantly switching between the foreground and a background mirror image. These subtle special effects are pulled off with amazing precision, and you really have to pay attention to who's center frame and how that plays into its complex, identity-toying storyline."

Another of the film's champions was *The Telegraph's* Robbie Collin, who called it "a riotous, rascally hybrid of a thing: part glittering love-letter to the disreputable nightlife district in which it takes place, part darting psychological thriller that rips up the letter as soon as it's written before tearfully torching the scraps. For a sense of its tone, imagine one of those playful-yet-cautionary postwar British dramas about innocent young women making their way in the big city—most of them seemed to star Rita Tushingham, who has a talismanic supporting role here as Eloise's grandmother—then refract it through the lurid crack-up horror lens of *Suspiria* or *Repulsion*."[3] Meanwhile, Mark Olson suggested that pop-culture enthusiasts seek it out, for its "dazzling re-creation of mid-'60s London. And while Edgar Wright's film is led by rising stars Thomasin McKenzie and Anya Taylor-Joy, it's the pivotal supporting turns from Terence Stamp, Rita Tushingham and Dame Diana Rigg . . . that draw more direct connections in the era." The *Hollywood Reporter's* David Rooney found *Last Night in Soho* to be "immensely pleasurable," singling out Steven Prince, whose score "gradually builds from ominous suspense into all-out Grand Guignol horror." Wright and editor Paul Machliss, adds Rooney, "zig and zag with dexterous vitality between the two eras."[4]

Like virtually all movies released between 2020 and 2022, *Soho*'s box-office take was adversely impacted by the COVID-19 pandemic. Despite that, Wright said that his life had been "forever enriched by having had the chance to work with Terence, Rita and Diana." Especially Diana, it seems. Working with her was, he said, "beyond a thrill." He added, "Honestly . . . the crush I had on her as a little kid never really went away."

• • •

Diana yearned to see more of the world while there was still time. "I've never seen myself as just an actor," she said, once enthusing about a trip to Bhutan: "It's got weed by the roadside. You can dry it, take it home, and smoke it. If I had my way, I'd spend the rest of my life doing that!"[5]

But tobacco, not marijuana, had been Diana's favorite vice since she was thirteen. Ray Austin recalls that during the filming of *The Avengers*, she "smoked all the time." He felt it was his duty as a friend to a least try to dissuade her from lighting up even one more cigarette. Austin had been profoundly affected by a hospital visit with a former stuntman who died a painful death from cancer; this moved Austin to throw away his stash and lighter, becoming a nonsmoker from that day forward. Patrick Macnee, who had managed to kick the habit as well, was also concerned about the potential risks to his costar's health and well-being. Ray and Patrick broached the topic with Diana on the set. Ray mentioned to her that he had recently been on the set of a British-made horror movie starring Bette Davis. "Davis smokes all the time," he told Diana. "*All the time.*" Diana, clearly unmoved, said simply, "Well, that's her right." She then stated rebelliously that she, too, could smoke if she wanted to, end of subject. Austin shrugged. "You just couldn't go there."[6]

When Rigg discovered her cancer was malignant, her daughter Rachael Stirling, in a chronicle for *The Guardian*, said that all the theaters were already dark.

According to Stirling, Rigg said, "Normally, when one gets bad news like this, one becomes the focus of attention, but in a pandemic, no one gives a fuck."

"Mum was ill, so of course there was an apocalypse," noted Stirling, who became her mother's caregiver in every capacity. Diana was so weakened that she refused to spend Easter with her family. "All over the country people are choosing not to visit their families," she said. "I want to honor their sacrifice."

Then, on Easter Sunday, Rigg fell and fractured her spine. "For the first time she complained of pain," Stirling said. "Knowing Ma's pain threshold this would be the equivalent of gratuitous medieval torture to you and me because she simply never complained about pain."

"Apart from anything else, darling," Rigg told her daughter, "it's just so boring."

Subsequently, a drive to the hospital with Stirling led to a devastating diagnosis: a fractured lumbar, and the spread of the cancer. Stirling paid close attention to her mother's face as the surgeon detailed the medical alternatives available at this tragic stage. "I knew she had no intention of enduring any more than she already had," Stirling said. "She told the doctor what I already knew."

The physician had the surname of a famed chutney, which inspired Rigg referred to him as "Lunch! Listen! Forgeddit! I've had enough!" Rigg agreed to cyberknife surgery, which was specific radiotherapy to the brain. According to Stirling, Rigg wanted to die "with all my grey matter intact, thank you!" That she did. Prior to the surgery, she promised the doctor she would deliver a post-surgery speech from *The Taming of the Shrew*. "And if I get a word wrong," she said, "I'll know you fucked it up!"

Later that week, Stirling arranged for an ambulance to bring Rigg to return home and die, surrounded by her family. "She had to be persuaded," Stirling said. "Not about the dying bit, she was resigned to that."

"Oh, but I've had such a life, Rachie!" Diana told her only child, who said, "She didn't like the loss of independence, hated the thought of being a burden, and flatly refused to use the doorbell that Guy had taped to her bedside table in case she needed helped. She also refused morphine as it dulled her brain."

"I had thirty alarms on my telephone for all the medications," Stirling said. "She called me Nurse Ratched," in reference to the character played by Louise Fletcher in the 1975 feature film, *One Flew Over the Cuckoo's Nest*.

"Dignity," that was "the most important thing . . . to preserve," Stirling said. To make certain Rigg was not in pain, and that she felt "comfortable, safe, and loved."

"We had Campari's [an Italian alcoholic liqueur] at four o'clock in the afternoon, every afternoon, right up until the day she died. I organized visitors when allowed; half an hour was about enough before she'd give the signal to usher them out. We laughed all the time at the darkest of things, of course. Death laughs are the best because nothing is off limits. I have a diary of her last six months that would make your eyeballs weep with laughter and wince with pain all at once. Though I can't bear to look at it."

Stirling said Rigg wanted to "fix things before she left, one of which was my beloved's health. One day, when I had accidentally given her double steroids, she fondly patted my husband's belly and said to him, 'Guy! Tell me the truth! When was the last time you saw your willy?'" To which Guy replied, "For reasons it wouldn't be appropriate to share with my mother-in-law, I have no problem seeing my willy."

"They howled at that," Stirling said. "Mama and Guy fell in love. He could finish off the last line of an obscure sea shanty she remembered, and they would sing old jazz numbers and recite poetry together. That was a glorious thing."

At one point, Diana asked, "Rachie, has anyone ever written a script about a mother who goes to live with her daughter, but then the son-in-law falls in love with her because she's much better in bed?"

"No, Ma," Stirling replied. "I don't think they have. After all, said daughter would probably medicate aforementioned mother so she never got out of said bed, again."

Stirling recalled her "Mother Ship" as the "least complaining, most courageous woman" she had ever known or "will ever know."

"She had not a trace of self-pity," Stirling said, nor would she put up with any bunk.

That included the thoughtless physician who attended Rigg in her final days. When Diana wondered how long she had left to live, the doctor began his reply with, "If I had a pound for every time . . ." But Rigg swiftly cut him off at the pass. "How fucking *dare* you patronize me or any dying person with that meeeaaaningless platitude," she screamed. "Get *out*!"

"Mama was a truth-teller," Stirling said. "She loathed lies and liars more than anything on Earth. Being caught telling an untruth by my mother was one of life's great humiliations. She would shame you to the core. Just like her secret daytime TV heroine, Judge Judy.

"She was also very naughty," Stirling continued. "I can't remember which poor actor it was that had to take her hand at the end of a play, after she'd copped it in the plot, and deliver a grief-stricken speech to the Corpse of Mother, but she had a warm wet frankfurter in her palm waiting for him."

Stirling admitted that she "didn't always get on" with her mother. "There was enormous love, but it was a painful relationship for both of us at times." When Stirling and her husband invited Rigg to live with them, according to Rachael, they had "no idea how hard it would be or how traumatic. Yet, it was the greatest privilege to help her to die as comfortably as I could, and she returned that kindness with a stoicism that shielded me from her darkest moments. We showed each other love without end, in the end. One day she said, 'Rachie, it's almost as if we are the same person.' And it was."

Rachael Stirling, Rigg's actress-daughter with theatrical producer Archibald Stirling, added, "She spent her last months, joyfully reflecting on her extraordinary life full of love, laughter and a deep pride in her profession."[7]

According to the *Daily Mail*, and what journalist Charlie Smith documented on the British website, express.co.uk, Rachael inherited a sizable amount of her mother's estate, valued at £3,368,886. This, after a "traumatic" time living with her mother before Diana died. As Smith continued to report, Rachael was one of the guests on the UK's Channel 4 weekly TV show, *Sunday Brunch* (hosted by Tim Lovejoy and Simon Rimmer). The London-born actress, married to Elbow frontman Guy Garvey, was set to appear in *Scandaltown*, at the Lyric Hammersmith Theatre April of 2022.

A portion of Diana's fortune was said to include properties in France and the United States. In her will, Diana was also said to have left a £5,000 gift to a beautician called Jessica from her local nail salon. She also donated approximately £280,500 to family and charities, including £50,000 for both Great Ormond Street Hospital and St. Christopher's Hospice.

"Following the huge outpouring of grief for Dame Diana in the wake of her death," Smith noted, "Rachael penned her own heartfelt tribute to her mother in a detailed article in October last year."

In a piece for *The Observer*, Rachael, who became her mother's caregiver, discussed Diana's remarkable life and their "traumatic" time living together after her cancer diagnosis.

In her essay, edited by screenwriter and director Edgar Wright, Rachael wrote how her mother "returned that kindness with a stoicism that shielded me from her darkest moments. We showed each other a love without end, in the end."

As Smith documented, "Rachael described how she cared for her mother, doing her cooking, shopping, handling her medication and taking her to and from radiotherapy and chemotherapy. She recalled how her mother was hospitalized with a fractured lumbar, when she was told by a surgeon that the cancer had spread through her body."

"After her hospital stay," Smith added, "Dame Diana was initially reluctant to move in with her daughter."

On September 10, 2020, Diana passed away at age eighty-two, peacefully at her home, surrounded by Rachael, and other family members.

Once the sad announcement hit the airwaves, there was an enormous outpouring of affection by those who had been fortunate to work with and know this great lady of the theater.

Said Edgar Wright, who had only recently directed Diana in *Last Night in Soho*: "Diana was forever Mrs. Emma Peel. But the image of the astonishingly lithe, cat-suited Avenger, gun in hand, comma of fringe over the eye, could never overshadow what a terrific actor she was . . . though Diana always resolutely referred to herself as an actress." Wright added that "the story of the film and the entire production has become both inextricably linked and achingly poignant to me . . . not least because Diana is no longer with us. I was working with her, and indeed laughing with her, right up a week or two before she passed away. She was a true delight to work with. . . . I feel somehow equally proud of the fact that she invited me to brunch with her after the shoot so we could talk about anything and everything."

In a fitting tribute, Wright dedicated the film to Diana's memory.

Thomasine McKenzie, who shared a pivotal scene in *Last Night in Soho* with Diana, was overwhelmed by losing her so soon after filming. "It's kind of hard to express," she said. "I feel very lucky to have been able to work with her. It is a beautiful role for her career to end on because she gave such a powerful performance. And I think everyone on set was very aware of how amazing she was and how lucky we all were to be working with Dame Diana." McKenzie was particularly impressed with the actress's professionalism. "She just arrived, and she got it done," she said. "I really admired her a lot. She was so strong and so into it and such a beautiful grand presence."

Susanne Simpson, executive producer of *Masterpiece*, released this heartfelt memorial: "The *Masterpiece* team was saddened today by the news of Dame Diana Rigg's death. She was an integral member of the *Masterpiece* team, serving for fifteen years as the host of *Mystery!*, where her elegant introductions made an indelible impression on US audiences. She won an Emmy for her performance in *Rebecca*, dazzled audiences in *Mother Love*, *Bleak House* and in her recent star turn in *Victoria*. In January, audiences will see her in *All Creatures Great and Small* in the role of the eccentric Mrs. Pumphrey. The British Grand Dame of Drama. Diana was one of a kind and we will miss her."

Paul Bond, a respected journalist, said that when it came to her actual performance technique, "Rigg's directness and coolness suited her admirably to early twentieth century authors like Ibsen, Anton Chekhov, and Shaw. They also fitted well the heightened rhetoric of the French classical authors and Greek tragedians."

David Suchet, who costarred with Diana in a 1996 West End production of Edward Albee's *Who's Afraid of Virginia Woolf?*, described his costar
as "very generous and warm." Suchet had first met Rigg in the rehearsal
room and recalled being intimated and anxiety-ridden. "She started as
she continued, with a hundred guns blazing, and was extremely powerful."
He also described her as having "a fierce intelligence and extraordinary
strength of passion."

Sir David Hare, the English playwright, screenwriter, and theater and
film director, commented on the scope of Diana's career. He recalled the
"dazzling change of direction in middle age as a great classical actor. . . .
When Emma Peel played Euripides' Medea, Albee's Martha and Brecht's
Mother Courage, she swept all before her."

Shortly after Diana passed away, Professor Gerry McCormac, the principal and vice-chancellor of the University of Stirling, paid tribute to her
on the university's official website, referencing her "long, distinguished and
award-winning career on stage, in film and on television.

"The University community is deeply saddened to learn of the passing of Dame Diana Rigg," McCormac continued. "We are grateful for the
unwavering support and commitment she showed during her tenure as
Chancellor. Her energy, charisma and pro-active nature will forever be
remembered, and she will always be a significant figure in our history."

Harry Adam, acting chair of the University Court, also paid tribute to
Diana on the site, posting, "I was a member of the University Court during
Dame Diana's tenure as Chancellor and have fond memories of her time
in post. As a great fan of *The Avengers*, I often thought that she brought
some of the spirit of her character, Emma Peel, to her chancellorship. She
was a very active and supportive Chancellor."

In his statement to the press, Samuel West, her adoring costar from *All
Creatures Great and Small*, said: "When I discovered that she died, I tweeted
that it was just an extraordinary surprise to think of her not being with
us, because she had such energy. She basically lived the hell out of all of
us. You meet people like that, and it doesn't really matter how old they
are—in her case, eighty going on seventeen. She was properly respected,
when she's on set, you know, and things happen with her in mind first,
and quite right, too."

In a collective statement to the press, Channel 5, which had aired *Creatures*, said: "We are terribly saddened to hear the news today of Dame
Diana's passing. She was a stage and screen icon, who most recently
starred as the loveable and eccentric Mrs. Pumphrey in our adaptation of
All Creatures Great and Small.

Sir Colin Callender, the executive producer of *Creatures,* added: "Dame Diana will be sorely missed across the creative industries and our thoughts go out to her friends and family at this time.

"All of us at *All Creatures Great and Small* are heartbroken by the passing of Dame Diana Rigg one the greats of British acting royalty. From day one we wanted Dame Diana to play James Herriot's iconic character Mrs. Pumphrey and we were thrilled when she said yes. She embraced the role with reckless abandon and brought to the screen enormous glamour, dignity and self-deprecating wit. We were deeply privileged to have worked with her. She will be deeply missed."

Barbara Barrie, the veteran character actress who maintained a friendship with Rigg many years after the two had worked together on the *Diana* sitcom, noted: "It was always so wonderful to be with her. She was so un-self-conscious, so modest, you know. She never acted like a great big star. She was such a joyful person. I didn't know she was sick, and I think she was sick when she was here [in New York] in *My Fair Lady.* But she didn't tell anybody. She was playing right up the street at Lincoln Center. And then we got together again. It was not like we stayed in constant contact. We never lost touch with each other and yet, we never stayed in daily contact. It wasn't that kind of relationship. But I always just thought of her as a lovely friend. She was an amazingly kind and joyful woman. And so funny."

Even James Bond actor George Lazenby, with whom she allegedly had a cantankerous association, released a statement to the press, which said: "Diana . . . undoubtedly raised my acting game when we made *On Her Majesty's Secret Service* together. Her depth of experience . . . helped me. We were good friends on set. As my new bride Tracy Bond, I wept for her loss. Now, upon hearing of Dame Diana's death, I weep again."

Actress Dana Delany summed it up nicely on Twitter, saying: "For a girl in the 1960s, Diana Rigg was the embodiment of power and allure. To see her on stage in *Medea* thirty years later was sheer terror. And the icing was *Game of Thrones.* She outplayed them all. A great grand actor."

Margaret Drabble, Diana's understudy from decades ago, shared with *The Guardian* her final memories of dear colleague: "After Stratford, I watched her on television and on the screen, admiring her meteoric rise in performances that didn't interest me so much: both she and Judi managed effortlessly to bridge the gulf between Shakespeare and James Bond, but I was never a Bond fan.

"The last time I saw her on stage was in a rather tired performance of *Pygmalion,*" Drabble concluded. "But I have much happier memories of our last ghostly meeting in the flesh. We were both washing our hands in some grand powder room, possibly at the Savoy, and our eyes met in the mirror, and we both laughed at the comedy of life. There was something strange and timeless and delightful about this mirror meeting. We are such stuff as dreams are made on."

In all, the great Dame Enid Diana Elizabeth Rigg received well-deserved praise and accolades from her colleagues, friends, fans, and members of the media. To the end, she lived life, yes . . . on her terms. It's a melo-dramatic cliché, but it's also the truth. She loved to act, was good at it, demanded respect because of it, and got it. She always acknowledged her good fortune and appreciated the fact that she was "still working" in her later years. She retained that regal breeding and elegant manner through-out her entire life, but she also liked to keep it real. She never forgot those days when there were no acting jobs, or when the phone didn't ring, or when her private life crumbled. She had few regrets, but only one that really stung—and that was with regard to her parents. As she told journalist Rosanna Greenstreet of *The Guardian*, Diana felt that she owed them one thing: "The belief in a happy marriage over many years. I didn't achieve it."

If she could have gone back in time, she would have visited the "Eliza-bethan era—the first," and her dream dinner party would have included "Elizabeth I and her ladies-in-waiting."

Like Sean Connery, an actor who at times felt stereotyped by play-ing superspy James Bond in the movies, Diana felt similarly confined by portraying the larger-than-life secret agent Emma Peel in *The Avengers* on TV. But whereas Connery failed to fully escape the link to his superspy persona, no matter what character he portrayed (even his William of Bakersfield in *The Name of the Rose* seemed to be the an alpha-male Bond in a monk's sheep clothing), with roles like Olena Tyrell in *Game of Thrones* Diana ultimately managed to create another iconic character memorable enough to come a close second in general recall.

Conversely, whereas Connery catered more diligently to his health in real life, and in the process, aged better in aesthetic terms, the ironically willful Diana simply could not muster the willpower to beat the severely debilitating addiction to cigarettes that did not serve her wellbeing or appearance. Some psychologists might decipher her excessive smoking as party to a subconscious act of self-destructive behavior and sabotage to distance herself from the immortal image of the eternally youthful and stout Emma Peel. Had Diana not smoked so obsessively, maybe her skin may have retained slightly more elasticity, her teeth might have remained a little whiter, and maybe she possibly would have lived a trifle longer. One will never know.

But either way, before she actually did pass away, the closest she came to death was, as she once recalled, "On a climb in Australia years ago. Ill-equipped, amateur and halfway up a chimney, I got stuck and thought I was going to fall to my death."

She named "no creaking joints" as the one single thing that would have improved her life. But she never told secrets, "mine or other people's." She "never really thought about" what her greatest achievement was or might have been because, she said, "I'm not into self-congratulation." And though she once cited her film career "or lack of it," as her biggest disappointment, she added, "but it's too late now."

However, that was remedied, if posthumously, with her compelling swan song performance in *Last Night in Soho*.

As to the song she would have liked played at her funeral? "Knockin' on Heaven's Door," by Bob Dylan, would have done it for her. Dylan, in general, is the ideal musical "voice" of the era in which Diana's iconic popularity on *The Avengers* was initially born. As one of Dylan's other classic tunes assail, "The Times They Are A-Changin'," indeed.

And as to being the feminist icon of the 1960s as Mrs. Emma Peel?

"I never was really," she said. In fact, she "preferred to keep my mouth shut for the most part."

"I've been through bad patches," she concluded another time. While, in the end, the *bad* was replaced by the *good*. The phone may have stopped ringing for a while, but it eventually once again ... and again ... and again ... began to ring off the hook.

And that's exactly how Diana Rigg, *one tough dame*, played at life.

In 2009, Diana is stage-struck once again, this time playing Judith Bliss in *Hay Fever*, Noël Coward's farce which is presented at the Chichester Festival Theatre, and costarring (among others) Laura Rogers and Sam Alexander as her children Sorel and Simon. Courtesy Classic TV Preservation Society (CTVPS).

On June 9, 2014, Diana reunited with Archie Stirling at Syria Trojan Women Project Party at Leighton House, Kensington, London, Britain, to the delight of their daughter, Rachael Stirling. Richard Young/ Shutterstock.

Diana returns to television on April 7, 2013, to thunderous audience applause and peer review as Olenna Tyrell in *Game of Thrones*. Courtesy Classic TV Preservation Society (CTVPS).

On May 4, 2013, Diana performed with daughter Rachael Stirling in "The Crimson Horror," their now-famous episode of *Dr. Who*. Courtesy Classic TV Preservation Society (CTVPS).

In her final performance on television, Diana portrays Mrs. Pumphrey in two episodes of the heralded PBS series, *All Creatures Great and Small*. The episode, "A Tricky Case," premieres January 1, 2021; the second segment, "Another Farnon," originally airs April 17, 2021; both are shown posthumously. Courtesy Classic TV Preservation Society (CTVPS).

Dame Diana Rigg delivers an enigmatic, near-hypnotic swan song, posthumous performance as Ms. Collins in Edgar Wright's horror flick, *Last Night in Soho*, released by Focus Features in 2021.

Courtesy Classic TV Preservation Society (CTVPS).

LIFE AND CAREER HIGHLIGHTS— A SELECTIVE TIMELINE

1903   June 21, Louis Rigg, Diana's father, is born.

1909   February 26, Beryl Hilda (Rigg), Diana's mother, is born.

1934   Hugh Rigg, Diana's brother, is born.

1938   July 20, Diana is born in Doncaster, then in West Riding of Yorkshire (now in South Yorkshire). The daughter of a railroad engineer, she moved with her family to India at the age of two months and resided there until she was eight (and learned to speak Hindi).

1955–1957   Attends and graduates from the Royal Academy of Dramatic Arts (RADA) in London, England; becomes an associate member. Classmates include Glenda Jackson and Sian Phillips.
Makes professional stage debut as Natella Abashwili in *The Caucasian Chalk Circle*, Theatre Royal, at the York Festival.

1959   Joins the Royal Shakespeare Company (RSC) with small roles in plays like *All's Well That Ends Well* and *A Midsummer's Night Dream*.

1960   Appears as one of the Attendants in *The Winter's Tale*; appears in *Troilus and Cressida*, and *The Duchess of Malfi*, all both performed by the RSC.

1961   Makes West End debut in Jean Giraudoux's *Ondine* (which is later included in *Theatre Night* series).

1962   Cast as Cordelia in *King Lear*, performed by the RSC

1963   Plays Helena in *A Midsummer Night's Dream* with the RSC.
Portrays Francy Wilde in the "A Very Desirable Plot" episode of the TV series *The Sentimental Agent*.
Considered for guest roles in *Doctor Who*:Kassia in "The Keeper of Traken," Todd in "Kinda," and Jane Humpden in "The Awakening."

1964   Portrays Cordelia in *King Lear* with RSC (European/US tour).
            Plays Anita Fender in "The Hothouse" episode of *Armchair
            Theatre*.
            Performs as Adriana in *The Comedy of Errors*.

1965   Appears as Bianca in Thomas Middleton's "Women Beware
            Women" episode of ITV's *Play of the Week*.

1965   Begins legendary role as Emma Peel on *The Avengers*; becomes
            feminist and fashion icon in the process.

1966   Appears as Viola in *Twelfth Night* with the RSC.
            Estimated on-set of romance with Philip Saville.

1967   Becomes an associate artist of the RSC, the first as such to later
            join the National Theatre of Great Britain (1971).
            Receives Emmy nomination for Outstanding Continued Per-
            formance by an Actress in a Leading Role in a Dramatic Series,
            The Avengers.
            Nominated for *Photoplay* Gold Medal Award for Favorite TV
            Program, *The Avengers* (shared with Patrick Macnee).

1968   Receives second Emmy nomination for Outstanding Continued
            Performance by an Actress in a Leading Role in a Dramatic
            Series, *The Avengers*.
            Portrays Helena in the film *A Midsummer Night's Dream*.
            Nominated for *Photoplay* Gold Medal Award as Favorite Female
            Star.
            Winner, Bravo Otto Award (Germany) for Best Female TV Star.
            July 9, Louis Rigg, Diana's father, dies at age sixty-five.

1969   Illness forces Rigg to reject the role of Elizabeth in the film, *Paint
            Your Wagon*, with Clint Eastwood. Jean Seberg replaces her.
            Delivers ground-breaking performance as Tracy Bond/Mrs.
            James Bond/Contessa Teresa di Vicenzo in *On Her Majesty's
            Secret Service*.
            A long outspoken critic of feminism, Rigg says, this year,
            "Women are in a much stronger position than men."
            Considered for role of Ursula Brangwen in *Women in Love*, but
            the part goes to Jennie Linden.
            Stars opposite Oliver Reed in the film *The Assassination Bureau*,
            as a journalist who uncovers contract killers.
            Appears in the film short, *Minikillers*.
            Wins Bravo Otto Award (Germany) for Best Female TV Star.

1970   Plays Liz Jardine in the "Married Alive" episode of ITV's *Sat-
            urday Night Theatre*.

Portrays Portia in the film *Julius Caesar*, opposite Jason Robards as Brutus. John Gielgud plays Caesar; movie also stars Charlton Heston and Christopher Lee.

Becomes first major actor (along with costar Keith Michell) to appear nude onstage (in the production of Ronald Miller's *Abelard and Heloise*, Wyndam's Theatre, London).

Nominated for Golden Laurel Award for Female New Face for performance as Sonya Winter in the film, *The Assassination Bureau*.

1971 Becomes first recipient of the associate artist of the Royal Shakespeare Company to join the National Theatre of Great Britain.

Makes Broadway debut, receives first of three Tony Award nominations for Best Actress in a Play for performance as Heloise in *Abelard and Heloise* at the Brooks Atkinson Theatre, New York.

Becomes Steve McQueen's first choice to play his love interest in the film *Le Mans*, but is unavailable. Elga Anderson is cast instead.

Is considered for the role of Amy Sumner in the film *Straw Dogs*, but the part goes to Susan George.

Is offered the starring role in the movie *Countess Dracula*, but rejects it. The role goes to Ingrid Pitt.

Portrays Barbara Drummond, love interest to George C. Scott's character, in the satirical film, *The Hospital*, which is selected for the National Film Registry by the Library of Congress as being "culturally, historically or aesthetically" significant; receives (in 1972) Golden Globe nomination for Best Supporting Actress (Motion Picture) her role as Drummond.

1972 Is now a member of National Theatre Company at the Old Vic Theatre in London; portrays Lady Macbeth in *Macbeth* opposite Anthony Hopkins.

Journalist and interviewer Michael Parkinson describes Diana as the most desirable woman he ever met, who "radiated a lustrous beauty."

1973 Portrays Edwina Lionheart in *Theatre of Blood*, which she later classifies as the favorite of her films.

Stars as Diana Smythe in NBC's short-lived *Diana* TV sitcom, in which she reunites with Patrick Macnee for the episode titled "You Can't Go Back"; is devastated when show is canceled.

Marries Menachem Guffen.

Plays Celimene in *The Misanthrope* at the Old Vic Theatre in London.

1974   Portrays Eliza Doolittle in *Pygmalion* at the Albery Theatre, London.

1975   Rejects role later played by Judy Geeson in *Brannigan*.

Portrays Celimene in *The Misanthrope* at St. James Theatre in New York ; receives second Tony Award nomination, this time for Best Actress in a Play; also receives Drama Desk Award nomination for Outstanding Actress in a Play.

Receives Emmy Nomination for Outstanding Lead Actress in a Special Program—Drama or Comedy for her portrayal of Philippa in the TV movie *In This House of Brede*.

Nominated for *Photoplay* Gold Medal Award as Favorite Female Star.

1976   Divorces Menachem Guffen.

Declines to reprise her role as Emma Peel in *The New Avengers* TV series reboot.

Nominated for *Photoplay* Gold Medal Award as Favorite Female Star.

1977   Portrays Countess Charlotte Mittelheim in the film *A Little Night Music*, in which she makes her on-screen singing debut.

May 30, gives birth to Rachael Stirling on in St. Marylebone, London.

1979   Portrays Clytemnestra in the three-part BBC miniseries *The Sea Serpent*, a TV adaptation of Aeschylus's Oresteia trilogy of Greek tragedies; Helen Mirren plays Cassandra.

1980   Cast as Mrs. Agnes Cromwell in the war film *The Sea Wolves* but drops out; the role goes to Barbara Kellerman.

Portrays Eloise in the TV movie *The Marquise*.

1981   March 25, Beryl Hilda Rigg, Diana's mother, passes away at age seventy-two.

June 26, Diana appears as Lady Holiday in *The Great Muppet Caper*, a family friendly comedy and a refreshing departure from Rigg's more dramatic roles.

Plays the lead in the Yorkshire TV production of Ibsen's *Hedda Gabler*.

1982   Weds Archie Stirling.

Takes the lead in a US national tour of the play *Colette*, which closes during the tour en route to Broadway.

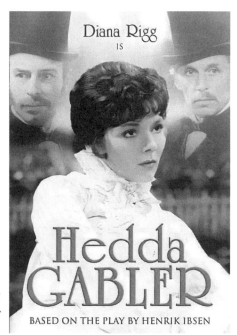

Courtesy Classic TV
Preservation Society
(CTVPS).

Courtesy Classic TV
Preservation Society
(CTVPS).

Portrays Rita Allmers in the "Little Eyof" episode of the *Play of the Month*.

Receives the Variety Club of Great Britain Award for Best Film Actress in Agatha Christie's *Evil Under the Sun*, in which she plays Arelena Marshall (opposite her character's old rival, played by Maggie Smith).

Publishes first edition of *No Turn Unstoned*, released by Elm Tree Books in the United Kingdom and Doubleday Books in the United States.

1983 Cast as Regan opposite Laurence Olivier in the Granada television production of *King Lear*.

Paperback edition of *No Turn Unstoned* is released.

1985 Stars as Cleopatra in *Antony & Cleopatra* at the Chichester Festival Theatre in the UK.

Plays Lady Honoria Deadlock opposite Denholm Elliott in the BBC's TV adaptation of Dickens's *Bleak House*.

1986 Portrays Miss Hardbroom in *The Worst Witch*.

1987 Plays the Evil Queen (Snow White's evil stepmother) in film adaptation of *Snow White*.

Cast as Lady Harriet Vulcan in the TV movie *A Hazard of Hearts*.

Performs in West End production of Stephen Sondheim's musical *Follies*.

1988 Named a Commander of the Order of the British Empire (CBE) in the New Year Honors List.

Receives Honorary Degree from the University of Stirling (November).

1989 Begins hosting the PBS TV series, *Mystery!*, broadcast in America by WGBH; replaces previous host Vincent Price, her costar from *Theatre of Blood*.

1989–1990 Receives the first of several awards for her role as Helena Vesey in the TV miniseries *Mother Love*, including BAFTA TV Award for Best Actress, and the Broadcasting Press Guild. As with each of her awards, it was well-deserved, though this was a particularly remarkable performance as an eccentric and often difficult woman utterly consumed by love for her son and vengeful hatred for his father.

1990 Receives the Best Actress Award from *The Evening Standard* for performance in *Medea*.

Winner, Broadcasting Press Guild Award as Best Actress for *Mother Love*.

Divorces Archie Stirling.

1991 Revised paperback edition of *No Turn Unstoned* is released by
    Silman James Press.

1992 Receives honorary degree from the University of Leeds.
    Plays Mme. Colbert opposite Angela Lansbury in the TV movie,
    Mrs. 'Aris Goes to Paris.

1992–1993 Stars in *Medea* at the Almeida Theatre and Wyndham's Theatre
    both in London; ends the run at the Longacre Theatre in New
    York.

1994 Receives additional accolades upon taking titular role on stage
    in *Medea*; the *Evening Standard* bestows upon her the Best Actress
    Award; receives the Tony Award for Best Actress in a Play.
    Plays Chole Fanshawe in Bruce Beresford's *A Good Man in Africa*,
    which proves to be another nice comedic screen departure, if
    not a box-office success. Costars with John Lithgow.
    In June, she's deemed a Dame Commander of the Order of the
    British Empire (DBE) by Queen Elizabeth II in the Honours List
    for her extensive contributions to theater and film.
    Receives the Drama Desk Award nomination as Best Actress;
    receives Olivier Award Nomination for Outstanding Actress in
    a Play.

1995 Portrays Mother Courage in *Mother Courage and Her Children* at
    the National Theatre in London.
    Receives honorary degree (doctor of literature) from the Uni-
    versity of Nottingham.
    Plays Evgenia, the main character's grandmother, in the TV
    adaptation of Danielle Steel's *Zoya.*
    Nominee, Cable ACE Award, Supporting Actress in a Movie or
    Miniseries, for "Genghis Cohn" episode of *Screen Two.*

1996 Receives honorary degree (doctor of literature) from the Lon-
    don South Bank University.
    Receives *Evening Standard* Theatre Award for Best Actress
    for her performances in *Who's Afraid of Virginia Woolf?* (at the
    Almedia Theatre, which transfers to the Aldwych Theatre in
    October 1996) and *Mother Courage* (at the National Theatre).
    Nominated for the Cable ACE Award as Supporting Actress in
    a Movie or Miniseries for *Screen Too.*
    Portrays Mrs. Grose in TV movie *The Haunting of Helen Walker.*
    Plays Mara in the TV movie *Samson and Delilah.*

1997 Stars as Martha in *Who's Afraid of Virginia Woolf?* at the Almeida
    Theatre and Aldwych Theatre, both located in London, for

which she receives Laurence Olivier Theatre Award for Best Actress in a Play.

Portrays vengeful housekeeper Mrs. Danvers opposite Emilia Fox as the second Mrs. de Winter and Charles Dance as Maxim in an acclaimed TV adaptation of Daphne du Maurier's gothic novel *Rebecca*. The performance earns her an Emmy Award for Outstanding Supporting Actress in a Miniseries or a Movie.

Cast as Mrs. Golightly in the PBS adaptation *The Fortunes of Misfortunes of Moll Flanders*.

1998   Begins ten-year term as chancellor of University of Stirling in Stirling, Scotland, UK.

Refuses to appear as Alice in the big-screen remake of *The Avengers*; the role goes to Dame Eileen Atkins.

Plays the lead in *Phaedra* at the Almeida at the Albery Theatre in London, and BAM in Brooklyn, New York.

Portrays Madame de Bellegarde in *The American*.

1999   Nominated for the Laurence Olivier Theatre Award for Best Actress for her performances in both *Britannicus* and *Phèdre*.

Appointed as Cameron Mackintosh Visiting Professor of Contemporary Theatre at St. Catherine College, Oxford, a one-year appointment.

Portrays Lisa in the film *Parting Shots*.

2000   Plays Dame Beatrice Adela Le Strange Bradley in the BBC series *The Mrs. Bradley Mysteries*; the series fails to win critical acclaim, and does not return for a second season.

Appears as Mature Rebeccah in the TV movie *In the Beginning*.

Wins Special BAFTA Award for *The Avengers* (shares with Honor Blackman, Joanna Lumley, and Linda Thorson).

2001   Appears in first of two television series about Queen Victoria: as Baroness Lehzen in *Victoria & Albert* (followed by her portrayal of the Duchess of Buccleuch in *Victoria*, 2016).

2002   Receives Emmy nomination as Outstanding Supporting Actress in a Miniseries or a Movie for *Victoria & Albert*.

2003   Ends her long run as the host of the PBS anthology series *Mystery!*

Appears as Jill Craig in the "Suicide" episode of *Murder in Mind*.

Plays Queen Henrietta Maria in TV miniseries *The Power and the Passion*.

October 20, the British courts award her $63,832 and $134,000 in court expenses in her libel suit against Britain's *Evening Standard* and *Daily Mail* newspapers (both of which referenced her as an embittered woman who held British men in low regard).

2004	Portrays Violet Venable in Sheffield Theatres' production of Tennessee Williams's play *Suddenly, Last Summer*, which tranfers to the Albery Theatre in London.
2005	Plays Grandmamma in the film *Heidi*.
2006	Appears at Wyndham Theatre in London's West End in the drama *Honour*, which has a limited but successful run.
	Portrays Mother Superior in the film *The Painted Veil*.
	Plays herself in the "Daniel Radcliffe" episode of TV's *Extras*.
2007	Portrays Huma Rojo in *All About My Mother* at the Old Vic Theatre in London.
2008	Portrays Ranyevskaya in *The Cherry Orchard* at the Chichester Festival Theatre in the UK.
	By this time, too, Diana is a patron of International Care and Relief and was for many years the public face of the charity's child sponsorship scheme.
2009	Returns to the Chichester Festival Theatre, to star as Judith Bliss in Noel Coward's farce *Hay Fever*.
	A smoker since eighteen, Rigg is by now still smoking twenty cigarettes a day
2011	Portrays Mrs. Higgins in *Pygmalion* at the Garrick Theatre in London, opposite Rupert Everett and Kara Tointon.
2013	Commences her iconic run as Olenna Tyrell in TV's *Game of Thrones*; receives Emmy nomination for Outstanding Actress in a Drama Series.
	Recipient of the *Doctor Who Magazine* Best Guest Actress for 2013 for her role as Mrs. Gillyflower in the *Doctor Who* episode "The Crimson Horror" (costarring her daughter Rachael).
	Wins OFTA Television Award for Best Guest Actress in a Drama Series for *Game of Thrones*.
	Wins Gold Derby TV Award for Drama Guest Actress of the Decade for *Game of Thrones*.
	Nominated for International Online Cinema Award (INOCA), Best Actress in a Drama or Comedy Series, *Game of Thrones*.
	Nominated for Critics' Choice TV Awards for Best Guest Performance in a Drama Series for *Game of Thrones*.
2014	Her smaller-than-usual role on *Detectorists* is explained by the fact that her character's daughter, the female lead on the series, is played by real-life daughter Rachael Stirling.
	Recipient of the Will Award presented by the Shakespeare Theatre Company (with other recepients Stacy Keach and John Hurt).

Nominated for Emmy, Outstanding Guest Actress in a Drama Series for playing Lady Olenna Tyrell in *Game of Thrones.*
Nominated for Critics' Choice TV Awards for Best Guest Performance in a Drama Series for *Game of Thrones.*
Wins OFTA Television Award for Best Guest Actress in a Drama Series for *Game of Thrones.*
Wins Gold Derby TV Award for Drama Guest Actress of the Decade for *Game of Thrones.*

2015   Marks fiftieth anniversary of her portrayal of Emma Peel on *The Avengers*; British Film Institute (BFI) screens an episode (on October 25), followed by an on-stage interview with Rigg about the show.
In June, gives interview to *The A. V. Club* website, during which she talks about her chemistry with Patrick Macnee.
Serves as the narrator of *The Honourable Rebel.*
Nominated for Emmy, Outstanding Guest Actress in a Drama Series for playing Lady Olenna Tyrell in *Game of Thrones.*
OFTA Television nomination for Best Guest Actress in a Drama Series for *Game of Thrones.*
Wins Gold Derby TV Award for Drama Guest Actress of the Decade for *Game of Thrones.*

2017   Grandson is born to Rachael Stirling and Guy Garvey.
Portrays Lady Neville in *Breathe.*
October, has cardiac arrest.
By December, Rigg has stopped smoking after serious illness leads to heart surgery. A devout Christian, she comments, "My heart had stopped ticking during the procedure, so I was up there and the Good Lord must have said, 'Send the old bag down again, I'm not having her yet!'"

2018   Returns to Broadway, in non-singing role of Mrs. Higgins in *My Fair Lady* at the Vivian Beaumont Theatre in New York; receives her fourth Tony nomination.
Nominated for Emmy, Outstanding Guest Actress in a Drama Series for playing Lady Olenna Tyrell in *Game of Thrones* episode, "The Queen's Justice."
Wins OFTA Television Award for Best Guest Actress in a Drama Series for *Game of Thrones.*
Wins Gold Derby TV Award for Drama Guest Actress of the Decade for *Game of Thrones.*

	Wins International Online Cinema Award (INOCA), Best Actress in a Drama or Comedy Series for *Game of Thrones*.
2019	April 6, receives Variety Icon Award in France. Wins Gold Derby TV Award for Drama Guest Actress of the Decade for *Game of Thrones*. July 4, Hugh Rigg, Diana's brother, an RAF test pilot, passes away at eighty-four. In the fall, films her role as Mrs. Pumphrey at Broughton Hall near Skipton for two episodes of the acclaimed PBS series *All Creatures Great and Small*. Films her role as Miss Collins in London for the horror movie *Last Night in Soho* (which is released in 2021).
2020	Wins CinEuphoria Merit—Honorary Award for *Game of Thrones* (shared with all associated the series). March, diagnosed with cancer. September 10, Diana Rigg, eighty-two, succumbs to cancer at her daughter Rachael Stirling's home in London. Upon her demise, she is cremated at Breakspear Crematorium in Ruislip, England. It's yet to be disclosed as to whether her cremains are either interred there or given to her family.*
2021	Rigg's final film, *Last Night in Soho*, is released with an on-screen dedication to her.

POSTHUMOUS ACCOLADES

| 2021 | Nominated for OFTA Television Award for Best Guest Actress in a Drama Series, *All Creatures Great and Small*. Nominated for Detroit Film Critics Society Award for Best Supporting Actress, *Last Night in Soho*. |
| 2022 | Nominated for EDA Special Mention Award for Actress Defying Age and Ageism, Alliance of Women Film Journalists. Nominated for Fangoria Chainsaw Award for Best Supporting Performance, *Last Night in Soho*. Nominated for Saturn Award for Best Supporting Actress, *Last Night in Soho*. Wins BloodGuts UK Horror Award for Best Supporting Actress, *Last Night in Soho*. |

* Additional Note: Diana passed away five months after Honor Blackman, whom she famously replaced on *The Avengers*. Also, both had portrayed big-screen "Bond women" who were older than their given Bond actor (George Lazenby for Diana, Sean Connery for Blackman).

On August 11, 1994, Diana smiles with glee outside Buckingham Palace after receiving her DBE as Dame Commander of the Order of the British Empire, the crowning glory of her countless just awards. PA Images / Alamy Stock Photo.

ACKNOWLEDGMENTS

A book is never the result of just one person. Several individuals are involved with the process, from start to finish, and this publication is no different. Deep gratitude is extended to the many fine people who contributed to the preparation and completion of this book.

Firstly, thank you to Ray Austin, Barbara Barrie, Bruce Beresford, Damon Evans, Bernie Kopell, Rupert Macnee, Juliet Mills, and Samuel West for sharing their personal memories and insight of Diana Rigg. Thank you to film historians Robert S. Ray, producer, director and James Bond documentarian David Naylor, actor John Schuck, and journalist/actress Andrea Whitcomb-May for offering their perspectives on Diana.

A special extra thank you to Mr. Austin and Mr. Macnee, each of whom generously provided very special opening remarks (in the foreword and introduction, respectively).

Deep gratitude to Lon and Debra Davis, and Wendy Hauk Kaiser, for their editorial expertise, input, and research assistance.

Thank you also to Ken Gehrig, Ashley Longmire, and Michael D. Williamson, for assisting with additional research and editing, and providing precise transcriptions of the various interviews.

Thank you as well to Frank Balkin, Bob Barnett, Terry Diorio, Roger Hyman, Christopher Pufall, Caryn Richman, Howard Richman, Nat Segaloff, and Frank Torchio, for supporting this project in ways too numerous to mention; Gregory L. Tanner, my attorney, for his superior skills and humanity; Lee Sobel, a remarkable agent whose enthusiasm and respect for my work generated the idea for this book.

A most special thank you to Emily Bandy, Peter Tonguette, Michael Martella, and all the terrific people at University Press of Mississippi who believed in this book from the beginning.

The cover photograph appears courtesy of mptvimages.com.

NOTES

CHAPTER 1. RIGGED

1. Sean Connery who, like Diana, was known as a fabricated international spy, hailed from that region as well.
2. A topee is a lightweight, helmet-shaped hat made of pith or cork.
3. "There is a sense": Trevor Fishlock, "India: Emma Peel and the Railway Sahib," *The Telegraph*, February 9, 2002.
4. "It's rather bewildering": Fishlock, "India."

CHAPTER 2. FIRST SIGNS OF ROYALTY

1. "I am terribly conscious": Fishlock, "India."
2. "I went to the town hall": University of Kent, "Gavin Esler in Conversation with Dame Diana Rigg," December 13, 2016.
3. "I don't know": University of Kent, "Gavin Esler."
4. "I do a lot of wrong things": Dominic Maxwell, "Diana Rigg Tribute: Six Decades of Delight on Stage and Screen," *Sunday Times*, September 10, 2020.
5. "a huge amount of ambition": "Gavin Eisler in Conversation with Diana Rigg," University of Kent, December 13, 2018.
6. "You have to work": Mary Parkinson interview with Diana Rigg, BBC-TV, 1974.
7. "A brilliantly skilled": Michael Parkinson interview with Diana Rigg, BBC-TV, 1972.
8. "was either a downfall": author telephone interview with Ray Austin, March 10, 2022.
9. "deep": "Gavin Eisler in Conversation," 2018.
10. "They simply could": "Dame Diana Rigg, Full Q and A," Oxford Union, March 8, 2019.
11. "I was supposed to play": "Dame Diana Rigg, Full Q and A."
12. "I was incredibly lucky": "Dame Diana Rigg, Full Q and A."
13. "Listening to that": "Gavin Eisler in Conversation," 2018.
14. "If you can imagine": "Gavin Eisler in Conversation."
15. "I was standing": "Gavin Eisler in Conversation."
16. "What happened": "Gavin Eisler in Conversation."
17. "don't exist anymore": "Gavin Eisler in Conversation."
18. "the desire to learn": "Gavin Eisler in Conversation."
19. "It's rubbish": "Gavin Eisler in Conversation."
20. "There were a lot": "Gavin Eisler in Conversation."
21. "Buy as many": "Gavin Eisler in Conversation."
22. "read as much": "Gavin Eisler in Conversation."

23. "Unless the young": "Gavin Eisler in Conversation."
24. "terribly important": "Dame Diana Rigg, Full Q and A," Oxford Union, March 8, 2019.
25. "Go there": "Dame Diana Rigg, Full Q and A."
26. "a nightmare": "Dame Diana Rigg, Full Q and A."
27. "She was extraordinary": "Dame Diana Rigg, Full Q and A."
28. "I think he must": "Gavin Eisler in Conversation," 2018.
29. "A wonderful actress": "Gavin Eisler in Conversation."

CHAPTER 3. GREAT EXPECTATIONS

1. "It was a wonderful": "Gavin Eisler in Conversation."
2. "a mermaid who": "Gavin Eisler in Conversation."
3. "was the only": "Gavin Eisler in Conversation."
4. "deeply, deeply unfortunate": "Gavin Eisler in Conversation."
5. "wildly handsome": "Gavin Eisler in Conversation."
6. "was looking at": "Gavin Eisler in Conversation."
7. "Diana, I hear you": "Gavin Eisler in Conversation."
8. "rather better than": "Gavin Eisler in Conversation."
9. "It was a wonderful": "Gavin Eisler in Conversation."
10. "a very chilly": "Gavin Eisler in Conversation."
11. "nearly every night": "Gavin Eisler in Conversation."
12. "too young": "Gavin Eisler in Conversation."
13. "It's a cliché: "Gavin Eisler in Conversation."
14. "We're at a stage": "Gavin Eisler in Conversation."
15. "I just love": "Gavin Eisler in Conversation."
16. "To be without money": "Gavin Eisler in Conversation."
17. "The trouble with": "Gavin Eisler in Conversation."

CHAPTER 4. EMBRACING EMMA

1. "The twain never": Robert Berkvist, "Nobody's Going to Typecast Diana Rigg," *New York Times*, March 9, 1975.
2. "As an actress": author telephone interview with Ray Austin, March 10, 2022.
3. "people's body English": author telephone interview with Austin.
4. "you expect an actor": author telephone interview with Austin.
5. "You haven't got": author telephone interview with Austin.
6. "a tall": Anita Gates, "Diana Rigg, Stylish Emma Peel of 'The Avengers,' Dies at 82," *New York Times*, September 10, 2020.
7. "Subliminally it was": David Story, *America on the Rerun: TV Shows That Never Die* (New York: Citadel Press, 1993), p. 211.
8. "a new type": Story, *America on the Rerun*, p. 211.
9. "But then we": Story, *America on the Rerun*, p. 212.
10. "terribly sweet": Story, *America on the Rerun*, p. 212.
11. "So, the jewel": Story, *America on the Rerun*, p. 212.
12. "dropped away at": "Gavin Eisler in Conversation," 2018.
13. "She's not a bad actress": Story, *America on the Rerun*, p. 212.
14. "a dazzling actress": Story, *America on the Rerun*, p. 212
15. "My dad grew up": author telephone interview with Rupert Macnee, February 8, 2022.
16. "The very first thing": Interview with Patrick Macnee, *The Lady* (magazine), 2014.

17. "The wonderful thing": Interview with Macnee, *The Lady*.
18. "I'm very proud": Interview with Macnee, *The Lady*.

CHAPTER 5. AVENGING ANGEL

1. "It was a wonderful part": "Gavin Eisler in Conversation," 2018.
2. "It helps if": "Gavin Eisler in Conversation."
3. "If you ask me": Story, *America on the Rerun*, p. 214.
4. "Quite often": Story, *America on the Rerun*, p. 214.
5. "There was great balance": Story, *America on the Rerun*, p. 214.
6. "was head and shoulders": Story, *America on the Rerun*, p. 214.
7. "I didn't have a telly": *TV Guide*.
8. "I hadn't seen Honor": Michael Parkinson interview with Diana Rigg, BBC-TV, 1972.
9. "the ideal interviewee": author telephone interview with Ray Austin, March 10, 2022.
10. "I don't like this outfit": author telephone interview with Austin.
11. "And that was": author telephone interview with Austin.
12. "an absolute nightmare": author telephone interview with Austin.
13. "No one in England": author telephone interview with Austin.
14. "I'd go down": author telephone interview with Austin.
15. "were terrible": author telephone interview with Austin.
16. "I suppose they would": author telephone interview with Austin.
17. "good . . . with long": author telephone interview with Austin.
18. "this little fight": author telephone interview with Austin.
19. "*More* than happy": author telephone interview with Austin.
20. "Brian said": author telephone interview with Austin.
21. "a load of bullshit": author telephone interview with Austin.
22. "she would have": author telephone interview with Austin.
23. "We got on": author telephone interview with Austin.

CHAPTER 6. DEFENDING MRS. PEEL

1. "Number one: they": author telephone interview with Austin.
2. "He was incredible": author telephone interview with Austin.
3. "There was no obvious": author telephone interview with Austin.
4. "This guy goes": author telephone interview with Austin.
5. "America *loved* it": author telephone interview with Austin.
6. "If a man": author telephone interview with Austin.
7. "very carefully": Story, *America on the Rerun*, p. 214.
8. "were getting a": Story, *America on the Rerun*, p. 214.
9. "Most importantly": author telephone interview with Ray Austin, March 10, 2022.
10. "Just silly fun": author telephone interview with Austin.
11. "I mean, how silly": author telephone interview with Austin.
12. "We're not going": author telephone interview with Austin.
13. "a heightened reality": author telephone interview with Austin.
14. "Then I put": author telephone interview with Austin.
15. "There were going": author telephone interview with Austin.
16. "they understood the": author telephone interview with Austin.
17. Dubbed "Emmapeelers": Story, *America on the Rerun*, p. 213.
18. "In those days": Oxford Union Q&A.

19. "hard to explain": Oxford Union Q&A.
20. "a choice": Oxford Union Q&A.
21. "I know it": "Gavin Esler in Conversation," 2018.
22. "little desire to": Story, *America on the Rerun*, p. 124.
23. "a very personal process": Michael Parkinson, interview with Diana Rigg, BBC-TV, 1972.
24. "You can have": Parkinson, interview with Diana Rigg.
25. "I don't mean": Parkinson, interview with Diana Rigg.
26. "The Paris Olympia": "Gavin Esler in Conversation," 2018.
27. "this extraordinary golden": "Gavin Esler in Conversation."
28. "I've come to": "Gavin Esler in Conversation."
29. Rigg asked, "Not": "Gavin Esler in Conversation."
30. "I love the": Story, *America on the Rerun*, p. 215.
31. When "Knot" premiered: Story, *America on the Rerun*, p. 215.
32. "forces outside": Story, *America on the Rerun*, p. 215.
33. "split, because on": "Gavin Esler in Conversation," 2018.
34. "considered to be": "Gavin Esler in Conversation."
35. "I felt like": "Gavin Esler in Conversation."

CHAPTER 7. FROM THE BUREAU TO BOND

1. "I'm not really": Mark Shivas, "Will Diana Ever Get It Together?," *New York Times*, February 2, 1969.
2. "the star business": Shivas, "Will Diana Ever Get It Together?"
3. "It just depends": "Dame Diana Rigg, Full Q and A," Oxford Union.
4. "stuck with the": Mark Shivas, "Will Diana Ever Get It Together?," *New York Times*, February 2, 1969.
5. "I can't tell": "Gavin Esler in Conversation," 2018.
6. "Oh, come on!": Anthony Mason, "Diana Rigg on Life Before and After 'The Avengers,'" CBS News, May 20, 2018.
7. "It's nice to": Vincent Canby, "Screen: British Murders Are Cute," *New York Times*, March 24, 1969.
8. "had been a": Canby, "Screen."
9. "I think the": "Gavin Esler in Conversation," 2018.
10. "a visual treat": Julia Sirmons, "Could *On Her Majesty's Secret Service* Be the Best Bond Film?," crimereads.com, October 8, 2021.
11. "We see Tracy's": Sirmons, "Could *On Her Majesty's Secret Service*."
12. "a poor-little-rich-girl": Sirmons, "Could *On Her Majesty's Secret Service*."
13. "Would you like": "Dame Diana Rigg, Full Q and A," Oxford Union.
14. "stunning": *Yours Retro Magazine: Celebrating the Stars We Love* (Media House, 2020).
15. "was probably not": Mark Altman and Ed Gross, *Nobody Does It Better: The Complete, Uncensored, Unauthorized Oral History of James Bond* (New York: Forge), 2020.
16. "the first real": Altman and Ed Gross, *Nobody Does It Better*.
17. "She's a totally": Altman and Ed Gross, *Nobody Does It Better*.
18. "They got me": Altman and Ed Gross, *Nobody Does It Better*.
19. "She wanted to": author telephone interview with Ray Austin, March 10, 2022.
20. "George had come": author telephone interview with Austin.
21. "George was a": author telephone interview with Austin.
22. "absolutely, 100 percent not": author telephone interview with Austin.

23. "knew exactly": "Dame Diana Rigg, Full Q and A," Oxford Union.
24. "much loved": "Dame Diana Rigg, Full Q and A."
25. "He'd really throw": Nichole Lambert, "I Don't Miss Romance," *Daily Mail Weekend*, October 21, 2015.
26. "And that's the first": Lambert, "I Don't Miss Romance."
27. "So, here she's": Lambert, "I Don't Miss Romance."
28. "Hey, George": Lambert, "I Don't Miss Romance."
29. "The press kept": Lambert, "I Don't Miss Romance."
30. "So, clearly, she": *The James Bond Film Guide: The Official Guide to All 25 Films* (London: Collector Books/Eaglemoss, Ltd., 2021).
31. "If you're an actor": *The James Bond Film Guide.*
32. "And then it just": *The James Bond Film Guide.*
33. "an incredible sport": *The James Bond Film Guide.*
34. "remarkably similar": Charles Helfenstein, *The Making of On Her Majesty's Secret Service* (London: Spies LLC, 2009).
35. "ran out of steam": "Gavin Esler in Conversation," 2018.

CHAPTER 8. HAILING CAESAR, THE HOSPITAL, AND BLOOD

1. "was alright": "Gavin Esler in Conversation."
2. "Paddy and I": "Gavin Esler in Conversation."
3. "a very good": "Gavin Esler in Conversation."
4. "I was in": *New York Times*, January 3, 1972.
5. "Arthur was the": *New York Times.*
6. "brilliant . . . so original": Dame Diana Rigg, Oxford Union full Q&A, March 8, 2019.
7. "I adored it": Rigg, Oxford Union full Q&A.
8. "Coral and Vincent": Rigg, Oxford Union full Q&A.

CHAPTER 9. WHEN DIANA MET *DIANA*

1. "And because it": Mary Parkinson interview with Diana Rigg, BBC-TV, 1974.
2. "I don't agree": Michael Parkinson interview with Diana Rigg, BBC-TV, 1972.
3. Rigg is making a reference to Belarusian-Israeli dancer and choreograph Valery Matvee-vich Panov (b. March 12, 1938) and his second wife, Galina, a ballerina at the Kirov. They came to international attention in 1972 when they applied for exit visas to emigrate to Israel, which they were given in 1974.
4. "because of all": Parkinson interview, 1972.
5. "I think you": Parkinson interview, 1972.
6. "Laughter is absolutely": Mary Parkinson interview with Diana Rigg, BBC-TV, 1974.
7. "a charming man": Parkinson interview, 1974.
8. "It was how": Parkinson interview, 1974.
9. "It was a": Parkinson interview, 1974.
10. "I think we're all": author telephone interview with Barbara Barrie, May 31, 2022.
11. "I was to be": author telephone interview with Bernie Kopell, February 22, 2022.
12. "Oh, he loved it!": author telephone interview with Rupert Macnee, February 8, 2022.

CHAPTER 10. HER CRAFT, UNSTONED

1. "The result is": Clive Barnes review of *The Misanthrope*, *New York Times*, March 13, 1975.
2. "built like a": John Simon review of *Abelard and Eloise*, *New York Times*, April 28, 1989.

3. "I come from": Michael Parkinson interview with Diana Rigg, BBC-TV, 1972.

4. "the daftest thing": "Gavin Esler in Conversation with Dame Diana Rigg," University of Kent, Dec. 13, 2016.

5. "very funny": author telephone interview with Rupert Macnee, February 8, 2022.

6. "literally what it": author telephone interview with Macnee.

7. "It was a": Norvel Rose television interview with Dame Diana Rigg, *Channel 4 (Denver) News*, n.d.

8. "That says it": Rose television interview.

9. "absolutely fascinating": Rose television interview.

10. "I put a": Rose television interview.

11. "Peter Hall said": "Gavin Esler in Conversation with Dame Diana Rigg," University of Kent, Dec. 13, 2016.

12. "would be sidetracked": Q&A, Oxford Union, March 8, 2019.

13. "Somebody said it": Q&A, Oxford Union.

14. "The cords have": Q&A, Oxford Union.

15. "It demanded the": Q&A, Oxford Union.

16. "Bit by bit": Oxford Union Q&A.

17. "We had that": Oxford Union Q&A.

18. "Diana Rigg, as": Richard Ellman review of *Phaedra*, *New York Times*, October 12, 1975.

19. "There was a": Oxford Union Q&A.

20. "*serve* the text": Oxford Union Q&A.

21. "Where would we": Oxford Union Q&A.

22. "urgency refashions a": Matt Wolfe review of *Mother Courage and Her Children*, *Variety*, November 26, 1995.

23. "For me, I": Oxford Union Q&A.

24. "*misery*. You just": Oxford Union Q&A.

25. "That's the point": Oxford Union Q&A.

26. "You must never": Oxford Union Q&A.

CHAPTER 11. A LITTLE NIGHT MUSIC WITH A THREE-PIECE SUITE, AND MORE

1. "Do you know": *Daily Mail*, c. 2019.

2. "She was passionately": *Los Angeles Examiner*, June 30, 1981.

3. "extremely promising sequence": Vincent Canby review of *Evil Under the Sun*, *New York Times*, March 5, 1982.

4. "I can observe": Roger Ebert review of *Evil Under the Sun*, *Chicago Sun Times*, January 1, 1982.

5. "stagey, showy, and": Paul Mavis, dvdtalk.com.

6. "a musical in": Norvel Rose, *Channel 4 (Denver) News*, 1982.

7. "We were all": "Gavin Esler in Conversation with Dame Diana Rigg," University of Kent, December 13, 2016.

8. "First of all": "Gavin Esler."

9. "Oh, absolutely don't": Oxford Union Q&A.

10. "Well, not *The*": Oxford Union Q&A.

11. "It was an": Oxford Union Q&A.

12. "so much more": *Telegraph*, April 8, 2017.

13. "I'm good at": *Telegraph*.

CHAPTER 12. THE BRADLEY BUNCH

1. "The shit hits": Louis Wise interview, 2019.
2. "I suppose so": Wise interview.
3. "And I mean": Wise interview.
4. "That wonderful voice": Wise interview.
5. "I realized that": author telephone interview with Bruce Beresford, November 29, 2020.
6. "A good book": Janet Maslin review of *A Good Man in Africa*, *New York Times*, September 9, 1994.
7. "'Medea started very": Oxford Union Q&A.
8. "independent, brave, and": *New York Times*, September 1994.
9. "I loved doing": Oxford Union Q&A.
10. In 2022, the *Guardian* named Diana Rigg as the sexiest British television star of all time.
11. "Adela Bradley doesn't": spoken introduction for "The Speedy Death," the 1999 pilot episode of the *Mrs. Bradley* series, broadcast on *Mystery!* on the BBC.
12. "Apparently, this particular": Paul Mavis, dvdtalk.com.
13. "triumph, complete with": "Crown, the Hollow," *Sydney Morning Herald*, May 30, 2002.
14. "the undisputed": "Crown, the Hollow."
15. "They just wrote": Oxford Union Q&A.
16. The Leveson Inquiry, chaired by Lord Justice Leveson and published in 2012, was a judicial public inquiry into the culture, practices, and ethics of the British press following the News International phone hacking scandal.
17. "Well, I think": Oxford Union Q&A.
18. Known in 2023 as the Noël Coward Theatre.
19. "I learnt, courtesy": Diana Rigg's email reprinted in the *New York Post*, July 5, 2018.
20. "They put a": Oxford Union Q&A.
21. "I'm flying the": Oxford Union Q&A.

CHAPTER 13. THE QUEEN OF THRONES AND THORNES

1. "I think what": "Gavin Esler in Conversation with Dame Diana Rigg."
2. "In fact, it": "Gavin Esler."
3. "It's known as": "Gavin Esler."
4. "What met first": "Diana Rigg Remembered by Mark Gatiss," *The Guardian*, December 13, 2020.
5. "She started off": author Zoom interview with Ray Austin.
6. "she was a": author Zoom interview with Austin.
7. "No, no, they": Oxford Union Q&A.
8. "I don't know": Oxford Union Q&A.
9. "Playing a baddie": Oxford Union Q&A.
10. "really lovely, meaty" Oxford Union Q&A.
11. "On these sets": Oxford Union Q&A.
12. "Only if they": Oxford Union Q&A.
13. "It would be": Oxford Union Q&A.
14. "Because it is video": Oxford Union Q&A.
15. "I'm sort of": *The Times (London)*, August 26, 2017.
16. "the mum from": Morgan Jeffrey, "Diana Rigg: 'It's Wonderful Being Glamorous—I'm an Old Bag on 'Game of Thrones," www.digitalspy.com, October 31, 2017.
17. "a really terrific": Valentine Low, "My Manner is: Don't Brook Any Argument—Good for Playing a Duchess," *The Times (London)*, August 26, 2017.

18. "In one priceless": Bill Young, www.tellyspotting.com, August 17, 2017.

19. "Well, they have": Valentine Low, "My Manner is . . .," *The Times (London)*, August 26, 2017.

20. "This is a": Brian Tallerico, editor of rogerebert.com, October 13, 2017.

21. "really self-respecting": Oxford Union Q&A.

22. "I didn't know": Nichole Lambert, "I Don't Miss Romance," *Daily Mail*, c. 2019.

23. "I would advise": Oxford Union Q&A.

CHAPTER 14. FINAL BOWS

1. "never relied on": Morgan Jeffrey, "It's Wonderful Being Glamorous," www.digitalspy.com, October 31, 2017.

2. "I have no": Jeffrey, "It's Wonderful Being Glamorous."

3. "For this one": On a special tribute page published on the PBS website, cast members from the BBC series *All Creatures Great and Small* share their memories of the late Dame Diana Rigg.

4. "It was a": special tribute page published on the PBS website.

5. "Obviously, we know": author Zoom interview with Samuel West, November 25, 2022.

6. "She made a": *All Creatures Great and Small* tribute page on the PBS website.

CHAPTER 15. ENCORE

1. "a surprising misfire": Guy Lodge, "'Last Night in Soho' Review: Edgar Wright's Retro Horror Has Its Heart in the Sixties and Its Head All Over the Place," *Variety*, September 4, 2021.

2. "In everything from": Mark Hanson, "Review: 'Last Night in Soho' Takes a Bold Swing at Retro Horror, and Mostly Misses," *Slant* magazine, September 12, 2021.

3. "a riotous rascally": Robbie Collin's review of 'Last Night in Soho,' *Telegraph*, October 21, 2021.

4. "immensely pleasurable": David Rooney, "Thomasin McKenzie and Anya Taylor-Joyce in Edgar Wright's 'Last Night in Soho' Film Review Venice 2021," *Hollywood Reporter*, September 4, 2021.

5. "I've never seen": Oxford Union Q&A.

6. "smoked all the": author Zoom interview with Ray Austin, November 25, 2022.

7. "Normally, when one": Rachael Stirling's comments about her mother's final days derive from an in-depth article in *The Guardian* at the time of Dame Diana Rigg's passing, on September 10, 2020.

BIBLIOGRAPHY

BOOKS

Altman, Mark, and Ed Gross. *Nobody Does It Better: The Complete, Uncensored, Unauthorized Oral History of James Bond*. New York: Forge, 2020.

Brooks, Tim, and Earle Marsh. *The Complete Directory to Prime-Time Network and Cable TV Shows, 1946 to Present*. New York: Ballantine Books, 2007.

Fox, Ken, and Maitland McDonagh. *TV Guide Film and Video Companion*. New York: Cinebooks, 2002.

Javna, John. *Cult TV: A Viewer's Guide to the Shows America Can't Live Without*. New York: St. Martin's Press, 1985.

Lawrence, Will. *The James Bond Film Guide: The Official Guide to All 25 Films*. London: Collector Books, 2021.

Maltin, Leonard. *Movie Guide 2014: The Modern Era*. New York: Plume, 2013.

Maltin, Leonard, ed. *Classic Movie Guide: From the Silent Era Through 1965* (2nd ed.). New York: Plume, 2010.

McNeil, Alex. *Total Television: A Comprehensive Guide to Programming 1948 to the Present*. New York: Penguin Books, 1991.

Pilato, Herbie J. *Glamour, Gidgets and the Girl Next Door: Television's Iconic Women From the '50s, '60s, and '70s*. Lanham, MD: Taylor Trade Publishing, 2013.

Rogers, Dave. *The Complete Avengers: The Full Story of Britain's Smash Crime-Fighting Team!* New York: St. Martin's Griffin, 1989. London: Boxtree, 1989; New York:

Rubin, Steven Jay. *The James Bond Movie Encyclopedia*. Chicago: Chicago Review Press, 2021.

Sackett, Susan. *The Hollywood Reporter Book of Box Office Hits* (revised ed.). New York: Billboard Books, 1996.

Sean Connery: Bond, and Beyond—The Characters He Created, The Movies He Made, The Life He Led. New York: Life Magazine, 2020.

Sean Connery: Tribute to a Legend—His Remarkable Life. New York: *Centennial*, 2020.

Sennett, Ted. *On-Screen Off-Screen Movie Guide*. New York: Fireside Books, 1993.

Simpson, Paul. *Bond vs. Bond: The Many Faces of 007*. New York: Race Point, 2020.

Smith, Ronald L. *Sweethearts of '60s TV*. New York: S. P. I. Books/Shapolsky Publishers, 1993.

Stamp, Gavin. *The Memorial to the Missing of the Somme* (2007 ed.). London: Profile Books, 2006 (2007, ed).

Story, David. *America on the Rerun: TV Shows That Never Die*. New York: Citadel Press, 1993.

Tracy, Kathleen. *Diana Rigg: The Biography*. New York: BenBella Books, 2004.

PERIODICALS

Barnes, Peter. "Leading British Theatre Director Whose Casting Coups Included First Serious Roles for Bob Dylan and Kenneth Branagh." *The Guardian*, November 22, 2022.

Berkvist, Robert. "Nobody's Going to Typecast Diana Rigg." *New York Times*, March 9, 1975.

Billington, Michael. "Perfect Theatrical Blend Marks Rigg as the Best." *Winnipeg (Canada) Free Press*, January 7, 1980, p. 24.

Billington, Michael. "Theatre Review: *All about My Mother*." *The Guardian*, September 5, 2007.

Billington, Michael. "Theatre Review: *Who's Afraid of Virginia Woolf?* Is a Misunderstood Masterpiece." *The Guardian*, September 16, 2016.

Bond, Paul. "British Actress Diana Rigg (1938–2020)." *World Socialist Web Site*, September 17, 2020.

Bradshaw, Peter. "*The Honourable Rebel* Review—Lustrous Life of an Aristo Adventuress." *The Guardian*, December 3, 2015.

Brown, Tracy. "Emmys 2014: Complete List of Nominees." *Los Angeles Times*, July 10, 2014.

Canby, Vincent. "Screen: British Murders Are Cute." *New York Times*, March 24, 1969.

Canby, Vincent. "'Evil Under Sun,' New Christie." *New York Times*, March 5, 1982.

Canby, Vincent. "Sunday View; Diana Rigg Is a Chilly, Elegant Medea." *New York Times*, April 17, 1994.

Carr, Flora. "What Time Is *The Goes Wrong Show* on TV?" *Radio Times*, January 31, 2020.

"Cast List, *The Cherry Orchard* (2008)." www.passiton.cft.org.uk.

Clarke, Stewart. "Diana Rigg, Terence Stamp Join Edgard Wright's *Last Night in Soho*." *Variety*, June 25, 2019.

Costa, Maddy. "Medea: The Mother of All Roles." *The Guardian*, October 2, 2012.

Coveney, Michael. "Television: Dame Diana Rigg Obituary." *The Guardian*, September 10, 2020.

"Crown, The Hollow." *Sydney Morning Herald*, May 30, 2002.

Crowther, Linnea. "Peter Brook (1925–2022), Tony Award-winning Theatre and Film Director." Legacy.com, July 6, 2022.

Curtis, Nick. "Rachael Stirling on Life as Diana Rigg's Daughter and Her Whirlwind Romance with Elbow's Guy Garvey." *Daily Telegraph*, April 8, 2017.

"Dame Diana Rigg Joins Season 3 of HBO's *Game of Thrones*." www.theplaylist.net, July 13, 2012.

Dargis, Manohla. "A Plague Infects the Land, as Passion Vexes Hearts." *New York Times*, December 20, 2006.

"Diana Rigg Gets New Star Role in Stirling & Chancellor." *The Herald*, November 21, 1997.

"Diana Rigg Joins the Cast of *Pygmalion* at Garrick, 12 May." *London Theatre Guide*, June 8, 2016.

"Diana Rigg on Life Before and After *The Avengers*" (featuring correspondent Anthony Mason). CBS News, May 20, 2018.

Drabble, Margaret. "As Diana Rigg's Understudy, I Never Tired of Watching Her. She Was Splendid." *The Guardian*, September 11, 2020.

Ellman, Richard. "*Phaedra* Spiced with Curry." *New York Times*, October 12, 1975.

"Enter Diana Rigg." *Pasadena (California) Star News*, October 7, 1973.

Farndale, Nigel. "Diana Rigg: Her Story." *Daily Telegraph*, August 17, 2008.

Fishlock, Trevor. "India: Emma Peel and the Railway Sahib." *The Telegraph*, February 9, 2002.

"Flashback: The Mrs. Bradley Mysteries." www.atvtoday.com, February 7, 2011.

Gates, Anita. "Diana Rigg, Emma Peel of *The Avengers*, Dies at 82." *New York Times*, September 10, 2020.

Gibbons, Fiachra. "Diana Rigg: Is She the Sexiest TV Star of All Time?" *The Guardian*, August 8, 1999.

Gilbert, Gerard. "The 6 Best TV Shows You Can Watch with Your Family This Christmas." *The Independent*, December 18, 2015.

Gillman, Ollie. "'Patrick Was a Very Dear Man and I Owe Him a Great Deal': Diana Rigg Pays Tribute to Her Avengers Co-star Who Died Yesterday, Aged 93." mailonline.com, June 26, 2015.

Gosling, Francesca. "My Heart Stopped Ticking During Operation—Dame Diana Rigg." *The Telegraph*, December 30, 2017.

Green, Jesse. "Review: Whose 'Fair Lady'? This Time, Eliza's in Charge." *New York Times*, July 7, 2019.

Greenstreet, Rosanna. "Q&A: Diana Rigg." *The Guardian*, April 21, 2007.

Griffiths, Eleanor Bley. "Meet the Voice Cast of *The Snail and the Whale*." *Radio Times*, January 1, 2020.

Hale, Mike. "*Black Narcissus* Review: Nuns, Mountains, High Passion." *New York Times*, November 22, 2020.

Hathaway, Benjamin, "Diana Rigg's 10 Best Movie & TV Roles, Ranked By IMDB." screenrant.com, November 1, 2021.

Hauptfuhrer, Fred. "Being Mr. Diana Rigg Was Too Much for Gueffen." *People*, July 15, 1974.

Hollywood Studio Magazine, 1971.

"'Honour' with Diana Rigg at Wyndham's." www.londontheatre.co.uk, February 7, 2006.

Huntman, Ruth. "Diana Rigg: Becoming a Sex Symbol Overnight Shocked Me." *The Guardian*, May 13, 2019.

Jacobs, Matthew. "Emmy Nominations 2014: *Breaking Bad*, *Orange Is the New Black* among Top Nominees," *Huffington Post*, July 11, 1984.

Jeffrey, Morgan. "Diana Rigg: 'It's Wonderful Being Glamorous—I'm an Old Bag on *Game of Thrones*.'" www.digitalspy.com, October 31, 2017.

Jeffries, Stuart. "Diana Rigg: 'Women of My Age Are Still Attractive. Men My Age Are Not.'" *The Guardian*, March 9, 2014.

Jones, Emma. "Why Diana Rigg 'Loves Being Disliked.'" BBC News, April 20, 2019.

"*King Lear, The Comedy of Errors*." *New York Times*, April 12, 1964.

Krebs, Albin, and Robert Mcg. Thomas Jr. "Notes on People; Diana Rigg Wed to Scottish Producer." *New York Times*, March 26, 1982.

Lambert, Nichole. "I Don't Miss Romance." *Daily Mail Weekend*, October 21, 2015.

Laurent, Lawrence. "Diana Rigg in TV Comedy." *Washington Post* (*Hamilton Journal News*), August 27, 1973.

Lawson, Carol. "Broadway; Diana Rigg to Play Title Role in Musical *Madame Colette*." *New York Times*, January 2, 1981.

Lefkowitz, Andy. "Diana Rigg to Exit Broadway Revival of *My Fair Lady*." www.broadway.com, July 18, 2018.

Low, Valentine. "Cover Story: 'My Manner Is: Don't Brook Any Argument—Good for Playing a Duchess.'" *The Times (London) Saturday Review*, August 26, 2017.

Lowry, Brian. "*You, Me, and the Apocalypse* Finale Runs into a Dead End." *Variety*, April 1, 2016.

Mandell, Jonathan. "Eliza Doolittle through the Century, in *My Fair Lady* and *Pygmalion*." www.newyorktheater.me, April 19, 2019.

Mason, Anthony. "Diana Rigg on Life before and after *The Avengers*." CBS News, May 20, 2018.

Mass Media and Violence Newsletter, 1965.

McBride, Walter. "Photo Throwback: Diana Rigg Rehearses for *Colette* in 1982." www .broadwayworld," September 11, 2020.

"*Mother Courage and Her Children* at the National Theatre/Review." *The Telegraph*.

"No Best Side, But Two Profiles." *Appleton (Wisconsin) Post Crescent*, February 9, 1969.

Norman, Dalton. "Diana Rigg's Role in *Doctor Who*, Explained." *ScreenRant*, March 1, 2023.

Olsen, Mark. "Diana Rigg's Poetic Final Screen Role." *Los Angeles Times*, August 29, 2021.

Pacheco, Adriana. "12 Famous Actors Who Guest Starred in *Road to Avonlea*." www.road toavonlea.com, February 27, 2020.

Paller, Rebecca. "UK's Almeida New Season Features *Phaedra* Starring Rigg." *Playbill*, February 17, 1998.

Paton, Maureen. "Dame Diana Rigg on the Day Her Heart Stopped and Being 'Incredibly Lucky.'" *The Telegraph*, December 23, 2017.

"*Penn Zero: Part Time Hero* to Premiere on Disney Channel and Disney XD February 13." www.laughingplace.com, January 12, 2015.

Percival, Ash. "Dame Diana Dies, Aged 82." *Huffington Post*, September 10, 2020.

Potter, Laura. "'My Body and Soul.' Diana Rigg, Actress, 70." *The Guardian*, March 18, 2019.

"Production Photograph, *Antony and Cleopatra* (1985)." www.PassItOn.cft.org.uk.

"Rachael Stirling Is a Rising Stage Star and She's in Love with Her Ass." www.standard .co.uk, April 10, 2012.

Rainho, Manny. "This Month in Movie History." *Classic Images*, March 2015.

"Review: *Taming of the Shrew*." *Variety*, October 4, 1961.

"Review: *A Midsummer's Night Dream*." *Variety*, July 3, 1963.

"Review: *The Comedy of Errors*." *Variety*, December 12, 1963.

Riedel, Michael. "Diana Rigg Annoyed that *My Fair Lady* Star Is Taking Sundays Off." *New York Post*, July 5, 2018.

Rogers, Buck. "Writer Lambastes Ghetto Sketch by 'Dawn.'" *Lubbock (Texas) Avalanche Journal*, February 20, 1975.

Rosenfeld, Megan. "*Zoya*: Russian through the Steel Mill." *Washington Post*, September 16, 1995.

Russell, Clive. "Diana Stuns Off the Screen." *San Antonio Light*, October 1, 1972.

Rutigliano, Olivia. "The Great Muppet Caper Is the Loveliest Crime Movie Ever." crimereads .com, June 26, 2020.

Saunders, Emily, and Molly Pike. "Diana Rigg Dead: *Game of Thrones* Star Dies after Secret Cancer Battle, Aged 82," *Daily Mirror*, September 10, 2020.

Sharbutt, Jay. "Diana Rigg Sticks to Stage." *Madison Wisconsin State Journal*, February 7, 1982.

Shivas, Mark. "Will Diana Ever Get It Together?" *New York Times*, February 2, 1969.

"Shows Abroad: *A Midsummer Night's Dream*." *Variety*, July 3, 1963.

"Shows Out of Town: *Comedy of Errors*." *Variety*, October 4, 1961.

Sirmons, Julia. "Could *On Her Majesty's Secret Service* Be the Best Bond Film?" crimereads .com, October 8, 2021.

Smith, Charlie, "Diana Rigg Left Daughter Rachael Huge Sum in Will after 'Traumtic' Time before Death." Express.co.uk, March 21, 2022.

Spencer, Charles. "*Mother Courage and Her Children* at the National Theatre, Review." *The Telegraph*, September 28, 2009.

"*Suddenly, Last Summer* Review." London Theatre Guide, June 8, 2016.

"Theatre: *Who's Afraid of Virginia Woolf?*" *The Independent*, September 27, 1996.

Trueman. "Mum's the Word: Helen McCrory and Diana Rigg on Playing Medea." *The Guardian*, August 27, 2014.

TV Week, October 7, 1973.

"UK's Almeida New Season Features *Phaedra* Starring Diana Rigg." playbill.com, February 17, 1998.

Whitmore, Greg. "Diana Rigg: A Life in Pictures." *The Guardian*, September 10, 2020.

"Why Is 1960s Female Icon Diana Rigg Now Laying into Other Women." *The Guardian*, April 30, 2013.

Wolf, Matt. "For Diana Rigg, Neurosis . . ." *New York Times*, April 3, 1994.

Wolf, Matt. "Mother Courage and Her Children," *Variety*, November 26, 1995.

Young, Bill. "Dame Diana Rigg Descends on Queen Victoria and Graces the Halls of Buckingham Palace in *Victoria* S2." www.tellyspotting.com, August 17, 2017.

Yours Retro Magazine: Celebrating the Stars We Love. Media House, 2020.

WEBSITES

dianarigg.net career: theatre

dianarigg.net

https://www.factinate.com/people/facts-diana-rigg/

nndb.com

www.aagpbl.org

www.bafta.org

www.birthdaywiki.com/diana-rigg

www.brucebrownfilms.com

www.catalog.afi.com

www.criterion.com

www.denofgeek.com

www.hollywoodreporter.com

www.huffpost.com

www.imdb.com

www.latimes.com

www.libraries.psu.edu

www.loc.gov

www.londontheatreguide.com

www.newyorktimes.com

www.npr.com

www.oscars.com

www.rogerebert.com

www.tcm.com

www.telegraph.co.uk

www.theagecom.au

www.theatricalia.com

www.thecut.com

www.tvtropes.com

www.variety.com

www.waybackmachine.com

www.wikipedia.com

VIDEO INTERVIEWS [VIA YOUTUBE]

Conrad, Barry. "Diana Rigg Interview on *Collette*," 1982: https://www.youtube.com/watch?v=mkqyIamkVYk.

"*Doctor Who* Diana Rigg on 'The Crimson Horror' including the Clip": https://www.youtube.com/watch?v=q5b67t65LsM.

Oxford Union. "Dame Diana Rigg | Full Q&A | Oxford Union," March 8, 2019: https://www.youtube.com/watch?app=desktop&v=L5-Aor8qUXE.

University of Kent. "Gavin Esler in Conversation with Dame Diana Rigg," December 13, 2016: https://www.youtube.com/watch?app=desktop&v=t_p1qf-xBJw.

HERBIE J PILATO INTERVIEWS

Ray Austin, via Zoom, November 25, 2022.
Barbara Barrie, via telephone, May 31, 2022.
Bruce Beresford, via telephone, November 29, 2020.
Damon Evans, via email, March 17, 2023.
Bernie Kopell, via telephone, February 22, 2022.
Rupert Macnee, via telephone, February 8, 2022.
Juliet Mills, via telephone, May 17, 2023.
Robert S. Ray, via telephone, March 17, 2023.
John Schuck, via email, March 17, 2023.
Samuel West, via Zoom, November 25, 2022.
Andrea Whitcomb-May, via email, March 26, 2023.

INDEX

Page numbers in **bold** refer to illustrations.

ABOUT THE AUTHOR

Herbie J Pilato. Credit: Dan Holm Photography.

Born and raised in Rochester, New York, HERBIE J PILATO is a Los Angeles-based writer, producer, director, actor, TV personality, and singer/songwriter. His eclectic list of critically acclaimed pop-culture/media tie-in books includes *Connery, Sean Connery: Before, During and After His Most Famous Role* (BearManor Media, 2023), *Retro Active Television: An In-Depth Perspective on Classic TV's Social Circuitry* (Headline Books, 2023, and which the Los Angeles Book Festival named "Book of the Year," and Pilato, "Author of the Year"), *The Bionic Book: The Six Million Dollar Man and the Bionic Woman Reconstructed*—"Special Commemorative Edition" (Bear-Manor Media, 2023), *The 12 Best Secrets of Christmas: A Treasure House of December Memories Revealed* (Archway Publishing, 2022), *Mary: The Mary Tyler Moore Story* (Jacobs Brown Press, 2019), *Dashing, Daring and Debonair: TV's Top Male Icons from the '50s, '60s, and '70s* (Taylor Trade, 2016), *Glamour, Gidgets and the Girl Next Door: Television's Iconic Women From the '50s, '60s, and '70s* (Taylor Trade, 2014), *The Essential Elizabeth Montgomery: A Guide to Her Magical Performances* (Taylor Trade, 2013), *Twitch Upon a Star: The Bewitched*

Life and Career of Elizabeth Montgomery (Taylor Trade, 2012), *NBC & ME: My Life as a Page in a Book* (Bear Manor Media, 2008), *The Bionic Book: The Six Million Dollar Man and the Bionic Woman Reconstructed* (Bear Manor Media, 2008), *The Kung Fu Book of Wisdom* (Tuttle, 1995), *The Kung Fu Book of Caine* (Tuttle, 1993), and *The Bewitched Book* (Dell, 1992).

Pilato has served as executive producer, director, writer, and on-screen cultural commentator for the heralded 2023 Reelz Channel TV documentary *Elizabeth Montgomery: A Bewitched Life*, as a consultant and audio commentator for the Saturn Award–nominated Blu-ray release of *The Six Million Dollar Man and the Bionic Woman*, and as a consultant and on-screen commentator for CNN's hit eight-part series, *History of the Sitcom*. He also worked on various other Blu-ray and DVD releases including those for *Bewitched*, as well as broadcast and cable TV documentaries such as Bravo's *100 Greatest TV Characters, Bewitched: The True Hollywood Story; David Carradine: The E! True Hollywood Story;* A&E's *Biography* of Lee Majors; TLC's *Behind the Fame* specials about *The Mary Tyler Moore Show* and *The Bob Newhart Show,* and *L.A. Law* and *Hill Street Blues;* the Syfy Channel's *Sciography* series; and the TV Guide Channel's hit five-part series, *100 Moments That Changed TV;* among others.

In addition to authoring his books, Pilato has written for the Television Academy at emmys.com and *Emmy Magazine,* and has contributed to several other media outlets, such as *Closer Magazine, Remind Magazine,* and tvwriter.com, for which he has served as contributing editor emeritus for over twenty-five years.

In 2010, Pilato established the Classic TV Preservation Society, a formal 501(c)3 nonprofit organization dedicated to the positive influence of classic television shows. In 2019, he pioneered the classic TV talk show format, serving as a host and an executive producer (with Joel Eisenberg) on *Then Again with Herbie J Pilato,* which premiered on Amazon Prime, Amazon Prime UK, and Shout! Factory TV.

For more information, visit herbiejpilato.com.

ABOUT THE CONTRIBUTORS

RUPERT MACNEE is a much-respected television producer, whose credits include the popular syndicated series *An Evening at the Improv* (fifteen seasons, 1981–1998) and *History's Mysteries* (sixteen seasons, 1998–2011). Macnee and his sister, Jenny Macnee, are the offspring of Patrick Macnee and Barbara Douglas.

RAY AUSTIN, aka the Baron of Delvin, was the distinguished director, producer, screenwriter, and novelist. Born in London and educated at Brighton College, Austin made his US feature film debut as a stuntman/bit player in *Spartacus* (1960). He also appeared in supporting roles on such television action shows as *Highway Patrol*, *Peter Gunn*, and *Have Gun Will Travel*. Following his return to the UK, he was appointed stunt director for the epic film *Cleopatra* and worked as a second-unit director/stunt coordinator on the Rome location. In 1970, Austin was named Outstanding Producer/Director and Writer of the Year by the London Film Festival for his short *The Perfumed Garden*. In 1978, he relocated to the United States, where he worked behind the scenes on scores of television shows through the 1990s. In recent years, he lectured on media studies at UCLA, the Actors Playhouse, and the London Film School. He was the author of several mystery novels. On May 17, 2023, Austin passed away at age ninety.